"The Bible is a treasu̱   ̦
TouchPoint will bring you to a deeper place of understanding
just how true that statement is. Bob's academic research and
Spirit-led inspiration will convince you that the Bible truly is the
greatest book of all books!

–Dale Adams
Lead Pastor
LifeSpring Christian Church
Greensburg, PA

Not just another book about The Book, but a theologically
sound, insightful explanation of how a person can discover the
real meaning of life. Bob Santos makes it perfectly clear that the
Word of God is living, active, a seed, a lamp, flawless, right and
true. Not only will it never pass away, but it must be the primary
"TouchPoint" of a life connected with God.

–Chris Ball
President
Elim Fellowship
Lima, NY

Ultimately, God's Word came to us so that we might know God
Himself, and few books illustrate this profound truth so well as
The TouchPoint. With candid brilliance and subtle eloquence,
Bob Santos proclaims the beauty, authenticity, and relevance of
the Christian Bible. I can't imagine anyone who will not benefit
from reading this book, and will heartily recommend it to all of
my students, colleagues, friends, and family.

–John Caton
Apologetics Director
Youth With A Mission
Boston, MA

In *The TouchPoint: Connecting with God through the Bible*, Bob Santos addresses the essential issues and topics that surround a proper understanding of God's Word. For decades I have taught seminars on how we got and why we trust the Bible, both entertaining questions and hearing challenges. These subjects arise repeatedly. Bob's book is a great starting place for evaluating the uniqueness of the Bible and understanding its themes. Through his encouragement, I hope you come to read it for all it's worth.

–Brent J. MacDonald
Executive Director
Cottage Cove's Discipleship Training Institute
and Lion Tracks Ministries
Nashville, TN

I thought *The TouchPoint* was beautifully done! I think that it will be equally encouraging and inspiring for a person who may be new to their faith, as well as someone who is farther along in their spiritual walk.

–Demi Richardson
English Major
Indiana University of Pennsylvania

In *The TouchPoint,* Bob has given a thoughtful, reverent, and accessible examination of the role of Scripture in the believer's life. His heart for helping others know Christ more deeply is evident on every page. Bob's passion is for every believer to experience the fullness of Christ, and in this book he has made a clear case for Scripture's vital role in that experience. *The TouchPoint* offers understanding for those just beginning their journey of faith and insight as well as encouragement for those who have journeyed long.

–Todd Stanley
Worship Pastor
The Summit Church
Indiana, PA

In this book, Bob, with surgical precision splits open long held assumptions of the Bible's place in society from a Christian worldview alongside other prevailing scientific thoughts and philosophies. He presents his Biblical perspective with grace while maintaining an absolute bond to the thrust of Christian living—knowing God personally through Jesus. The reader is taken beyond mere arguments about the Bible and invited to have an encounter with the God who inspired its writing. Highly recommended reading!

–Judah Thomas
Lead Pastor
Word of Grace Fellowship
Indiana, PA

Once again, Bob Santos has produced a very readable book which entreats non-Christian and Christian alike to get informed about life's big picture, and that the Bible deserves prime place in our search for truth. Basic issues of life are considered, and our response to hot topics like Islam and sexuality are not avoided. This book does a great job of presenting the Bible as an inspired "*TouchPoint*" and abounds in common-sense sound mindedness.

–Philip Underwood
Pastor
New Life Church
Vorhees, NJ
Cornerstone Christian Church
Broomall, PA

The TouchPoint is a must read for those who have questions about the Bible and about what being a Christian really means. Bob's informal conversational style delivers the message clearly and is very "user-friendly."

–Dr. Ruiess Van Fossen Bravo
Retired Chemistry Faculty
Indiana, PA

THE
TOUCHPOINT

THE
TOUCHPOINT
CONNECTING WITH GOD THROUGH THE BIBLE

BOB SANTOS

SEARCH FOR ME MINISTRIES, INC.
INDIANA, PA

The TouchPoint: Connecting with God through the Bible
By Bob Santos

Copyright © 2016 by Search for Me Ministries, Inc.

Cover Design: Steve Margita and Sean McGaughran
Front Cover Background: Designed by Freepik
Interior Design: Sean McGaughran
Editor: Nat Davis

Published by SfMe Media
A Division of Search for Me Ministries, Inc.
865 School Street
Indiana, PA 15701
www.searchforme.info
www.sfme.org

Printed in the United States of America

Library of Congress Control Number: 2016903017

ISBN: 978-1-937956-06-6
ePub ISBN: 978-1-937956-11-0
Mobi ISBN: 978-1-937956-10-3

In honor of all who have devoted their lives to making God's eternal Word available for others.

Contents

Introduction   13

1. The Bible as Our TouchPoint   17

2. The Mystery of the Bible   33

3. Preparing Our Hearts   49

4. The Authority of the Scriptures   65

5. A Brief Overview of the Bible   81

6. Incredibly Credible   97

7. What About Science?   117

8. Credibly Incredible   135

9. The Favorable Influence of the Gospel   151

10. Inspiration from Heaven   171

11. Understanding the Bible   187

12. Cracking the Book   205

13. Knowing God   223

14. The TouchPoint of Everlasting Hope   241

Acknowledgements   257

INTRODUCTION

"I hate God!" Appalled at hearing her five-year-old son utter these dreadful words as the family prepared for church, the Christian mother quickly reprimanded the little guy. But after a little thought, she felt inclined to dig deeper into his reasoning. Only a couple of questions revealed that her son didn't hate God at all—he hated church. Actually, church wasn't the problem. Dancing—and probably doing coordinated gestures—during the children's service was the real culprit.

The mother's explanation of this incident with her son caught my attention for one simple reason: I've seen far too many people reject God for reasons that had little or nothing to do with God Himself. Guilt by association, misunderstanding our Creator's character, and addiction to human approval are all factors that can taint our views of the Divine. And while the Bible can provide significant answers to our struggles, the words on its pages don't always make obvious sense.

The Bible is a mysterious book, and differing opinions of it abound. Some view it as a rulebook for life. Others think it to be nothing more than the product of human imagination. In the course of my Christian experience, I've encountered a wide array of perspectives, but sometimes the most important purpose is the least realized. The Christian Bible is, first and foremost, a book of *relationship*. From beginning to end, its key themes center around the eternal Creator's relationship—or lack thereof—with the human race. Without a vital connection to the God who designed and created us, our lives are but a shell of what He intends them to be.

One of the biggest challenges we face in relating to God is that, though He created the human race in His image, our current ability to see and understand His ways is severely lacking. God functions primarily on a spiritual plane, while our sensory perceptions and ways of thinking knit us into the physical realm. It pains me to admit it, but the more I've discovered about the God who created all things, the more I've learned how much I am *unlike* Him.

We desperately need the Bible as our *TouchPoint*—that connecting place where we develop a clearer understanding of God, and just as importantly, learn how to relate to Him according to His design. I didn't write *The TouchPoint* for the person who is simply looking to add more knowledge to his or her information arsenal. Instead, this work flows from the realization that our Creator gifted the Bible to humanity as a means of connecting with Him.

Only through the Bible's influence do we begin to realize that knowing God is as much about the state of a person's heart as it is about the capabilities of his or her brain. At the same time, knowledge matters, so I've included a good deal of foundational information for those who have an interest in the Bible but aren't sure where to begin.

As with the five-year-old who thought he hated God, we're also influenced by seemingly indirect issues that affect a meaningful relationship with our heavenly Creator. Because having confidence in the Bible can powerfully influence our day-to-day lives, I've also included a section about its authenticity. The information I've provided is by no means exhaustive, but it does provide a good overview of this all-important issue.

As much as avoiding the subject of the Bible's credibility would have made this project easier, no relationship can be healthy without trust, and trust is impossible without credibility. The Bible will never be our *TouchPoint* for connecting with God if we lack the confidence that He is the true inspiration behind its written text.

I freely admit that this book is limited in scope and that many of the ideas presented can be found in any number of excellent works. But I also believe that my condensed arguments and relational perspective will enrich those who, with honest hearts, are pursuing God and His eternal truth.

Regardless of whether the topic is the state of a person's heart, the credibility of the Bible, or the importance of context, I hope to convey one prevailing truth: your heart can brim with hope because you are passionately loved and highly valued by the Creator who ever seeks to draw you near. In this, I see the Bible as a profound book filled with living warmth in a very cold world.

God deeply desires to know you experientially, and with equal passion, wants you to know Him. This timeless truth continually bleeds through the pages of the Bible. And while the circumstances of your life may not always seem to confirm His love, a clearer understanding of God, as discovered through the Christian Bible, will help you personally experience the reality of His goodness.

1

THE BIBLE AS OUR TOUCHPOINT

We look upon prayer as a means of getting things for ourselves; the Bible idea of prayer is that we may get to know God Himself.

- Oswald Chambers

Then Jesus cried out in the temple, teaching and saying, "You both know Me and know where I am from; and I have not come of Myself, but He who sent Me is true, whom you do not know. I know Him, because I am from Him, and He sent Me."

John 7:28-29

If war can be described as *a bloody hell*, then the WWII battle for the Pacific island of Okinawa fits the description well. Heavy monsoon rains knew neither friend nor foe as they turned the tropical battlefield into a muddy caldron of death. Decaying bodies, engulfed by the muck, then created a noxious, inescapable stench. Most certainly, the Pacific War had taken its grueling toll.

Surrounded by destruction, death, and misery, war correspondent Clarence W. Hall encountered an extraordinary scene that would remain forever embedded in his memory. Riding with an advance patrol to investigate a local village, Hall was stunned by what he described as, "Shimabuku, the strangest and most inspiring community I ever saw." It was a jewel of humanity fixed in a setting of human wretchedness.

THE TOUCHPOINT

As they approached the village, the wary soldiers were met by Mojun Nakamura, the mayor, and Shosei Kina, the schoolmaster, one of whom was holding a well-worn Bible. Thirty years prior, the two local leaders explained, an American missionary on his way to Japan had visited the village. The strange visitor stayed long enough only to introduce these men to Jesus Christ, teach a couple of hymns, and leave them with a Bible. Despite the brevity of the missionary's stay, the village was profoundly impacted. To Hall and the battle-worn soldiers he accompanied, the contrast between Shimabuku and the surrounding villages could not have been more extreme.

> We'd seen other Okinawan villages, uniformly down-at-the-heels and despairing; by contrast, this one shone like a diamond in a dung heap. Everywhere we were greeted by smiles and dignified bows.
>
> Proudly the two old men showed us their spotless homes, their terraced fields, fertile and neat, their storehouses and granaries, their prized sugar mill. . . .
>
> Nurtured on this Book, a whole generation of Shimabukans had drawn from it their ideas of human dignity and of the rights and responsibilities of citizenship. The result was plain to see. Shimabuku for years had had no jail, no brothel, no drunkenness, no divorce; there was a high level of health and happiness.[1]

Intrigued by what he had seen and experienced, Hall felt compelled to return, so he requested a driver who could translate the local tongue. Soon they were strolling "the quiet village streets, soaking up Shimabuku's calm." The pleasant sound of singing led the duo to a local religious service. What they saw next left the war-hardened men nearly speechless. A well-worn Bible had been integral in preserving that isolated village from the decay of human conflict and devastation.

> The book's imitation-leather cover was cracked and worn, its pages stained and dog-eared from 30 years' constant use. Kina

---

1. Clarence W. Hall, "The Village That Lived by the Bible," *The Heartbeat of the Remnant 11, no.6* (2005), 31-32.

held it with the reverent care one would use in handling the original Magna Carta.

The service over, we waited as the crowd moved out, and my driver whispered hoarsely, "So this is what comes out of only a Bible and a couple of old guys who wanted to live like Jesus!" Then, with a glance at a shell-hole, he murmured, "Maybe we're using the wrong kind of weapons."

Time had dimmed the Shimabukans' memory of the missionary; neither Kina nor Nakamura could recall his name. They did remember his parting statement. As expressed by Nakamura, it was: "Study this Book well. It will give you strong faith. And when faith is strong, everything is strong."[2]

It's unlikely that the villagers of Shimabuku had the full understanding of doctrine (teaching; instruction) that many traditional Christians have come to expect, but somehow, without Bible school or scholarly resource, a single copy of the Bible had brought a taste of paradise to one of the most hellish places on earth.

OUR TOUCHPOINT

The more I understand about the Bible, the more I appreciate its beauty, unity, and yes, even complexity. Though penned long before the idea of a computer was ever conceived, its truths challenge the greatest depths of human intellect, its sweetness brightens the wearied soul, and its insight provides real significance in an often meaningless world. Although once a skeptic, I now believe, along with a multitude of others, that the Bible is the most amazing book ever written.

There have been very few days over the past thirty years when I haven't read at least a little of the Bible, and it has impacted virtually every aspect of my existence. Before the *Book of books* became integral to my life, I often felt like I was alone and adrift in a vast sea of human selfishness. That's not to say that everyone I knew was entirely self-absorbed, or that I have lived a "rose garden" existence since—I certainly have my share of challenges and struggles—but my life now has meaning and purpose even in the worst of circumstances.

2. Ibid., 32.

THE TOUCHPOINT

When I mention reading the Bible virtually every day, I'm providing a personal reflection—not making a boast. You see, I've come to understand that the Bible is our *TouchPoint* for life—that conduit where people of all races and strata can touch the warmth of heavenly love. It's our connecting point to divine hope.

Overstating the importance of this dynamic is nothing short of impossible. All that we have and all that we are proceeds from our Creator, and so the full meaning of our lives can only be discovered in relationship with Him. Whether we feel that we're among the least of the least or the greatest of the great, we all find ourselves on equal footing as we seek to connect with the One who despises elitism.

Moreover, if our Creator is the phenomenal Being that many of us believe, we need something more than our own musings to understand Him and His ways. Throughout my life, I've encountered no small number of people who find the idea of a relationship with God appealing, but more or less demand that He cater to their terms. Most of us, I believe, desire a "manageable" God who exists to serve human desires. The Creator of the Universe, though, will have nothing of it.

Why is the Bible necessary to a healthy relationship with God? It teaches us what we need to know—not simply what we want to hear. Through its pages, we discover a God who is rich and complex in character, and very much unlike any government ruler who ever lived. Few issues are as important as our perspective of God because who we perceive Him to be, and what we believe He thinks about us, will impact the entire course of our lives.

God's person consists of many different characteristics and attributes seamlessly interwoven in an entirely congruent manner. Our eternal Creator, for example, is both loving and just in all He does. His love cannot be separated from His sense of justice, nor His justice from His love. Consistent and objective Bible reading helps to remind us of these things, thus minimizing the natural temptation to "recreate" God according to our own imaginations. Without the Bible as our *TouchPoint*, reality-based faith quickly morphs into a sort of earthly-minded mythology.

GRASPING GOD

God is *transcendent*—meaning that He exists outside of the range of our natural human senses. We can't gaze into His eyes, measure His height, or hear Him expound deep mysteries over a morning cup of coffee. This spiritual nature of God leads some people to believe that He doesn't exist.

I once attended a college campus debate in which an atheist speaker adamantly contended that, because we cannot measure God, He cannot possibly exist. I was astounded to see him employ such a weak argument in a university debate. Having doubts about God is one thing; conclusively denying His existence because of our limited human capabilities is another. There was a day when humankind lacked the technical expertise to measure radiation, but our inability did nothing to change the reality of uranium-238!

The truth is that no human will ever be able to entirely "grasp" God. How can the finite fully comprehend the infinite? How can infinitesimal humans on a minuscule planet in a tiny solar system expect to unpack all of the deep mysteries of the universe? Are we so arrogant as to believe human intelligence reigns supreme above all else?

Merely contemplating the transcendence of God can make a person feel painfully small and insignificant. We may, in fact, begin to believe we can never truly know *anything* about Him. "Perhaps," our doubts badger us, "we're nothing more than wayward souls hopelessly adrift in a nebulous existence." Such might be the case if not for one exciting (and amazing) fact: our Creator loves us so much that He *deeply desires* to reveal Himself to us. How do we know? Jesus Christ came to earth so we could see the personality of God in human form.

The Architect of the Universe wants us to know Him, but doing so involves a journey of profound discovery that will stretch the limits of both heart and mind. More than once, I have found myself in awe of His magnificence. Bowing low to worship makes much more sense as the veil of obscurity is removed, and we begin to see our Creator for His true self.

We can employ various methods to learn about the existence and nature of God. To begin, we need simply to observe the material world around us. I took an interest in science at a young age, eventually majoring in chemistry on a university level. When examining the scientific and aesthetic wonders of our material existence, I am compelled to agree with many of the great scientific minds of old that the nonexistence of God seems beyond imagination. I realize that naturalists see things differently, but the idea of billions of massive galaxies, with billions of stars in each, simply popping into existence without cause has little, if any, scientific merit.

On every level, from minuscule to ginormous, we are struck by the beauty, order, and complexity of our natural world. This evidence points us toward a Creator who is artistic, powerful, and highly intelligent. And though God is massive beyond thought, amazingly, He also concerns Himself with the smallest of details. The crystalline structure of a grain of salt is as much an act of God as the Milky Way galaxy. Beyond all of these things, we must consider not only the existence of life, but also the mysterious complexities of human emotion, conscience, and intelligence, not to mention our deep-rooted desires for freedom and justice. No naturalistic theory of creation comes close to providing an adequate explanation for all of these wonders.

Also, in addition to clues about God's existence, we find embedded within our natural world hidden treasures of wisdom—the life and death cycle of seeded fruit, for example—that help to reveal His way of thinking. Humanity is immersed in a world of profound insight and eternal wisdom, but unless our hearts and minds are tuned to heaven's "frequency," we remain oblivious to the spiritual world thriving beyond the scope of our natural existence. In other words, we can't, by human intellectual ability, figure out God's majestic ways. We need His help!

IT'S ALL ABOUT RELATIONSHIP

If an invisible God exists outside the measurable realm of natural law, how can we definitively understand anything about Him? We can't—unless He chooses to reveal the reality of Himself. And thankfully for us, there are few things He wants more.

In its essence, *truth is nothing more than reality exposed.* And what could be more real than the One who brought the heavens into existence? Any God powerful and intelligent enough to create our immense galactic wonder must certainly be able to give us glimpses of His spiritual reality. This potential is evidenced by the fact that the Bible repeatedly encourages us to seek God wholeheartedly (Deuteronomy 4:29; Isaiah 55:6; and Hebrews 11:6).

The Biblical call to seek God provides an awesome message of hope for those who dwell in a pain-filled world! The eternal Creator of our universe strongly desires that we know Him and His ways. In fact, He delights in revealing Himself to us. Such awesome knowledge, however, can never be a matter of a simple download accomplished with the press of a button. The process goes beyond casual seeking; Our Lord values us and expects us to value Him and His truth in return.

Furthermore, if we are to genuinely know God, we need a reliable way to discover and discern His true character. Such a realization brings us to two primary connecting points of revelation that our Creator has graciously provided for us: *the Bible* and the presence of *the Holy Spirit*. The Bible lays out for us the knowledge of God's character, and just as importantly, an understanding of how we can relate to Him. The dynamics of this relationship are almost beyond belief as the Holy Spirit—God Himself—comes to dwell in the hearts of those who become His children.

Some people perceive the Holy Spirit to be an impersonal force similar to that in the *Star Wars* series. On the contrary, He is the *third person of the Trinity.* Mere words are insufficient to express the sheer wonder of God's presence dwelling in human hearts. It is through this intimate connection that our journey of amazing discovery truly begins, for as we learn to align our ways with His, the Holy Spirit delights in revealing Himself to us.

Not only is it necessary for us to make the Bible integral to our daily lives, it's also essential that we look to the Holy Spirit for an accurate understanding of the truths contained within its pages. Even though the Book of books is a gift of God's design graciously given to humanity, it was *never* intended to substitute for a relationship with God. If we try to comprehend the Bible without the help of the One who inspired its writing, we will, without question, distort its intended meaning.

It is a sad fact that a person can spend an entire lifetime reading and studying the Bible and still not know his or her Creator. If the Spirit of God does not open our eyes to understand Biblical truth, selfish and prideful motives will soon distort the power and beauty of its inspiration. This book given for the benefit of humanity will then be used in destructive ways contrary to our Creator's intent—a fact confirmed by centuries of religious history. I sometimes wonder, how many well-intentioned people have had a relationship with the Bible but not with the God who brought it into being?

If I could draw a contrast that has proven invaluable to me, it would clearly delineate the difference between living out of a vital relationship with God and attempting to serve Him by our own abilities. Almost from the beginning of its history, humanity—even in its efforts to appease Him—has sought *independence* from God. It is in this sense that we often view the Bible as a "rule book" or "road map" for life that can be employed, through self-effort, to help us reach a desirable destination. This tendency, though quite common and potentially beneficial, can also have *deadly* consequences.

True life finds its source in the God who created us. He may allow us to momentarily walk this earth independent of a vital relationship with Him, but such a life is little more than a hollow shell of all that it could be. As much as I live with purpose, and as much as I look forward to an awesome eternity in heaven, I'm also aware of the glory of the journey. Eternity begins today, and life is but a stepping stone as we walk with God toward a greater tomorrow.

OUR BIGGEST OBSTACLE

One of the more significant problems that we face in understanding God's ways has nothing to do with the Bible and everything to do with *us*. Most of us expect to live according to *our own way*—as becomes quickly apparent not long after birth. Anyone who has ever reared or worked with children understands the battle of the human will that begins almost in infancy. Let's face it, even the cutest of kids wants to rule the world. If this tendency isn't wisely and lovingly addressed, the child will eventually grow into a larger expression of the temper tantrum. Society can (begrudgingly) manage a toddler throwing a selfish fit, but give his adult version some power, and trouble begins to flow like water!

I wish I could say that the issue of self-will is limited to those who categorically reject Christianity, but even devoted followers of God fall prey to selfish mindsets. Regardless of what we profess, living according to our desires is as easy as falling asleep while reading a boring book. (Did I really use that example?) All too often, we throw in a few religious trappings—going to church, putting money in the offering, helping someone in need, reading our obligatory devotions—and then feel that the "Big Guy in the Sky" is obligated to bless our lives.

Is it unreasonable that the Creator of all things would expect us to live on His terms? I think not, considering that He brought the entire universe into existence. Subsequently, He owns *all* of the rights. If you conceived and labored over a masterpiece of art, would you not expect to own the rights? Would it be fair for a greed-driven company to reprint the image you created and make millions without compensating you? In a very real sense, God owns the copyright on creation. The fact that He has blessed us with the freedom of will in no way means that He has abdicated His right of ownership.

I'm not suggesting that we're required to jettison all personal desires and become mindless zombies in order to know God, but that our true identities can be found only as we learn to connect with our Creator according to His design. Jesus completely yielded Himself to the heavenly Father, and yet, I see Him as one of the most passionate people to have ever lived. But while Christ's was a pure passion driven by pure love, selfishness often taints even our noblest desires.

When the Bible becomes a tool for selfish purposes, a host of significant problems result—only two of which I will briefly address. First, life becomes about *us*. Have you ever noticed that the Earth revolves around the Sun? Too often, though, we live as though the

Sun orbits the Earth. More specifically, we expect the Son of God to cater to our earthly expectations. The problem is that if our desires are misdirected, we'll totally miss the reality of who He is.

In search of a friend, I recently walked up to the balcony of our church. I had just seen Frank go up the steps, but as I looked around, he was nowhere to be found. Meanwhile, a couple of other friends—Arch and Jamie—saw me and waved. Intent on finding Frank, I ignored them until the reality of their presence took hold. How rude! It wasn't that I didn't care; my attention was simply preoccupied.

My experience with Arch and Jamie is consistent with what happens to many of us as we open the pages of the Bible. Looking to meet needs and fulfill personal desires, we miss a wealth of treasure. If we see the Bible simply as a means of finding peace, hope, strength, or direction, we'll remain oblivious to a meaningful relationship with the divine personality who provides all of those things. No doubt, we should seek God with specific needs, but there is much, much more to a relationship with our loving Lord. *The Bible is for us, but it isn't about us.* The sooner we grasp this reality, the better off we will be.

Second, we unjustly blame God when things don't go as expected. When we act as the kings and queens of our own lofty domains, we mistakenly begin to feel that God exists as a personal attendant to ensure the happiness of our short stay on earth. Then, when He doesn't bless according to our preconceived expectations, we inexplicably find Him to be at fault. A person can be clueless about what it means to walk with God and align with His ways, and yet, he or she still expects the sovereign King of the Universe to provide a happy and pain-free journey through life. Seriously?

I can't begin to count the number of people I encounter who are angry with God because they feel as though He let them down. Perhaps a loved one died prematurely, or life took an undesirable turn. It can be any number of things. While I won't begin to question either the sincerity or depth of their pain, few of these people seem to show any significant concern about walking with God prior to their trauma. The Sun does not revolve around the Earth; the Earth orbits the Sun.

Admittedly, there is a lot in this world that I don't understand. Even a person who lives near to God can experience extreme measures of pain and sorrow. There, however, is one thing I do get: *God is good, through and through.* If we've experienced some sort of pain or tragedy, attempting to throw blame on our Creator will never improve our circumstances. Furthermore, healing and transformation come only as we draw near to our heavenly Father—not as we keep Him at arm's length.

GOD'S GOOD PLANS

It is impossible to have a meaningful relationship with God apart from *faith.* It is through trust that relationships thrive, and it is in this realm that many of our struggles are rooted. Life in this world isn't terribly conducive to a vibrant belief in God. All too often, human voices assault the reality of our loving Creator. In addition, the pain of our personal experiences causes us to feel that either we are beyond hope, or God's character is somehow flawed. Conversely, a clear understanding of the Bible helps us to see God's goodness and its relevance to our lives.

Jeremiah 29:11, for example, stands as a favorite passage for no small number of people. I too value this verse and have found it to be an awesome source of encouragement during dark times:

> *"For I know the plans that I have for you," declares the LORD, "plans for welfare and not for calamity to give you a future and a hope." Jeremiah 29:11*

The Bible is amazing because God is amazing. If our hearts are in tune, we can sense eternal love seeping through every page. During Jeremiah's time, for example, the covenant people of God found themselves oppressed in exile because of their own stubborn sin, but amazingly, the sovereign Lord still had good plans and purposes for their lives. Many of us can relate to their circumstances. When we've dug ourselves into an inescapable pit, few promises are as sweet to the ear.

Problematically, Jeremiah 29:11 is frequently applied *out of context* (an issue I more thoroughly address in chapter eleven). In particular, verse eleven means little without the two verses that follow:

"Then you will call upon Me and come and pray to Me, and I will listen to you. You will seek Me and find Me when you search for Me with all your heart." Jeremiah 29:12-13

Our relationship with God is to be one of mutual devotion. He does indeed have good plans for each and every one of us; we, however, play a vital role in the process by searching for Him with our entire being. Only with this mindset of wholeheartedly seeking God will the Bible make its full impact in our lives. In other words, we can't expect the fulfillment of Jeremiah 29:11 if we aren't willing to practically apply Jeremiah 29:12-13.

The Bible is a treasure chest full of invaluable truths intended to bless abundantly, but it will not yield its precious wealth to the casual seeker. Even though God has taken repeated steps in our direction, and even though He seeks to bless us with the riches of heaven, those desiring to extract eternal wealth and rich blessings from the Bible *must* go after them—and on God's terms.

IF / THEN

Postmodern thought tends to dislike absolute words such as *must*, but that is to our detriment. A few of God's promises are *unconditional*. Regardless of what we do, for example, He will never flood the entire earth again (Genesis 9:11). But many more of God's promises are *conditional*. If we do what He commands, His blessings will come along in tow. The following are a few if/then statements made by Jesus and recorded in the Gospel of John:

"My teaching is not Mine, but His who sent Me. If anyone is willing to do His will, he will know of the teaching, whether it is of God or whether I speak from Myself." John 7:16b-17

"If you continue in My word, then you are truly disciples of Mine; and you will know the truth, and the truth will make you free." John 8:31b-32

"Truly, truly, I say to you, unless a grain of wheat falls into the earth and dies, it remains alone; but if it dies, it bears much fruit. He who loves his life loses it, and he who hates his life in

this world will keep it to life eternal. If anyone serves Me, he must follow Me; and where I am, there My servant will be also; if anyone serves Me, the Father will honor him." John 12:24-26

"If you know these things, you are blessed if you do them." John 13:17

Since Jesus is seated "far above all rule and authority and power and dominion" (Ephesians 1:20-22), His words are *authoritative*. We are not our own gods; instead we are subject to the one sovereign and eternal God. This is the way that it *must* be. God is who He is regardless of our opinions. All-knowing. Eternal. Unchangeable. He will never conform to human mindsets, nor should we want Him to. His ways alone are pure, holy, full of freedom, and overflowing with life.

I don't suppose that presenting this type of if/then proposition is the most effective way to entice continued reading, but I've never been one to sugarcoat Christianity. Experience has taught me that the Bible offers little of lasting value if we aren't willing to wrestle with issues that don't appeal to our desires. Human domination always leads to corruption of one form or another. As much as we all want the world to revolve around us, neither we nor the world would benefit. If we are to experience God's blessed best, His will must hold sway over our lives.

Do we want the good "thens" that result from knowing God's truth? Those who seek to experience His freedom, want to be confirmed as His true disciples, wish to abide in His eternal life, long to be honored by the heavenly Father, and hope to reap His rich blessings dare not ignore the "ifs" expected by Jesus.

In no way am I suggesting we attempt to earn heaven's favor through sacrificial effort. Our good works are the *result*—not the cause—of our acceptance with God. But genuine faith and love produce far more than simply a passive acceptance of what God has done for us; they call us to active devotion as the only reasonable response to His gracious gifts.

The Bible plays an essential role in the if/then scenario of heavenly blessing. How can we walk with God if we don't understand what He values or how He relates to humanity? The Jeremiah 29:11 message of

God's good plans to a captive people would have been unnecessary had the people of ancient Israel heeded their Lord's warnings to know and obey His commands. Notice the connection between God's promises to Joshua (and the Israelites) and the admonishment to honor His law:

> *"No man will be able to stand before you all the days of your life. Just as I have been with Moses, I will be with you; I will not fail you or forsake you." Joshua 1:5*

> *"This book of the law shall not depart from your mouth, but you shall meditate on it day and night, so that you may be careful to do according to all that is written in it; for then you will make your way prosperous, and then you will have success." Joshua 1:8*

The dynamics of relating to God have changed since Joshua's time, but the basic principles have not. If we neglect God's Word, we will pay a steep price for the resulting ignorance of His ways. Opening the Bible might be only a first step in walking with God, but I can guarantee it to be a necessary one.

A LIFELONG ADVENTURE

Learning to know God and fully align with His ways is a lifelong adventure that involves a basic five-part process we continually repeat:

1. We seek to know God and His ways.
2. He reveals Himself and His truth.
3. We come to a deeper level of knowing.
4. We align our ways with His.
5. We taste the fruit of His kingdom.

The basic dynamics of this process generally hold true, but the steps involved don't always flow in this exact order. Sometimes, God reveals Himself for reasons known only to Him. Furthermore, He will often call us to steps of obedience before giving us deeper levels of revelation. The knowing will eventually come, but only after the obeying.

One thing is certain: the development and perfection of our faith is woven into every facet of our growth. This fact is *inescapable!* If having a relationship with God matters, then trusting God matters. Intimacy is impossible without trust. Accordingly, our loving Father will go to great lengths to firmly establish our faith. But if we are ignorant of God's ways, we will mistake this faith-building process for a lack of love.

I might also note that aligning with God can require varied responses. He might simply call us to correct a wrong way of thinking, or perhaps, adjust an unfavorable attitude. Of course, there are times when behavioral changes are necessary. Sometimes our adjustments come quickly, and we see radical changes almost instantly. In other cases, the growth process seems painfully slow. How I wish that transformation were always instantaneous! So ingrained are our natural ways that the slow process of change can at times feel like being stuck in rush-hour traffic with no sign of movement for what seems like years.

Thankfully, God patiently works to transform even the root levels of our existence. If we persist in pursuing our loving King and submitting to His ways, over time, we'll learn to walk with Him, grow in His grace, and make a viable difference in this world. A life's journey, inspired and led by God, that begins with hopeful anticipation will end with greater hope fulfilled. Still, the road between beginning and end may have the feel of a wild roller coaster ride.

CHAPTER WRAP-UP

At first glance, the Bible may seem impossible to comprehend, but with a little help and some deliberate effort, you'll find it blessing your soul, strengthening your spirit, and guiding your steps. At times, though, it will also pierce your heart.

> *For the word of God is living and active and sharper than any two-edged sword, and piercing as far as the division of soul and spirit, of both joints and marrow, and able to judge the thoughts and intentions of the heart. Hebrews 4:12*

Make no mistake: humanity is subject to the living power of God's eternal Word—not vice versa. I fully realize I've taken a strong stand regarding our need to submit to His ways, but the Christian faith doesn't seem to work any other way. Thankfully, our heavenly Father cares about us more than we can fathom. We may feel at times like His truth is "working us over," but our lives will be forever enriched through the process.

I sincerely hope that what I have learned over the past thirty-five or more years will somehow help and bless those who read these pages. God has placed teachers in the body of Christ not to replace the role of the Holy Spirit, but to help people better understand His ways. May we never forget the goal of our learning. Our loving Creator has gifted us with the Bible as a necessary *TouchPoint* so that we may intimately know Him and live in the abundance of His dynamic presence.

2

THE MYSTERY OF THE BIBLE

The Bible is a supernatural book and can be understood only by supernatural aid.

—A.W. Tozer

Trust God from the bottom of your heart;
 don't try to figure out everything on your own.
Listen for God's voice in everything you do, everywhere you go;
 he's the one who will keep you on track.

Proverbs 3:5-6 (MSG)

Have you ever gazed into the sky on a clear night and considered the immensity of it all? One summer, while on a trip to South Dakota, our family had an opportunity to see the beauty of the Badlands Wilderness Area. But our visit didn't go as expected—unforeseen difficulties delayed our arrival until after the sun had set. Most scenic wonders aren't nearly as scenic after nightfall.

Surprisingly, our disappointment turned to wonder as we stopped straining to see the darkness-clad landscape and turned our gaze to the stars above. With minimal pollution and no man-made lights, the brilliant night sky made us feel as though we were standing in the heavens—and considering the infinitesimal place we occupy in the universe, indeed we were! A meteor shower only added to our delight.

Even though awed by the immensity of the cosmos, we'd like to think we have our natural world figured out. The truth, however, is that mystery abounds. There is *far more* that we don't know than we do know. In spite of millions of man-hours and billions of dollars invested in study and exploration, we remain largely ignorant of our greater universe. The same can be said for our spiritual world. It is a realm that can't readily be seen, heard, or touched with our natural senses.

Theodore Roosevelt—the twenty-sixth president of the United States—once stated, "A thorough knowledge of the Bible is worth more than a college education." Considering how much money, time, and effort people invest in a college degree, that's saying a lot! A thorough knowledge of the Bible, however, is not easily gained. Just as many aspects of our natural world remain shrouded in mystery, God's kingdom functions by a mindset that is entirely beyond natural human thought.

We'll address the credibility of the Bible in the future, but for now, I want to lay a foundation so that we can establish a better understanding of God's perspective in light of humanity's. This is an often ignored but nonetheless vital step in our efforts to utilize the Bible as God intends.

If God's mindset inherently differs from that of humankind, it's entirely reasonable that we would struggle to understand how natural words on man-made paper might be impregnated with spiritual wisdom and life. Furthermore, this *TouchPoint* between the spiritual and natural worlds is filled with metaphors, cryptic sayings, and figures of speech. A person cannot expect to open the Bible and immediately comprehend the deep mysteries of the universe. Thankfully, even though grasping a thorough understanding of the Bible may be beyond our natural reach, our loving Creator provides the opportunity for us to comprehend many of His ways.

One of the keys to knowing God is to align our lives with His master plan for humanity. In this, ignorance is our archenemy. We can't align ourselves with God's design while being oblivious to His eternal mindset. All too often, we erroneously assume that God thinks the way we think. But He doesn't! And sometimes, the difference is *extreme*.

GOD'S WAYS ARE HIGHER!

In his first epistle (letter) to the Corinthian church, the apostle Paul wrote, "A natural man does not accept the things of the Spirit of God, for they are foolishness to him; and he cannot understand them, because they are spiritually appraised" (1 Corinthians 2:14). We can't say for sure, but it's entirely possible that Paul had the following passage from Isaiah in mind when he penned his letter:

> Seek the LORD while He may be found;
> Call upon Him while He is near.
> Let the wicked forsake his way
> And the unrighteous man his thoughts;
> And let him return to the LORD,
> And He will have compassion on him,
> And to our God,
> For He will abundantly pardon.
> "For My thoughts are not your thoughts,
> Nor are your ways My ways," declares the LORD.
> "For as the heavens are higher than the earth,
> So are My ways higher than your ways
> And My thoughts than your thoughts."
> Isaiah 55:6-9

This single passage—four simple verses—opens our eyes to a reality that few people want to accept: *God's way of thinking is far beyond our own.* Three primary observations further help us gain eternal perspective:

1. **God's foundational level of thought isn't just different from ours—it is diametrically opposed.** How high are the heavens above the earth? The matter is not simply one of physical distance but of *contrast.* God's intellect and our human reasoning function on two entirely different planes.

   Our world, for example, is driven by *outward appearances.* We tend to define people by how they measure up to the standards of today's "fashion police." Consequently, internal beauty ranks terribly low on our priority list. In contrast, God cares virtually nothing about physical appearance but is intensely concerned about the state of human hearts (see 1 Samuel 16:1-7).

2. **God desires that His compassion find expression in our lives.** The Bible wasn't written to condemn us, but to help us. It's all too common for people to confuse *truth and honesty* with *judgment and condemnation*. Truth can be compared to a sharp scalpel in the hands of a skilled surgeon. God will sometimes "wound" us with His truth, but only to cut away spiritual cancers in restoring us to health and wholeness.

3. **The Creator of our universe calls us to seek Him while we have the opportunity to do so.** Accordingly, *we* play an essential role in coming to know God and His ways. We seek Him. We call upon Him. We forsake our wicked ways. We return to Him. Once again, we are confronted by the if/then proposition that defines the nature of our Christian experience.

If our lives were skyscrapers, each of these truths would be a pillar embedded in the bedrock far below our surface existence. Many storms of life are unavoidable. But when the clouds burst and winds swirl, we can stand tall and unshaken knowing that our God has answers where none can be seen, that He has gone to great lengths to free us from the crushing burden of condemnation, and that we remain secure amidst the shifting sands of human opinion.

GOD REVEALS AND ILLUMINATES

God desires good for us regardless of our past failures. Apart from the Bible, though, we'd have no sure way of knowing where we stand with the King of Heaven. I'm not referring to the need for some sort of unquestionable dogma, but rather a comprehension of truth rooted in a clear perspective of God's reality. Ignorance of His eternal character and wise design for humanity will leave us anxious and wanting in the end.

We need not be lost in a world of vague ideas and nebulous concepts. We can know what is true because the King of Heaven wants to disclose Himself to us. Otherwise, we muddle along the adversity-ridden trails of life with little or no hope.

The past thirty-five years of my life, for the most part, have been spent seeking a deeper understanding of God's ways. As a teacher at heart, my personal quest for truth has compelled me to invest in others the things that God has given me. In the process, I learn all the more. What a pleasure it's been to see God radically change human lives through this learning/teaching/learning cycle!

I've also been blessed to network with other Christians who are pursuing God and His truth. And while no two people agree on everything, many of us have arrived at the same basic understanding of who God is and how He works. One specific truth has prevailed through this experience: *people are separated when they champion ideologies, but the pursuit of truth causes hearts to converge in unity.* How much of our worldly conflict would simply vaporize if more people valued truth over their personal agendas?

The pursuit of truth is by no means arbitrary. To gain God's perspective, we all start with our necessary *TouchPoint*—the Bible—where we can connect with our Creator and better understand His mindset. Our passage from Isaiah 55 continues with:

"For as the rain and the snow come down from heaven,
And do not return there without watering the earth
And making it bear and sprout,
And furnishing seed to the sower and bread to the eater;
So will My word be which goes forth from My mouth;
It will not return to Me empty,
Without accomplishing what I desire,
And without succeeding in the matter for which I sent it."
Isaiah 55:10-11

What a powerful reality for us to grasp! God speaks into our human realm to accomplish specific plans and purposes according to His desires. We all have opinions, but accurately discerning God's eternal truth goes far beyond personal agendas and natural thought processes. Biblical interpretation, then, is never a matter of human opinion or intellect, but of *revelation* and *illumination* from the sovereign King of the Universe.

It's not worth splitting hairs, but these two concepts—revelation and illumination—while closely related, can sometimes differ slightly. Jesus, for example, was revealed from heaven as the Son of God, but not everyone's eyes were illuminated so as to recognize the fullness of His identity.

On the road to Emmaus, as He explained the seemingly bizarre story of His death and resurrection, a fascinating occurrence took place:

> *When He had reclined at the table with them, He took the bread and blessed it, and breaking it, He began giving it to them. Then their eyes were opened and they recognized Him; and He vanished from their sight. Luke 24:30-31*

This passage is huge! Jesus was speaking to two disciples who knew Him well—and who had been immersed in practically every facet of His life—but their spiritual vision was still lacking. Until the risen Christ opened their eyes to see, these faithful followers remained blind to the essence of His marvelous work on earth. Continued reading in the same chapter shows a similar occurrence with the other disciples. In flesh and blood, the King of kings and Lord of lords walked and talked with them, and yet, they could not see or understand the fullness of His person. Right there! He was right there! They saw, but they couldn't see.

Similarly, the Biblical text is pregnant with life, but we won't see or experience that life apart from God's enabling. Spiritual blindness is our "default mode" (see John 3:3). Not until the Holy Spirit opens our eyes and shines His light into our hearts are we able to see God's spiritual reality. A person can read the same Bible verse a hundred times over and get almost nothing out of it. Then, one day those words will suddenly burst from the page, and the individual will be forever changed.

Furthermore, truth often has multiple layers. As we "peel back" each layer, we begin to understand that there is more depth to God's truth than previously realized. Probably, hundreds of thousands of sermons have been preached from the Bible, and yet, its supply of insight is never exhausted. At the same time, apart from God's illuminating grace, the combined power of human intellect barely scratches the surface of Biblical wisdom.

I once watched a television show in which a couple of thieves robbed a train and stole a safe full of money. No matter how hard they tried, they couldn't open the thick steel door. A few sticks of dynamite blew the heavy vault into the air, after which it dangerously fell back to the ground still closed tight. Rather than kill themselves trying to get the cash, the frustrated bandits finally gave up trying.

Practically anyone can glean wise sayings and noble ideas from the Bible, but knowing God's mind is an entirely different matter. Spiritual truth belongs to the eternal King; all of the force and intelligence of humanity cannot unlock the mysteries of His written Word. An intimate understanding of His ways comes only as the One who inspired the Bible reveals and illuminates, layer by layer, His reality.

At that time Jesus said, "I praise You, Father, Lord of heaven and earth, that You have hidden these things from the wise and intelligent and have revealed them to infants. Yes, Father, for this way was well-pleasing in Your sight. All things have been handed over to Me by My Father; and no one knows the Son except the Father; nor does anyone know the Father except the Son, and anyone to whom the Son wills to reveal Him." Matthew 11:25-27

Talk about an affront to the human ego! Considering these words in their context, we realize that *intellectual pride*—not a lack of intelligence—is the primary barrier to knowing God's ways. When our confidence rests in our own cranial ability to figure out God's truth, we are in trouble. I cannot state this point strongly enough: *our own intellectual arrogance is the uncrackable lock preventing us from deciphering the mysteries of the Bible.*

Unfortunately, neither can proud hearts admit their desperate need for help. More often than not, rather than coming to grips with our spiritual blindness, like frustrated and disgruntled bandits, we assail the Bible as an outdated and nonsensical book, held in esteem only by intellectual morons. Such attitudes, though, only intensify—if that's at all possible—our blindness.

When it comes to understanding the Bible, the state of a person's heart matters *more* than the capabilities of his or her mind. Heaven knows how hard I've tried to figure God out and how badly I've failed. It's not that we're called to embrace ignorance and become mindless zombies, but that we must come to grips with the fact that God operates on a level beyond our natural reach.

Our world is full of intellectually brilliant people who don't have a clue about God's ways because their highbrow attitudes undermine their ability to understand. Try as they might, they can never truly grasp God's wisdom. Comprehension of truth comes by way of revelation and illumination—not by intellectual prowess. A measure of mental capability is needed to understand the Bible, but intellect alone will never suffice. Spiritual truth must be revealed and illuminated by God, and He will divulge His mysteries only to those who esteem their value.

THE MYSTERY OF PARABLES

Have you ever wondered why Jesus frequently spoke in *parables*? The common answer is that the Son of God used such stories so that people could better understand spiritual concepts. But that is only part of the picture! Consider carefully the following quote taken from the parable of the sower as recorded in Matthew 13:

> *And the disciples came and said to Him, "Why do You speak to them in parables?" Jesus answered them, "To you it has been granted to know the mysteries of the kingdom of heaven, but to them it has not been granted. For whoever has, to him more shall be given, and he will have an abundance; but whoever does not have, even what he has shall be taken away from him. Therefore I speak to them in parables; because while seeing they do not see, and while hearing they do not hear, nor do they understand. In their case the prophecy of Isaiah is being fulfilled, which says,*
>
> *'YOU WILL KEEP ON HEARING, BUT WILL NOT UNDERSTAND;*
>
> *YOU WILL KEEP ON SEEING, BUT WILL NOT PERCEIVE;*
>
> *FOR THE HEART OF THIS PEOPLE HAS BECOME DULL,*
>
> *WITH THEIR EARS THEY SCARCELY HEAR,*

AND THEY HAVE CLOSED THEIR EYES,
OTHERWISE THEY WOULD SEE WITH THEIR EYES,
HEAR WITH THEIR EARS,
AND UNDERSTAND WITH THEIR HEART AND RETURN,
AND I WOULD HEAL THEM.'"
Matthew 13:10-15

Why did Jesus say He spoke in parables? Both to reveal *and* conceal truth. The Son of God often employed parables as "screening tools" to separate casual onlookers from passionate seekers of truth.

"Now, wait a minute!" you may be thinking. "Didn't you claim that God wants us to know His ways?" He absolutely does, but our Creator also values wisdom as *eternal treasure*. He will not entrust such wealth to those who treat gems like dirt. (Have you ever lent out a valuable item and had it returned ruined?) Herein, we uncover a primary reason we are encouraged to seek after God and the knowledge of His ways.

To whom did Jesus reveal the mysteries of truth? His disciples. What do we know about His disciples? They not only believed in Jesus as the Christ, they sacrificially sought after Him. In contrast, who received His parables as little more than nice stories? The crowds. And what do we know about the crowds? They followed Jesus from a distance, drawing near mostly to receive benefits such as healing, deliverance, and food. The disciples paid a price to know Jesus while the crowds, mostly motivated by self-interest, did far more receiving than giving.

How do we show that we value God's truth? Mostly by how we respond to it. Heaven's eyes search for people who are hungry for truth, who value what God says and are willing to humble their hearts. If we ignore this dynamic of heavenly wisdom, the comprehension of eternal truth will remain forever sealed in an impenetrable vault.

A HEART TUNED TO HEAVEN

King David is one of the most beloved persons in the Old Testament. David was no saint—to put it mildly—but he loved God deeply. Consider his following words from Psalm 138:6:

THE TOUCHPOINT

For though the LORD is exalted,
Yet He regards the lowly,
But the haughty He knows from afar.

This verse cuts against the grain of our natural thought. As humans, we regard celebrities and ignore—or even despise—the lowly. If I go to a professional ball game, it's not the grounds crew whose autographs I stand in line to receive. In contrast, God cares nothing about a person's fame or ability; humility is what excites His heart.

Many of us are familiar with the story of David and Bathsheba (2 Samuel 11). One evening, when his army was out to war, David walked out onto his roof and spied a beautiful woman, Bathsheba, bathing. Overcome by desire, the king sent for and slept with the woman even though she was married to Uriah—one of his most faithful and valiant warriors. Bathsheba conceived. Unable to convince the loyal soldier to sleep with his wife during a time of war, David engineered the circumstances to have Uriah killed in battle. The drama was nothing short of soap operaesque.

Not until confronted by the prophet Nathan did David at last own up to his horrid sin. Still, even through a moral failure of epic proportions, David oriented his heart toward the Lord:

For You do not delight in sacrifice, otherwise I would give it;
You are not pleased with burnt offering.
The sacrifices of God are a broken spirit;
A broken and a contrite heart, O God, You will not despise.
Psalms 51:16-17

As terrible as David's actions were, his story shines hope into many a darkened soul. If religion were simply about meeting moral standards, King David's name would be etched in infamy; no number of sacrificial offerings could have atoned for his actions. But David knew something about God that many of us miss—the sovereign King of the Universe will never despise a humble heart. A sinful act need not be the end of a person, but stubborn pride will be. If we are willing to humble ourselves and confess our waywardness, God is willing to forgive and embrace.

The state of the heart means *everything* to God. Consequently, our attitudes deeply affect our ability to understand the Bible. Spiritual blindness is preserved through a hardened heart marked by a complex mix of pride, callousness, stubbornness, and unbelief (see Ephesians 4:17-18). I find it nearly impossible to know where one "anti-virtue" ends and another begins. A hard, prideful heart is not only desensitized to knowing God's ways, it also resists the various workings of His Spirit. Blended into the mix is an inability—or unwillingness—to trust Him.

Especially deceptive is the fact that we can be in the middle of God's work and still be out of step with His ways. Consider the following passage from the book of Hebrews:

Therefore, just as the Holy Spirit says,

"TODAY IF YOU HEAR HIS VOICE,

DO NOT HARDEN YOUR HEARTS AS WHEN THEY PROVOKED ME,

AS IN THE DAY OF TRIAL IN THE WILDERNESS,

WHERE YOUR FATHERS TRIED ME BY TESTING ME,

AND SAW MY WORKS FOR FORTY YEARS.

THEREFORE I WAS ANGRY WITH THIS GENERATION,

AND SAID, 'THEY ALWAYS GO ASTRAY IN THEIR HEART,

AND THEY DID NOT KNOW MY WAYS';

AS I SWORE IN MY WRATH,

'THEY SHALL NOT ENTER MY REST.'"

Take care, brethren, that there not be in any one of you an evil, unbelieving heart that falls away from the living God. But encourage one another day after day, as long as it is still called "Today," so that none of you will be hardened by the deceitfulness of sin. Hebrews 3:7-13

This passage is quite unpleasant, but rather than ignoring its challenging message, we would do well to heed the warning. Not only should we carefully guard our hearts against hardness, we need to work hard to create safe and uplifting church environments for those who might be wavering in their faith. Preventing hardened hearts is an endeavor that succeeds only through a combination of individual and corporate effort.

I would never suggest that a church relax moral standards to accommodate the surrounding culture. At the same time, we all struggle to live in victory over sin. I can't imagine where I would be today if I didn't have the support of loving people during seasons of extreme vulnerability. At the same time, I can't help but wonder how many others have walked away from the Christian faith because of a church environment that resembled a mixed martial arts ring more than a triage center.

THE MISSING PIECE

Imagine working on a giant jigsaw puzzle that represents all we need to know about walking with God and living on earth. Depending on where you are in your Christian experience, the picture may be mostly complete, mostly empty, or somewhere in between. As we stand gazing at the puzzle, two primary realizations begin to emerge.

First, we see how interconnected everything is. For some, this is a major revelation in itself. Well into my Christian experience, I attended church, listened to messages, and read books without developing a firm grasp of the "big picture." I knew truths but didn't see their connection to one another. I can't pinpoint the exact timing, but one day it dawned on me that concepts such as faith, grace, love, and humility are not isolated ideas; instead, they are intricately related. "Lord, help me see how these things fit together," became one of my prayers.

Second, looking at our mega-puzzle, we realize that pieces are missing. But it's not a completely lost type of missing. In fact, the pieces are sitting right beside the puzzle. For some unknown reason, though, these "missing" pieces aren't being used. We might call them *virtual* pieces; we know they exist, but live like they don't.

I was born and raised in Pennsylvania—also known as *The Keystone State*. The nickname has multiple layers. As residents, we like to remind everyone that Pennsylvania played a crucial role in the founding of our nation. My perspective of the title, however, has always been a little different. I grew up near the site of the old Allegheny Portage Railroad, and *arch* bridges were part of the historical landscape. At the top of each arch rested a uniquely shaped keystone that held everything together. Remove the keystone, and the entire bridge would collapse.

More often than not, a humble and tender heart is the keystone conspicuously missing as we try in vain to assemble the puzzle we call Christianity. We read about humility in the Bible and readily agree on its importance, but all too often, we give the concept little more than lip service. (How we love to rail against those who disagree with our viewpoints!) Humility is not only desirable, it is *necessary* for those who seek to walk with God and comprehend His ways.

The writer of Hebrews 3:7-11 was quoting Psalm 95, which tells of God's frustration with the exodus generation of Israelites that refused to believe His promises, dying in the wilderness as a result. In the NASB version of the Bible, verse 10 of Psalm 95 reads, "For forty years I loathed that generation, and said they are a people who err in their heart, and they do not know My ways." Ouch! When it comes to knowing and honoring God, ignorance is *never* bliss.

Notice that the letter to the Hebrews was written to *Christians*. Yes, it's possible even for a Christian to become hardened as he or she lives by the old fleshly nature rather than by the Spirit of God. If we truly want to connect with God, we must prepare our hearts. There is no way around it. Let's not delude ourselves; the state of a person's heart makes a huge difference when it comes to knowing God and understanding spiritual truth.

Christians who are involved in the political arena should take special note of this issue. Seeking to influence government for the sake of righteousness is indeed noble, but to be consumed by the nasty mindsets of political "warfare" is spiritually deadly.

WRITABLE HEARTS

Understanding the nature of a hardened heart may help to illuminate some of our personal struggles. We humans are a hard-headed lot, and sometimes we need to be softened up a bit before we realize how life really works. All too often, though, we get caught up in our circumstances and fail to realize that there are underlying currents in just about every situation. Regardless of how adversity comes into our lives, God often allows it to help prepare our hearts so that we can better connect with Him. Unfortunately, the same situation meant to soften and bless us can also result in our hardening. The difference lies in how we respond.

These concepts are worth pondering. In practically every difficulty, two opposing dynamics create an uncomfortable tension: *the powers of evil work to harden us while God seeks to soften us.* If our faith is weak and we fail to see God at work, we're likely to yield to the darkness. This single truth is worth the weight of this book in gold—and more! If we can grasp the importance of this vital issue, it will change our perspective of difficult—and even unjust—circumstances.

I began learning about the dangers of a hardened heart in the early 1990s. Since then, I've encountered dozens of situations—some fairly extreme—that tempted me toward hardness and unbelief. There were undoubtedly times when, instead of trying to prove my rightness and significance, I should have been cultivating faith and humility. Thankfully, I've grown along the way, but the struggle against a hardened heart has been far more rigorous than I ever anticipated.

Stepping out of the apparent security of a career in the field of chemistry, I began to navigate an uncertain future through various avenues of ministry. Along the way, I have at times felt neglected, overwhelmed, and even betrayed. During my journey, I've watched other people in ministry navigate similar spiritual terrain—and I've seen many of them become jaded and cynical. A person with amazing potential would fizzle like a fuel-spent rocket as faith was lost and another well-intentioned heart hardened.

I think we often fail to understand that the same qualities that make a heart open to receive God's truth also make it "writable." What I mean is that Christianity is not about obeying lists of rules. God seeks to write His laws *on our hearts* so that we can live from the inside out:

"FOR THIS IS THE COVENANT THAT I WILL MAKE WITH THE HOUSE OF ISRAEL

AFTER THOSE DAYS, SAYS THE LORD:

I WILL PUT MY LAWS INTO THEIR MINDS,

AND I WILL WRITE THEM ON THEIR HEARTS.

AND I WILL BE THEIR GOD,

AND THEY SHALL BE MY PEOPLE.

AND THEY SHALL NOT TEACH EVERYONE HIS FELLOW CITIZEN,

AND EVERYONE HIS BROTHER, SAYING, 'KNOW THE LORD,'

FOR ALL WILL KNOW ME,

FROM THE LEAST TO THE GREATEST OF THEM.

FOR I WILL BE MERCIFUL TO THEIR INIQUITIES,

AND I WILL REMEMBER THEIR SINS NO MORE."

Hebrews 8:10-12 (ESV)

While the Ten Commandments—representative of the old covenant law—were recorded on tablets of cold, hard stone, God's new covenant law of love is engraved on malleable human hearts (Exodus 34:1-27 and Hebrews 10:16). Only on humble, tender hearts will our Savior write His *royal law of liberty* (James 1:25 and 2:8) and instill a motivating passion to impact our world. If our hearts aren't writable, it's impossible to make the gospel fully applicable. How many lives would be radically changed if more people understood the importance of this dynamic?

Spiritual insight never flourishes due to status, intelligence, education, or pedigree, but because hearts are humble, tender, and believing. Those people who "get it"—who truly understand the gospel and abide in God's life-giving grace—will walk with their heavenly Father and set an example for the ages by living out of His passions. For them, the mysteries of God create no sense of angst, but of awesome wonder.

CHAPTER WRAP-UP

The God who created the cosmos functions on a plane entirely different from our own. Thankfully, He wants to draw us near to Himself through the revelation and illumination of His ways. The issue is not so much of intellectual ability as it is the state of our hearts. "For though the Lord is exalted, yet He regards the lowly, but the haughty He knows from afar" (Psalms 138:6). If we can lay hold this eternal reality, the Creator of all things will open our eyes to an unseen world!

3

PREPARING OUR HEARTS

The condition of an enlightened mind is a surrendered heart.

—Alan Redpath

Watch over your heart with all diligence,
For from it flow the springs of life.

Proverbs 4:23

There are times when life can seem terribly unjust. Such was the case during my teenage years. I hated almost everything about my earthly existence. Our housing project neighborhood, life on the edge of poverty, my lack of athletic ability, and a dysfunctional home all contributed to my misery. By the time I turned sixteen, a hard, multi-layered crust had formed over my heart. Only God's grace, as expressed through the influence of a few caring people, kept me from traveling far down the roads of crime and substance abuse.

When the loving Lord of the Universe finally apprehended my heart, it resembled an old beat up car that needed major investments of time, money, and labor just to make it usable. But our Creator, I discovered, is more than a master mechanic seeking to restore beat up junkers; He is a *heavenly Father* who delights in making broken people whole. It's difficult for some people to grasp in our dysfunctional world, but *loving* and *giving* are two words that describe true fatherhood best.

God immediately began to work on softening my heart, and I didn't like it one bit. My hardness, you see, was intentional. I had erected walls of self-protection in a futile effort to avoid further emotional pain. Problematically, the same walls that promised protection also kept me imprisoned in misery. As the King of Heaven began to take His rightful place in my heart, I instinctively knew that those walls had to come down. More often than not, demolition must precede reconstruction, and on an emotional level, the process is rarely pain free.

THE REAL BATTLE

We want to think that people and circumstances are our enemies, but the Bible communicates a different story. In his letter to the Ephesian church, the apostle Paul penned the following:

Finally, be strong in the Lord and in the strength of His might. Put on the full armor of God, so that you will be able to stand firm against the schemes of the devil. For our struggle is not against flesh and blood, but against the rulers, against the powers, against the world forces of this darkness, against the spiritual forces of wickedness in the heavenly places. Ephesians 6:10-12

As much as we prefer to think only angels and cute little cherubs populate the spiritual world, reality speaks differently. Fallen angels—the Devil and his foul demons—seek to corrupt and destroy all that is good. The existence of dark forces is sometimes difficult to comprehend, but we can develop at least a basic understanding of their tactics.

Demonic spirits—our true enemies—forever seek to corrupt our ability to see and understand God not only by enticing us to sin, but also by hardening our hearts. At the same time, and often through the very same circumstances, our heavenly Father seeks to soften us so that He might disclose a precious and unique understanding of Himself.

As I began to grasp the true nature of the battle for and within my heart, the importance of faith became all the more evident. Unbelief and hardness, I discovered, go hand-in-hand. What choice did I have but to somehow, even if haltingly, walk out the life that my heavenly Father was calling me to experience?

The full blessings of God don't mystically sprinkle over our lives simply because we attend church or respond to a call to receive Jesus as our Savior. The Christian life begins with a decision to fully embrace God's will and receive His forgiveness, but that is only the first of many steps to be taken in a heavenly direction. The richness of the Christian life, with all of its meaning, purpose, and love, only increases as we align our hearts with God's eternal design through even the darkest of times.

The Bible provides us with many valuable things—inspiration, direction, correction, wisdom, perspective, etc.—but most of all, the Bible is the *TouchPoint* where we connect with our Creator. I refer to a coveted place of intimacy to which none of us entirely arrives on this side of heaven. Ironically, the more significant our challenges, the greater the potential for a deeper revelation of God's heart and character. Leave it to our Creator to bring life, glory, and hope out of adversity, heartbreak, and pain.

Concealed within every trial is an opportunity to grow and draw nearer to the God who loves us. Our real battles in life aren't against people or circumstances but against the influences that would harden and corrupt our hearts. Thankfully, we can take several practical steps to prepare our hearts so we can draw nearer to God and better understand His ways. The following list is by no means comprehensive, but provides a good start in the transformational process nonetheless:

1. **Be honest.** The first move toward favorable change almost always begins by honoring one specific virtue—*honesty*—and more specifically, *self-honesty*. The Greek orator Demosthenes once said, "Nothing is easier than self-deceit. For what each man wishes, that he also believes to be true." The always thoughtful Soren Kierkegaard later followed with, "There are two ways to be fooled. One is to believe what isn't true; the other is to refuse to believe what is true."

   Honesty about oneself is the first step toward humility. The starting point for all of us, then, is to humble our hearts by admitting that we don't see as we should. Getting started is really that simple, even though it may not be easy.

Why do we so frequently lie to ourselves? Pain. On almost any level, dealing with the reality of our human brokenness is rarely pleasant, and acknowledging personal fault or failure cuts like a knife through the heart of a proud person.

Bringing this concept into the overall context of this book, I've met people who are antagonistic toward the Bible primarily for personal reasons. A rotten childhood, hypocritical role models, and the loss of a loved one are just some of the reasons people use to justify their hatred of all things Christian. In reality, these issues have little to do with the Bible and everything to do with misguided perceptions of God. Simply acknowledging this fact can be a significant step in the right direction.

2. **Choose to value God's truth.** Truth will cost a person, at times exacting a considerable price. Far too often, we want the positive changes that come with Biblical truth, but aren't willing to pay the price that truth may require. In a world where public opinion establishes the order of the day, truth is often regarded as toxic sludge. Consequently, the few who wholeheartedly pursue truth risk sacrificing the temporal quality of their lives as they seek after something greater than this world can offer.

At some point, a person must ask, "Do I genuinely want God, or am I just looking for a better life?" Jesus didn't promise a better life (by human standards), but He did promise divine blessings. The problem is that a blessed life doesn't always fit our definition of "better." Do we truly value the words spoken by Jesus, or do we silently ignore the truths that are less than convenient?

> *"Blessed are those who have been persecuted for the sake of righteousness, for theirs is the kingdom of heaven.*
>
> *Blessed are you when people insult you and persecute you, and falsely say all kinds of evil against you because of Me. Rejoice and be glad, for your reward in heaven is great; for in the same way they persecuted the prophets who were before you."*
> *Matthew 5:10-12*

At least four different times (Matthew 11:15, 13:9, 13:43, and Luke 14:35), Jesus said, "He who has an ear, let him hear." Similarly, toward the close of each of the seven letters in Revelation 2-3, He added, "He who has an ear, let him hear what the Spirit says to the churches." What was Jesus implying? *Not everyone who wants to follow God is willing to accept the difficult things He says.*

Are we willing to admit when we are wrong? Are we willing to exchange earthly success for eternal blessings? Are we willing to be hated by people we love for no reason other than our pursuit of truth? We don't always know what truth will cost us, but taking the time to contemplate the potential price of loving truth is a wise course of action. Life altering decisions won't be quite as difficult if we make them *before* they have to be made.

3. **Ask.** In many ways, seeking truth involves asking. We ask God to open our eyes and teach us His ways; we implore Him to soften us and cleanse our unbelief. Some such requests may spawn anxiety in our hearts because we can't control how God answers, but we should ask regardless.

In addition, we must ask questions about what we read and what we are taught. Sadly, in some Christian circles, this type of approach is often viewed as adversarial. I'm not suggesting that we become antagonists who bombard pastors with hard-nosed challenges, but that we search the Scriptures to confirm the Biblical accuracy of church teachings. Real spiritual learning always involves thoughtfully contemplating what's being taught in light of Scriptural truth.

> *The brethren immediately sent Paul and Silas away by night to Berea, and when they arrived, they went into the synagogue of the Jews. Now these were more noble-minded than those in Thessalonica, for they received the word with great eagerness, examining the Scriptures daily to see whether these things were so. Therefore many of them believed, along with a number of prominent Greek women and men. Acts 17:10-12*

God's kingdom operates by faith, but that doesn't mean we blindly accept anything taught in the name of Christ. I see a distinct difference between asking questions to understand an issue better and launching a doubt-driven attack. If we are to delve deeper into God's realm, asking questions must become a way of life. Let's ask, however, with open and not stubborn hearts, with graciousness and not jadedness, with humility and not a sense of entitlement.

I can't guarantee that every question will be answered in a satisfactory manner—some mysteries are reserved for eternity—but I can promise that God will reveal more than enough if we passionately seek Him with humble hearts.

4. **Fully surrender your will to God.** Although the dynamics are very different, the general principles of grasping God's truth are the same for Christians and non-Christians. Both involve an essential surrender of the will. This, at least in part, is why wisdom is as much a matter of the heart as the intellect.

A Christian has the Holy Spirit dwelling in his or her heart; therefore, the "mind of Christ" is already present in any true believer (1 Corinthians 2:16). In a very real sense, we are starting from a place of privilege. Still, even a Christian can become hardened, so the state of our hearts always matters regardless how far we progress in our spiritual journey.

The non-Christian, on the other hand, is at a distinct disadvantage. The lack of a personal relationship with God leaves a person running blind. I can remember a time in my early exploration of Christianity when a friend and I were trying to understand a passage from Ephesians. The text seemed stupid to our skeptical hearts. Mysteriously, I read that same passage after becoming a Christian and couldn't believe that I hadn't understood it sooner.

> *Jesus answered and said to him, "Truly, truly, I say to you, unless one is born again [born from above] he cannot see the kingdom of God." John 3:3*

54

If an understanding of the Scriptures comes through a personal relationship with God, and you lack such a relationship, what are you to do? What if you want to dig deeper into the Christian faith, but aren't quite ready to take the plunge—to fully surrender your life to Jesus as both Lord and Savior?

Begin by realizing that God wants you to know Him and His ways, but that it has to be on His terms. On the day that you create your own universe, you can set your own conditions, but for now, God is the one who gets the final say. I suggest that you posture yourself by asking Him to open the eyes of your heart to see and understand His truth. From what I have seen and experienced, as long as a person is willing to move forward with an honest desire, God will reveal His truth in limited measures.

You can expect, eventually, to reach an impasse where you must decide between your will and His will. Such a crisis point is unavoidable. The natural bent of the human heart always runs against the grain of God's ways. If you want to know and experience kingdom reality, a prayerful surrender of your will is *necessary*. Ideally, this would happen at the time of salvation when you come to acknowledge His truth and yield yourself fully to Him. Some of the most miserable people on earth are those who profess to seek God's will while living for their own.

God will lead you to His saving grace in His time, and I won't pressure you with the process. I will say, however, that if you reach a place where you refuse to respond to what He reveals, your forward progress will stop until you become willing—if you get that opportunity. We are the ones who are debtors. The Creator of the Universe owes us nothing—not even the opportunity to embrace His eternal truth.

The first real surrender is usually the most difficult. I say "first" because yielding to God's will can never be a one-time experience; it must become a way of life. Again, the Bible will only yield its treasures when we approach it on God's terms. The King of kings and Lord of lords is not stubborn or selfish, but neither is He ever wrong. The sooner we come to accept this reality, the better off we'll be.

5. **Forgive others.** On a surface-level, our hearts harden quickly. All it takes is for someone to look, talk, or act the "wrong" way (by "wrong" I mean virtually anything we find disagreeable), and we develop an immediate dislike for that person. Even though this type of hardness may be relatively minor, the long-term cumulative effect adversely impacts our spiritual well-being.

I enjoy watching professional football—U.S.A. football, not the "real" football (i.e. soccer)—and being that we live near Pittsburgh, the Steelers are my team of choice. Donning the mantle of a Steelers' fan generally means embracing a strong dislike for the archrival Baltimore Ravens. What a dilemma I face upon hearing that a despised Raven is a faithful Christian! It's equally difficult to learn that a respected friend in Christ champions the Ravens. Thankfully, I don't have many friends who are fans of the New England Patriots.

Take a few seconds to think about people or sports teams you strongly dislike. Why do you feel this way? This type of disdain is so natural that it almost seems weird to question. If you secretly—or not so secretly—hope that a hated player will break a leg, how do you reconcile your attitude with God's love?

Taking the concept of hardness deeper, the effort by various groups—on both sides of the political spectrum—to shape public opinion involves the creation of maligned stereotypes we are then conditioned to despise. Thus, every religious conservative is cast as a hateful and extremist homophobe while every practicing homosexual must be a militant God-hater.[1] No doubt, these characterizations hold true for small numbers of people, but on a broader scale, the practice of stereotyping for political purposes tends to harden those who swallow the lie.

---

1. The term "conservative" can mean many things. We must be careful to distinguish between *theological* conservatives (my predominant emphasis in this book) and *political* conservatives. While there is often overlap between the two groups, I see more and more of a divergence developing.

On a deeper level still, we can become terribly bitter when someone unjustly (or perceived as so) harms us or our loved ones. The greater the loss or pain inflicted, the more difficult it is to let go of the offense. And while the pain may be quite real, refusing to forgive the perpetrator(s) only serves to hinder any potential for healing.

Bitterness, on any level, is a form of control that will, without question, harden our hearts. If we genuinely want to know God's ways, forgiving others—regardless of how deep the offense goes—is *never* optional (Matthew 18:21-35). If we value God's wisdom, we will value what God values. And God always values people—even the most despicable.

As much as I want to believe differently, professing Christ as Lord and Savior is not a magic antidote against the plague of bitterness. I've struggled at times to forgive, and I've watched many more faithful servants of Christ succumb to the wily temptation of an embittered heart. Forgiving may take some time, but God always provides the necessary grace.

Finally, be advised, the Bible is a dangerous tool in the hands of a bitter person. In the name of redemption, he or she will wield the sword of God's Word to hack people's lives to pieces. God doesn't call us to be mad at the world but to reconcile precious lives to Himself.

6. **Regardless of who caused the initial offense, attempt to reconcile broken or strained relationships.** If we want to walk with God and know His ways, we can never ignore the unjust hurt we may have inflicted on others (Matthew 5:23-24). There are, therefore, times when we need to humble ourselves and ask others for forgiveness. Connections with family members and other Christians are especially important.

Sometimes, people take offense at us through no fault of our own. For the sake of love and unity, we should do what we can to reconcile the damaged relationship. We don't need to apologize for wrongs we haven't committed, but we can humbly initiate honest discussion. "I feel terrible that things aren't better between us," might be a good place to start.

I won't paint an unrealistic picture by claiming that our efforts toward reconciliation will always meet with success. To be honest, I've had both positive and negative experiences. Some situations have worked out beautifully, others not so well. We can't control how a person will respond to our reconciliatory efforts, but we can honor God and align our hearts with His design by doing our part to put things right.

7. **Fast and pray.** If we truly want to ramp up our insight into God's Word, searching the Scriptures while fasting and praying for wisdom and understanding can be an exciting step to take. There is something about fasting (with the right motives) that sensitizes our hearts to receive from God's Spirit. Ideally, this should be done at a time when we also put aside unnecessary distractions (e.g. TV, social media) to more effectively pray and draw upon God's Word. Modified "Daniel fasts" (meats, sugars, and other foods are avoided) have also become increasingly popular.

For some people, fasting is an amazing experience. Others may experience little more than misery while attempting to deny fleshly appetites. In all likelihood, a rich flow of life will come later. Many times I have fasted with little recognizable benefit. Still, I persisted in my fast and cried out to God for a deeper understanding of His ways. Then, just as I returned to my normal routine, kaboom! It was as though the heavens opened and God began to flood my heart with insight like never before.

I don't entirely understand why, but fasting provides a powerful avenue by which we can gain a deeper understanding of God's ways. Certain medical conditions and eating disorders may be exacerbated by fasting food, so it's wise to pick up a good book *and* consult your medical expert on the subject before trying it yourself. For those who are able, fasting can be nothing short of life-changing!

EFFECTIVE DIALOGUE

Many of us care deeply about people who, due to the hardness of their hearts, are far from God. Reconciling others to Christ often requires a combination of wisdom and a multifaceted approach. Accordingly, understanding the dynamics of spiritual hardness will go a long way in helping us reach loved ones with the reality of God's love.

Regardless of outward appearances, many people are looking for answers. They want to know if God is real, and if so, what He's all about. They want to know the meaning of their existence, why things are the way they are, how they can overcome their issues, and how they can help to make the world a better place. Those of us who are Christians can play a powerful role in helping them.

Sadly, some of the outreach efforts done in the name of Christ needlessly harden people, thus increasing their resistance to God's life-changing gospel. If we truly want to help others connect with God, we must exercise wisdom in dealing with their hearts as well as our own.

People tend to be repulsed by dogmatic attitudes. Arguing for a set of beliefs that no one is allowed to question almost always proves counterproductive. Sadly, I've met more than one professing Christian who seemed more concerned about proving how right he was than about the soul of the person to whom he was "witnessing."

Over the past two centuries, we've seen Christian scholarship rise to new heights in combating widespread antagonism against the Bible. *Apologetics* is the word that we use to describe this type of effort. It comes from the Greek word, *apologian,* which means "to speak on behalf of oneself or of others against accusations presumed to be false— 'to defend oneself.'"[2]

> But sanctify Christ as Lord in your hearts, always being ready
> to make a defense [apologian] to everyone who asks you to give
> an account for the hope that is in you, yet with gentleness and
> reverence. 1 Peter 3:15

---

2. Johannes P. Louw and Eugene Albert Nida, *Greek-English Lexicon of the New Testament: Based on Semantic Domains* (New York: United Bible Societies, 1996), 437.

Notice that Peter includes "with gentleness and reverence [respect]" in his exhortation to make a defense of our Christian beliefs. This passage speaks of genuine humility combined with a profound respect for God and man. Why does Peter add these qualifications? When dealing with issues of religion and intellect, we're often tempted to become arrogant and argumentative—both of which are counterproductive to advancing God's purposes on earth.

Effective outreach doesn't flow from our simply being right; it involves presenting Biblical truth with hearts of love and in a Christ-like manner. Do we need accurate *theology* (the study of God)? Absolutely! But without a loving heart, our supposedly sound doctrine crumbles like dry bread crumbs stuck in the bottom of a well-used toaster.

Hardened attitudes, I believe, have significantly undermined the mission of the church in recent years. The mere accumulation of knowledge, no matter how good that knowledge may be, tends to inflate our pride, subsequently alienating others from the true substance of our message (see also 1 Corinthians 8:1). If those of us who profess Christ genuinely care about introducing others to our Lord and Savior, we will strive to boldly present truth while treating those who oppose us with gentleness and respect.

A LIFE-CHANGING EXPERIENCE

An experience on Halloween night of 1991 forever changed me. Having been invited to a student club meeting of the "Freezone" on the campus of Indiana University of Pennsylvania (IUP) for a "discussion" about the occult, I was one of three panelists representing a Christian perspective. Three other members were advocating for paganism and witchcraft. The bulk of the audience consisted of college students—many of whom held strong views opposing the Christian faith.

As I sat down at the table next to a practicing Wiccan, I felt the Holy Spirit prompt me to pull out her chair as a courtesy. Even though the young woman's lifestyle was in many ways at odds with God, He still wanted to express His love for her through me. Much to my regret, I was so intimidated by the near-overwhelming nature of the experience that I quietly ignored His promptings.

The meeting began, and I listened intently as each panelist presented his or her opinion on the matter. It wasn't long before a sense of disappointment settled into my heart. Recognizing the edgy attitude of the audience, the other two Christian panelists carefully sidestepped the primary issue at hand. In the end, they spoke well but provided few substantive arguments. And while I don't seek to antagonize people intentionally, I also understand that we can't help others without the risk of offending them.

When my opportunity to speak arrived, I explained that the Bible strictly forbids involvement with the occult because of the spiritual damage that it does. My comments were straightforward, but by no means harsh. Even so, it was as though I lobbed a smoke bomb into a hornet's nest! During the question and answer session that followed, a long line of students formed to state their opinions and to ask questions—or more appropriately—to *demand* answers. Not only was the hostility evident, their adversarial sights were zeroed in on one specific person—*me!*

Most of the interaction remains blurred in my memory, but I can still recall one particular blond girl screaming at the top of her lungs. Evidently, I was being hateful for claiming that involvement with the occult is dangerous. Surprisingly, I wasn't the least bit unnerved—a minor miracle considering I'm not a very public person and certainly not confrontational.

Drawing upon God's amazing grace, I did my best to address, gently and lovingly, each person's questions and concerns. That—and a bunch of friends' prayers—managed to take the edge off of the crowd. Genuine and meaningful dialogue began to follow, and the previously hostile crowd soon became inquisitive.

Do you know what happened in the midst of the discussion? The young lady beside me—the one dressed in black who had presented the case in favor of witchcraft—started asking me sincere questions about my Christian faith. In spite of my earlier failure, the Holy Spirit was doing a powerful work in her heart! What an odd sight that was—one panelist publicly questioning another in an honest search for answers.

My Halloween experience at the Freezone initiated a long involvement with campus ministry at IUP. And as part of my outreach efforts, I later began to consistently attend the weekly Freezone meetings. Another breakthrough came when, utilizing volunteers from several different churches, we organized and provided a mouth-watering Thanksgiving dinner at about the time the students were salivating for home cooking. The event became an annual tradition and opened many doors for honest and effective dialogue about spiritual matters.

I'll never, this side of heaven, know the full fruit of that Halloween night on the IUP college campus, but I will always remember how God's love quieted and touched a group of belligerent young people. Their actions typified rebellion, but they just wanted to be heard and loved. Since that time, I've often wondered how many more of them are out there. On the surface, they oppose the Christian faith, but deep down, they're just looking for something of genuine substance in which they can believe.

If my own heart had not been properly prepared that evening, my message would have never found its mark. Not only does God seek to mold our hearts for our own benefit, He also wants to make His children more effective in reaching out to others. Effective dialogue isn't just about *what* we say; it's also about *how* we say it. The attitudes that seep through our actions really do matter, and they matter *a lot.*

CHAPTER WRAP-UP

God's ultimate desire is for all people to know Him and His ways. Therefore, as Christians, we are compelled to guard and prepare our hearts so that we can more effectively receive His truth. I'm not claiming any sort of inability on God's part, but rather the importance of aligning ourselves with His design.

If we want to know God and His ways, we must begin by preparing our own hearts. If we want others to embrace fully the truth that we so deeply value, we cannot help but present truth in a wise, humble, and loving manner. Unless we learn how to reach our religious and political enemies through attitudes and methods that reflect the love of Christ, we will lose the battle for the coming generations—no matter how right our opinions and beliefs may be. Hardness of heart is the order of the day in our tit-for-tat world, and the only way for the cycle of hardness to be broken is for the people of God to jump off of the hard-hearted unmerry-go-ground. If we can't "talk religion or politics" without becoming angry, something inside us is off-kilter.

An amazing world of insight and wisdom surrounds us, and the God who created the cosmos longs to lavish His eternal riches upon precious human souls. Knowing Him is not a matter of intellect, title, or pedigree, but of aligning our hearts with His eternal design. The Creator of all things wants all people to know His ways, but that can happen only on His terms—through humble, tender, and believing hearts.

THE TOUCHPOINT

4

THE AUTHORITY OF THE SCRIPTURES

What is truth? said jesting Pilate, and would not stay for an answer.

—Francis Bacon

"Your word is truth."

John 17:17b

You've probably seen them—those nicely dressed missionaries from the Church of Jesus Christ of Latter Day Saints. I would also guess that many of us close the doors and step away from the window as we spy them working their way through the neighborhood in an attempt to convert others to Mormonism. I guess I'm not like most people. If the local "elders" (they're usually rather young) happen to show up on a day when I have time, I'll engage in dialogue. Although, past conversations have at times been lively, they've never gotten heated. Mormons are usually very nice people, and I've never had a time when they disrespected me.

Interestingly, Mormonism teaches that God the Father was once a man like any other man. But by purifying Himself, the Father rose to a place of supremacy over His own unique cosmic sphere. There's an old Mormon saying that states, "As man is, God once was. As God is, man may become." Mormons further believe that Jesus and Lucifer were God's children—"spirit brothers," if you will. Jesus, we are told,

65

was chosen to become the God of our planet Earth, which made Lucifer intensely jealous. Such envy led him to oppose Christ and receive a new moniker, *Satan*, which means "adversary."[1]

Although Mormonism claims to be "the Church of Jesus Christ," these beliefs blatantly oppose what the Bible teaches. To my frustration, Mormon missionaries don't like to talk about such issues, so by the time we reach this level of discussion they're looking for a polite way to exit the conversation.

If the missionaries choose to continue, I'll sometimes steer the conversation toward the Book of Mormon's lack of credibility. This issue is also out of bounds, and so the young elders will usually counter by presenting what I call, "The Mormon Challenge." They'll go on to explain that knowing the truth of Mormonism does not come by human reason, but by divine revelation. Thus, the only way for me to grasp the Book of Mormon's spiritual significance is not to examine its credibility, but to ask the Holy Ghost, "Is the Book of Mormon true?" Invariably, one of the guys will say that God "warmed his heart" when he lifted up this prayer, and so no amount of reasoning will ever convince him otherwise. Conversation over. "Have a nice day!"

Both Christians and Mormons place significant emphasis on the importance of spiritual illumination. Subsequently, the question at hand involves identifying the *source* of that illumination. As we'll soon explore, Jesus said that the Holy Spirit would guide His followers "into all truth" (John 16:13). However, learning to discern how the Spirit works and speaks is a *subjective* process. One person might feel that the Spirit is saying one thing and another the opposite. Therefore, we also need *objective* standards of truth that stand on their own merits regardless of personal opinions.

Christian tradition esteems the Bible as *the* objective standard of spiritual truth, and though certain parts of the Bible are cloaked in mystery, many of its primary teachings are clearly communicated. We don't find any wiggle room, for example, in identifying greed as being offensive to God (Colossians 3:5).

1. Johannes P. Louw and Eugene Albert Nida, *Greek-English Lexicon of the New Testament: Based on Semantic Domains* (New York: United Bible Societies, 1996), 829.

We are hard pressed to find a point of contact between God and humanity that is more important than the Bible. Upon it, Christianity rises or falls. Attempts to "recreate" Christianity apart from Scriptural authority tend to be expressions of humanism more than divine inspiration. Consequently, the Bible is the primary *TouchPoint* for all who seek to connect with our Creator. Without the Book of books, what would we know of the Christian faith?

Our next step is to explore the Book's authoritative nature. If we are to walk with God and align with His ways, we need a basic understanding of who He is and how He thinks. And because an overwhelming number of ideas about God exist, we find ourselves adrift without a reliable way to navigate the often-contradictory waters of human opinion. In this, the Bible is uniquely qualified to stand as the *authoritative standard* for objective truth by which all spiritual ideas are measured.

THE WORD OF GOD

A *word* is a means of communication. The Bible teaches that Jesus was the *Word of God incarnate*—that is the expressed intelligence of God embodied in human flesh.

In the beginning was the Word, and the Word was with God, and the Word was God. He was in the beginning with God. John 1:1-2

Jesus is the living Word of God (John 1:14). He is the One we worship and serve. In a very real sense, the Bible is our written expression of "the Expression." We often call the Bible the "Word of God," which is entirely appropriate. However, the Bible is not God—we won't find the angels of heaven singing praise to a book sitting on a throne. The point being that a person can highly esteem the Scriptures without ever developing a relationship with the God who inspired their writing. How easy it is for the well-meaning Christian to see the Bible as an end in itself!

Herein, the mystery of the Bible is compounded. How, exactly, are we to explain the Word of God as written text on a printed (or digital) page? Truth be told, I'm not sure any of us can entirely grasp this mystery. Still, we can build a foundation for understanding the written Word based on what the Bible says about itself.

All Scripture is inspired by God and profitable for teaching, for reproof, for correction, for training in righteousness; so that the man of God may be adequate, equipped for every good work.
2 Timothy 3:16-17

All Scripture is "inspired by God"—that is *God-breathed.*[2] On a rare occasion, God audibly spoke to a person who recorded the conversation (e.g. Moses and the burning bush in Exodus 3:1-6). At other times, an eyewitness passed along a historical account of our Creator's dealings with humanity (e.g. the Gospel of John). And probably most often, the Holy Spirit mysteriously spoke to a human heart to communicate an intended message (e.g. the New Testament letters). Regardless of the methodology used, God Himself was the source of the inspiration.

In short, the Bible is authoritative because God is the highest authority in the universe. Therefore, those who wish to question the authority of the Scriptures must first begin by questioning whether or not they recognize the authority of God to rule over human affairs. What a sticking point this is! For the person unwilling to yield to divine authority, no amount of evidence will make the Bible credible.

If we choose to reject God's sovereign authority, the Bible becomes a story of brutality on one end of the spectrum and a buffet of proverbial wisdom on the other. We freely pick and choose whatever delights the spiritual palate. But if we recognize the absolute sovereignty of God, our task is to determine whether or not the Bible—and the Bible alone—stands as the written expression of God's authority over human matters.

Words such as *authoritative* and *absolute* cause many in our Western cultures to cringe, but as much as we may dislike these concepts, our lives are built on shifting sand apart from them. Is it possible that our unwillingness to embrace theological certainty is directly linked to the rising tide of anxiety now enveloping our world?

The heavenly Father is absolutely devoted to His children, and in this we find comfort and security. If not for the Lord's unwavering faithfulness, in what can we trust? In our world's economies? In our

---

2. Robert L. Thomas, *New American Standard Hebrew-Aramaic and Greek Dictionaries: Updated Edition* (Anaheim: Foundation Publications, Inc., 1998).

human governments? In our friends? In ourselves? Every source of human "security"—including ourselves—will eventually let us down in one way or another. God is the only true "rock" to which the human soul can anchor during uncertain times (Psalm 18:1-3). We can work to do away with absolutes if we want, but we'll find ourselves anxious and alone in the end.

THE STANDARD FOR SPIRITUAL TRUTH

When Jesus walked on earth, the term *Scripture* referred to the *Hebrew Bible*—what many now call the *Old Testament*. To the Jewish religious mind, the Scriptures had been given by God and were highly esteemed as integral to Jewish life. A similar mindset then characterized the early Christian church that was primarily Jewish in its origins. The following quote states the importance of the Hebrew Bible well:

> From start to finish, the New Testament contains quotations, references, allusions and paraphrases of the Old Testament. Sometimes the New Testament follows the Hebrew text; in other cases it more closely follows the translation into Greek of the Old Testament called the Septuagint.[3]

The writers of the New Testament (NT) drew upon the authority of the Old Testament (OT) hundreds—if not thousands—of times. Sometimes they quoted almost verbatim from the original Hebrew and sometimes from the Greek Septuagint. Also, they routinely paraphrased passages or simply alluded to the Jewish Scriptures that were central to their cultural practices.

As highlighted by the following passages, the New Testament writers held true to the Son of God's attitude toward the sacred Scriptures. When beginning His ministry, Jesus used the book of Isaiah to identify Himself:

> *And the book of the prophet Isaiah was handed to Him. And He opened the book and found the place where it was written,*

---

3. Rich Robinson, "Jesus' References to Old Testament Scriptures," *Jews for Jesus* website (San Francisco: © 2015 Jews for Jesus, May, 2008) http://www.jewsforjesus.org/publications/newsletter/september-2008/05 <February 11, 2016>

"THE SPIRIT OF THE LORD IS UPON ME,

BECAUSE HE ANOINTED ME TO PREACH THE GOSPEL TO THE POOR.

HE HAS SENT ME TO PROCLAIM RELEASE TO THE CAPTIVES,

AND RECOVERY OF SIGHT TO THE BLIND,

TO SET FREE THOSE WHO ARE OPPRESSED,

TO PROCLAIM THE FAVORABLE YEAR OF THE LORD."
Luke 4:17-19

Later, when bringing a heavy hand of correction upon the Pharisees, the Son of God contrasted the importance of the Scriptures as opposed to man-made theological constructs:

And He answered and said to them, "Why do you yourselves transgress the commandment of God for the sake of your tradition?" Matthew 15:3

The time Jesus tangled with the Devil in the wilderness also speaks volumes. Interestingly, both of them employed the Jewish Scriptures in their spiritual wrestling match:

Then Jesus was led up by the Spirit into the wilderness to be tempted by the devil. And after He had fasted forty days and forty nights, He then became hungry. And the tempter came and said to Him, "If You are the Son of God, command that these stones become bread." But He answered and said, "It is written, 'MAN SHALL NOT LIVE ON BREAD ALONE, BUT ON EVERY WORD THAT PROCEEDS OUT OF THE MOUTH OF GOD.'"

Then the devil took Him into the holy city and had Him stand on the pinnacle of the temple, and said to Him, "If You are the Son of God, throw Yourself down; for it is written,

'HE WILL COMMAND HIS ANGELS CONCERNING YOU';

and

'ON their HANDS THEY WILL BEAR YOU UP,

SO THAT YOU WILL NOT STRIKE YOUR FOOT AGAINST A STONE.'"

Jesus said to him, "On the other hand, it is written, 'YOU SHALL NOT PUT THE LORD YOUR GOD TO THE TEST.'"

Again, the devil took Him to a very high mountain and showed Him all the kingdoms of the world and their glory; and he said to Him, "All these things I will give You, if You fall down and worship me." Then Jesus said to him, "Go, Satan! For it is written, 'YOU SHALL WORSHIP THE LORD YOUR GOD, AND SERVE HIM ONLY.'" Then the devil left Him; and behold, angels came and began to minister to Him. Matthew 4:1-11

These passages—and many others—convey a mindset that characterized the sovereign Son of God and, therefore, the early church. The Jewish and early Christian cultures considered the sacred Scriptures to be more than suggested reading for a happier lifestyle; they represented rock-solid standards for truth and guidance in practically all facets of life.

The idea of spiritual truth as a sort of fuzzy uncertainty was entirely foreign to all that Jesus said and taught. The Son of Man spoke with a sense of confident authority that few—if any—others possessed (see Matthew 7:29 and Luke 4:31-32). Jesus lived as though He understood truth, as though the Scriptures set the standard for truth, and as though He had the right to proclaim truth. *Never* do we find the Word of God in human flesh communicating the idea that a vague sense of belief is the best we can hope to attain.

TRUTH AS AN EXPRESSION OF REALITY

Some people argue that it doesn't matter what we believe about God as long as we believe. Such a statement may carry a noble air, but it fails to mesh with reality. If God is merely the product of human thinking, truth can be anything we want it to be. But if God is whatever we want God to be, then truth and divinity are nothing more than the creative fruits of our own human imaginations. Let's not be duped—reality is what it is regardless of what we think. Furthermore, the burden falls upon us to align our lives with that reality.

My office sits adjacent to our local university, and I think our street holds the town record for the number of cars that get "booted" due to unpaid parking tickets. For those unfamiliar with the terminology, a *boot* is a large metal contraption that local authorities lock onto the front wheel of a car so that it can't be moved until all outstanding fines are paid. I usually feel bad for the owners of the booted cars, but on one occasion, I laughed out loud. While a bright orange metal boot secured the front wheel, a rear bumper sticker—with a picture of Albert Einstein—read, "Imagination is more important than knowledge."

If I read it right, Einstein intended these words to open minds to a reality beyond our limited field of knowledge. When taken out of context, however, Einstein's ideas can be used as a weak excuse to justify our personal perspectives through the use of imagination. But all of the creative thinking in the world wasn't going to free that young lady's car until she aligned herself with the reality of our local governing authorities by paying her parking tickets. How much more must we align our lives with the expectations of the sovereign God who created the entire cosmos?

That which seems appealing and reasonable in the classroom doesn't always translate into real life. For example, let someone steal everything you own, destroy your reputation, and kill every person that matters to you. Then, in your hurt, anger, and frustration, try embracing the idea that absolute justice is nothing more than an old-fashioned ideal. To claim that there are no absolutes is nothing short of absurd.

The fact that we can use human imagination to create virtual realities does nothing to negate reality itself. If I choose to deny, albeit creatively, the existence of gravity and walk off the edge of a cliff, my lack of respect for natural laws will cost me dearly.

In a similar vein, our beliefs do nothing to invalidate the unseen spiritual reality around us. Time will eventually make God's existence clear, but we don't have the luxury of waiting until after death to make that discovery. If our Creator is a real entity with a real personality—as many of us contend that He is—our beliefs will have good and bad consequences depending on how they align with His absolute reality.

As challenging as it may sometimes be to understand the Bible, trying to navigate our unseen spiritual world without its sacred text will put us at odds with forces far more powerful than we can begin to fathom.

WHICH GOD(S) IS SOVEREIGN?

The dynamics of religious belief are generally built around the issue of *sovereignty*. At stake is the recognition of who has the highest level of authority, determining what is and isn't morally acceptable—or if morality even matters.

Essentially, we can condense the issue of sovereignty to one of four primary options:

1. The Christian God is sovereign.
2. The God of another belief system is sovereign.
3. Multiple Gods are sovereign.
4. Humans are sovereign.

The effort to determine which of these four options is true amounts to nothing more than seeking to discern the unseen reality surrounding us. At the core of our quest is the search for *truth*. We're not trying to support personal belief systems; we're seeking to understand the reality of God and the true nature of our existence.

One of our more significant errors, and one that fosters division of all sorts, is that we tend to argue in favor of our individual ideologies rather than pursuing truth. I am a Christian, not because I believe in an ideal, but because I have found the Bible to be true.

In studying the life of Jesus through the Gospels, I see that His ideology flowed out of an emphasis on truth—not the other way around. Faith, according to Jesus, was not a blind belief in a spiritual ideal, but a confident trust in a very real—albeit unseen—God. Our quest at hand, then, is to discover which deity is the real God.[4] We can authenticate such truth, however, only as we exalt the pursuit of truth above our individual and community preferences.

---

4. In the coming chapters, I provide several arguments supporting the credibility of the Bible, and thus, the sovereignty of the Biblical God.

Some people, of course, reject the authority of a monotheistic God, instead embracing the concepts of religious pluralism that contend either there are many gods, or all paths ultimately lead to the same God. At the risk of offending those who may disagree, basic logic compels me to reject this option.

If God is real, He is who He is regardless of what any of us believes. Furthermore, God, by His very nature, is the highest authority in the universe. If two differing perceptions of God contradict one another, at least one of them must be wrong. Once again, ideas that sound noble and reasonable in a classroom or coffee shop cannot possibly translate into reality. They are ideas, while reality is, well, reality. If God exists, He is the highest authority in existence, and no amount of human imagination, speculation, or manipulation is going to make Him anything less.

Finally, the idea of human sovereignty is nothing more than wishful thinking. Humanity plays a minuscule role in our massive cosmos. We are all subject to forces and laws beyond our control, and in this sense, there is no such thing as a person controlling his or her destiny. Any one of us might die tomorrow of a heart attack. Or the stock market could crash and throw the world's financial systems in chaos. Or maybe an asteroid will come out of deep space and destroy the entire Earth. God invested us with authority to make our own decisions and control our own actions, but beyond that, we are much more subject to external forces than we care to admit.

That we have honest questions about God and the Bible is understandable. But the human condition involves much more than some unanswered questions. We are a prideful lot, wanting to rule ourselves with no divine interference—unless our definition of divinity is embodied within ourselves. The quest for control is almost always at the center of our human conflicts, including religious controversies. Many of the moral issues we struggle with in Western culture can be boiled down to an intense struggle for human sovereignty because we innately detest the thought of being accountable to an authority higher than ourselves. In the end, choosing to reject the authority of the Bible because we want to control our own lives will reap a pitiful harvest of painful consequences.

GOD—ACCORDING TO THE BIBLE

The Bible teaches that the God who created all things is the *supreme authority* of all that exists. *No* human or supposed deity has the power or right to question His eternal authority. None. Sooner or later, each of us will go to the grave, and eventually, the fateful day will arrive when the eternal Judge calls every thought, word, and deed into account. We can kick, scream, and pout all we want, but the clock continues to tick, and we are powerless to keep the hands of time from moving forward.

The idea of a sovereign God accountable to no one might sound scary to some, but it doesn't have to be. Perhaps we've seen too many movies with super-powered villains motivated by twisted egos. Because our Creator is righteous, just, and characterized by love, we can rest assured that everything He does will be good—even if certain issues don't make sense at a given moment. Furthermore, we have the opportunity to seek God, to learn His truths, and to align our lives accordingly. Only when we stubbornly persist in our own selfish and prideful ways should the idea of an all-powerful Creator become truly frightening.

I do not expect you, the reader, to take my word on the matter of God's supremacy. That's an issue that you'll have to explore for yourself. I simply seek to present a perspective of reality that once eluded me. We all own the rights to our individual opinions, but what we believe doesn't change the truth of who God is. Allowing myself to accept this realization has radically changed the course of my life.

INSPIRED, INFALLIBLE, AND AUTHORITATIVE

Spiritual truth is an expression of spiritual reality, and it is on the basis of such a reality that we establish the authority of the Bible. If the Creator of the Universe is truly sovereign, the authority of His Word far surpasses anything said or written out of human reasoning. John 10:35 records Jesus saying that "the Scripture cannot be broken." In a sense, Jesus was stating, "This reality cannot be altered." In Matthew 5:17-19, the Son of God communicates the same message more forcefully:

"Do not think that I came to abolish the Law or the Prophets; I did not come to abolish but to fulfill. For truly I say to you, until heaven and earth pass away, not the smallest letter or stroke shall pass from the Law until all is accomplished. Whoever then annuls one of the least of these commandments, and teaches others to do the same, shall be called least in the kingdom of heaven; but whoever keeps and teaches them, he shall be called great in the kingdom of heaven." Matthew 5:17-19

If you ever wonder why so many Christians make such a big deal about the significance of the Bible, herein lies your answer. Jesus treated the Scriptures with the highest regard. His followers did the same. If we want to walk with God, we'll follow carefully their well-worn path.

For this reason, orthodox Christians contend the Bible to be the *inspired, infallible,* and *authoritative* Word of God to which all of humanity is subject.[5] If the Bible is not inspired by God, then it's just another expression of human ideas. But if, on the other hand, the Bible is the inspired written Word of God, all of humanity is accountable to its teachings. Once again, Christianity rises or falls upon the inspired nature of God's written Word.

The following three statements help lay the foundation for this all-important claim:

1. **The Bible is *inspired* because it is God-breathed.** The Holy Spirit moved on human hearts to communicate eternal truth.

2. **The Bible is *infallible* because it cannot fail.** God has spoken through His Word for a variety of reasons—to give wisdom, to provide direction, to correct, to rebuke, to encourage, to instill hope, to prepare us for what lies ahead, etc. As individuals, we may not always understand what the Bible is communicating, but the Word of God will never fail to hold true in light of the purposes for which God sends it.

3. **The Bible is *authoritative* because the One who inspired it is the highest authority in the universe.** Consequently, we are *all*

---

5. By "orthodox," I refer not to the official Orthodox Church but as conforming to the historical beliefs that have been passed to us from the early church.

accountable to what the Scriptures teach. Spiritual truth matters, and the implications are eternal.

I freely admit that we face several challenges ascertaining and understanding the original text of the Scriptures, but that doesn't give us the freedom to pick and choose what we want to believe. Either the Bible is a humanly conceived fraud, or it is the inspired, infallible, and authoritative Word of God. Thus, we are compelled to either embrace the Bible as being inspired and authoritative or to reject its authority over our lives.

The Bible's authority is an issue that we must each settle for ourselves, and though the pressure of human opinion might compel us to believe differently, trying to avoid the matter gets us nowhere good. To reject the authority of the Bible is to reject the authority of God, and to reject the authority of God is to alienate ourselves from any meaningful relationship with the One who possesses all we need.

I fully realize that these are lofty claims and understand that some readers will bristle in response. There was a time when I felt similarly, but the more I sought to understand the Bible, the more my perspective changed. To be honest, what troubles me most is that some people might never wrestle with this issue. It breaks my heart when the Bible is dismissed as outdated and meaningless without its claims or credibility being fully investigated. A callous—or even casual—attitude toward the Scriptures will leave a person *outside* the sphere of a meaningful relationship with the Lord of all things.

INFALLIBILITY AND INERRANCY

One of the more formidable challenges we face regarding the Bible centers on the issue of *inerrancy*. People who embrace the authenticity of the Christian Bible often proclaim its inerrancy, but problematically, the term *inerrant* is easily misunderstood. Consequently, I prefer to speak of the Bible as being *infallible* rather than *inerrant*. The Word of God will never fail to accomplish the purposes for which God sent it.

The word inerrancy is generally utilized to mean that the *original texts* of the Bible were without error. Many people don't realize this and find themselves struggling with the numerous *differences and errors* (*variants*) found in manuscript copies. Moreover, it's easy to wonder how far the claim of inerrancy reaches. Were there no spelling or grammatical errors in the original writings? Several of the New Testament writers— Peter, for example—were mostly uneducated. I doubt that Peter's letters would have gotten A+ grades in a college writing class.

It's not that I think the Bible is full of errors, but that focusing on inerrancy creates unnecessary diversions. If our goal is to connect with God and ponder the core issues of life, we want to do our best to minimize distractions. I feel that avoiding the term inerrant and instead proclaiming the inspired, infallible, and authoritative nature of God's Word better helps us stay on point while avoiding peripheral issues.

We face a very real danger of being trapped in a "minutiae syndrome" of sorts. It happens when we think that the Bible's credibility depends on our ability to explain *every* difficulty that it presents. As a result, theological conservatives often try to resolve questions that can't be adequately explained and argue points that lead to fruitless controversy. In the process, not only is their credibility undermined, they also stray from the more central issues.

We might, as a case in point, get caught up in the difference between the statement in Matthew 27:32 that Simon the Cyrene was enlisted to help Jesus carry His cross, and John's seemingly intentional point that Jesus carried His own cross (John 19:17). The real issue at hand, though, is that Jesus was crucified on the cross for the sins of all humanity. If our focus is diverted by what may simply be a difference of perspective, we never come face to face with the most significant event (apart from Christ's birth) in history. In a similar vein, we can stress over how many angels the Gospel writers record as present at the empty tomb, when what truly matters is that Christ's grave was indeed *empty*.

The sovereignty of God, the divinity of Jesus, and the historical reality of the resurrection are the core issues that help us recognize the authority of the Scriptures. And when it comes to how we live, *faith*, *grace*, *love*, and *covenant*—not distracting arguments—stand out as the central concepts that I believe should occupy the bulk of our attention.

Sadly, I've watched scores of people fall by the spiritual wayside because they lost sight of what truly matters in the grand scheme of reality.

Obviously, it would be difficult to establish the infallibility of the Bible if the book were full of errors. In this regard, conservative scholars squarely place their understanding of inerrancy on the original text of the Bible which, to the best of our knowledge, no longer exists.

One of the better explanations I've seen regarding inerrancy comes from Brent MacDonald of Lion Tracks Ministries and reads as follows:

> God accurately had everything that He intended written down in a fashion that its meaning and intent would be preserved and transmitted to future generations including through translation into other languages. The emphasis is not on the exact words or even a particular spelling. Unquestionably the meaning and intent of the message has been carried to us—this is inerrancy in action.[6]

While Brent and I may sometimes disagree on semantics, we share common ground by esteeming the authority of the Bible as it flows from the intent of what God seeks to communicate. God's intent—not distracting controversies over minor issues—represents the true heart of the matter.

CHAPTER WRAP-UP

If you struggle to understand fully all that's written in the Bible, consider yourself part of a rather large fellowship. Furthermore, we can disagree as we seek to grasp various truths conveyed through the pages of the Bible, but a confident belief in the inspirational, infallible, and authoritative nature of our sacred text is integral to the Christian faith. Only after these things are set firmly in place can we effectively "hash out" the specific truths that God is communicating through various passages.

---

6. Brent MacDonald, Executive Director of Lion Tracks Ministries, (personal correspondence; June 6, 2015).

THE TOUCHPOINT

5

A BRIEF OVERVIEW OF THE BIBLE

No other work of man in any language even faintly resembles the intricate structure and design of the Bible. The fact remains—only an infinite mind could have devised this Book of books.

—Winkie Pratney

And according to Paul's custom, he went to them, and for three Sabbaths reasoned with them from the Scriptures.

Acts 17:2

We sometimes struggle to grasp the inspirational nature of God's written Word—the place where divinity and humanity meet to produce almost mystical results. "How," we wonder, "can God speak a perfectly accurate message through such imperfect people?" Peter, for example, proved at times to be a buffoon, and yet, the Lord of Heaven used him powerfully. Consider what Peter wrote about Spirit-inspired prophecy:

For we did not follow cleverly devised tales when we made known to you the power and coming of our Lord Jesus Christ, but we were eyewitnesses of His majesty. For when He received honor and glory from God the Father, such an utterance as this was made to Him by the Majestic Glory, "This is My beloved Son with whom I am well-pleased"—and we ourselves heard this utterance made from heaven when we were with Him on the holy mountain.

So we have the prophetic word made more sure, to which you do well to pay attention as to a lamp shining in a dark place, until the day dawns and the morning star arises in your hearts. But know this first of all, that no prophecy of Scripture is a matter of one's own interpretation, for no prophecy was ever made by an act of human will, but men moved by the Holy Spirit spoke from God. 2 Peter 1:16-21

I doubt that Peter realized his letters would one day be added to the sacred Scriptures. He did, however, understand that God spoke to and through flawed—and often uneducated—men to communicate eternal truth. The inspirational nature of the Bible is quite mysterious, I'll give you that. But if God is indeed the source of its inspiration, the Bible is more than the work of mortals, and understanding its content is never simply a matter of human interpretation.

When it comes to God's written Word, we must remember that the power, intelligence, and perfection of our all-powerful Creator supersede any measure of human imperfection. God inspired the authors of Scripture to write, and consequently, He is able to open the eyes of our hearts as we read and study. The process, while seemingly imperfect, is highly relational—and that is what the Bible is all about.

OBJECTIVITY VERSUS SUBJECTIVITY

God has gifted us with the Bible so that we might know and relate to Him. Its pages overflow with spiritual truths that transcend our human opinions. But because many Biblical concepts—such as salvation by faith as opposed to works—are shrouded in mystery, it falls upon us to seek an accurate understanding of what our Creator intends to communicate through the Scriptures. In doing so, we forever strike a delicate balance between the *objectivity* and *subjectivity* introduced in the previous chapter.

During my years in the field of chemistry, the importance of objective scientific investigation became ingrained in my thinking. Subjective opinions play a necessary role in developing scientific thought and exploration, but real scientific fact is established in the realm of unbiased experimentation, testing, and verification.

Surprising to some, when it comes to objective truth, science and theology are quite similar. Both fields involve a focused effort to understand the reality around us. The difference—and I acknowledge that it's a big one—is that *science* focuses on the realm of our *natural* existence while *theology* focuses on an unseen, *supernatural* (*spiritual*) reality. Because God is a spiritual Being who operates beyond our natural senses, theology often has a subjective feel—even though the spiritual reality surrounding us may be of a higher order and greater permanence than our physical reality. More specifically, if an unchangeable God created our constantly changing universe, then a powerful realm lies beyond the physical world that captivates our natural senses.

Not everyone appreciates science, but we're all bound by some basic scientific principles. I've already used the existence of gravity as an example; those who attempt to ignore the law of gravity generally don't live long and prosper on this earth. Similarly, most people have formulated basic theological opinions that govern their day-to-day actions. But significant problems result when our perspectives of God are forged within the depths of our own human imaginations.

I once had a co-worker, Linda, who liked to tell me that God grew a little more loving with each passing day. Linda's life was out of control, but she still wanted to feel approved by God. The idea of a Savior who loved her a little more each day fit perfectly with her wild behavior, but it didn't come from the Bible. While failing to grasp the Biblical reality of God's perfect—and just—love, Linda's homegrown theology helped to foster a lifestyle that put her outside the sphere of God's blessing. Only after a personal trauma were her eyes finally opened.

Whether navigating the realm of science or theology, we face a significant need for objectivity because the ultimate goal is to allow reality (truth) to speak for itself. In either case, it's all too easy for us to skew our perception for personal reasons. Ego, money, emotional pain, and personal agendas of various sorts all can influence how we define or attempt to modify truth. And not only should we be aware of such biases, we also err when we fail to establish our personal subjective experiences within a framework of objective truth.

SKIN AND BONES

The human body provides an excellent illustration to help explain the relationship between subjectivity and objectivity. The adult body contains 206 bones intricately fit together to provide a person's basic shape. Built upon the objective framework of the human skeleton, we find subjective layers of muscle and skin. The skin is pliable and can be shaped with body piercings and such while the basic structure of the bones remains mostly fixed. Without the skeleton, the body would ooze along as a useless blob of flesh, but without the muscle mass and skin, it would resemble the lifeless displays found in medical classrooms.

Similarly, the Bible contains an objective framework of truth upon which we build our subjective experiences. Those who focus only on the objective truth of Scripture suffer the effects of a spiritually dry existence. But the ones who live only in the realm of subjective experiences and desires, fail to achieve the plans and purposes for which they were created. For our spiritual selves to be fully alive and fully functioning, we need to blend the dynamics of objective truth and subjective experience. Furthermore, if we want our subjective experiences to align with God's loving design, it's essential that we develop an accurate understanding of the objective framework of truth He has established for our benefit.

Most of us have watched a disturbing news report about a parent who killed his or her children because, "God said to do it." On what grounds do we claim such actions to be wrong? What justification do we have for committing the parent to jail or a mental institution? Murdering a child is wrong because it conflicts with the objective truth of Scripture—embodied by the Ten Commandments—which teaches us to value human life. The Holy Spirit is the *Spirit of Truth*, and as a general rule, the things we think we hear Him saying should align with the objective principles of His written Word.

THE BACKGROUND OF THE BIBLE

Our objective framework of Scriptural truth is established on a foundational level as we seek to understand the background of the Bible. Even though this process is not limited to studying the Scriptures themselves, it helps us grasp the bigger picture of what the Bible is all about. And because the readers of this book probably come from a wide variety of backgrounds, experience has shown that it's worth taking the time to start on a basic level.

The English word, *Bible*, finds its origins in the Greek term *biblos*—the name given to the spongy center of the papyrus reed once used to make a primitive form of paper (called *papyrus*) in Egypt.[1] An industry developed around the production of papyrus, and for centuries it was the dominant writing material used in the ancient world. Over time, the Christian Scriptures became known as *the books* and eventually *the Bible*. A massive number of people consider it to be *the Book*—or the *Book of books*, if you will.

In Old Testament times, a piece of reed was used as a measuring tool. The Hebrew word for reed (or rod), *kaneh*, was used originally to identify a measuring rod. It is from this Hebrew term that the Greek word *kanon* probably derived.[2] Eventually, the term *canon* "signified any standard by which anything could be measured, specifically, the standard by which the authenticity or spuriousness of a literary document could be evaluated."[3] The Hebrew and Christian Scriptures, then, include only ancient writings recognized by the covenant people of God as being *canonical* in that they alone set the standard for spiritual truth.

About forty different authors penned the Bible over a span of around 1,500 years. The first five books of the Bible, known as *the Pentateuch* (meaning "five-volumed"), usually are attributed to Moses as the writer. According to many conservative scholars, these books date from around 1440 to 1400 BC.[4] The last New Testament book, Revelation, was written by the Apostle John no later than AD 96.[5]

1. J. Harold Greenlee, *Introduction to New Testament Textual Criticism* (Peabody, MA: Hendrickson Publishers, 1995), 9-10.
2. Norman L. Geisler and William E. Nix, *A General Introduction to the Bible* (Chicago: Moody Press, 1986), 203-204.
3. Eugene H. Merrill, *An Historical Survey of the Old Testament*, 2nd Edition (Grand Rapids, MI: Baker Book House, 1991), 17.
4. *New International Version; Archaeological Study Bible: An Illustrated Walk Through Biblical History and Culture* (Grand Rapids, MI: Zondervan Publishing House, 2005), 2, 84, 155, 194, 252.
5. Ibid., 2043.

The writing of the Scriptures took place on three continents (Asia, Africa, and Europe) and utilized three languages (Hebrew, Aramaic, and Greek). Its diversity of authors came from the ranks of kings, government officials, priests, prophets, musicians, fishermen, shepherds, tax collectors, and doctors. Furthermore, the words of this amazing book were crafted in a wide variety of settings such as palaces, prisons, and tents, and in many different styles including poetry, law, prophecy, and historical narrative.[6]

That the Bible has any sense of continuity is powerful evidence of its validity. The more a person understands the Scriptures, the more he or she realizes they form a unified work. We don't study the Bible as a compilation of sixty-six different texts, but as *one* book intricately woven together by God Himself. The Book may have been penned by men, but the fact that its sixty-six distinct writings tell a single story reveals a source of inspiration beyond our natural world. The Bible's unified nature, historical accuracy, and overall manuscript support far outweigh what any other sacred text has to offer.

The Scriptures are comprised of two primary sections known as the *Old Testament* and *New Testament*. I feel the use of the word *testament* is quite unfortunate as it can foster a subconscious mentality that God has died and left us to follow His written will. When referring to the two major divisions of the Bible, the Hebrew word for testament, *berith*, is better translated as "covenant."[7] From a Biblical perspective, a *covenant* can be defined as "a binding pact or treaty between parties."[8] Thus, the Bible is not just a guide, but the primary *TouchPoint* for a real, loving, and devoted relationship with the living God who created us.

THE OLD TESTAMENT

The first few chapters of the book of *Genesis*—meaning "beginning"— tell the story of creation and the early history of humankind. The remaining thirty-eight Old Testament books focus on God's interaction

---

6. Josh McDowell, *The New Evidence That Demands a Verdict* (Nashville, TN: Thomas Nelson Publishers, 1999), 3-7.
7. Geisler and Nix, *A General Introduction to the Bible*, 21.
8. Elmer B. Smick, "282 הרב," ed. R. Laird Harris, Gleason L. Archer Jr., and Bruce K. Waltke, *Theological Wordbook of the Old Testament* (Chicago: Moody Press, 1999), 128.

with a man named *Abraham* (or *Abram*) and his descendants, and more specifically, the nation of Israel.

Jacob was Abraham's grandson, and God renamed him *Israel* (meaning "one who strives with God") after he wrestled with an angel and refused to give up (Genesis 32:24-32).[9] Jacob and his descendants were far from perfect (they did some pretty nasty things), but God favored Jacob's lineage because of the covenant relationship He had established with Abraham.

The thirty-nine books of the Old Testament, as listed in the Protestant Bible, are often broken down as:

- *The Law:* Genesis, Exodus, Leviticus, Numbers, and Deuteronomy (5 books)

- *History:* Joshua, Judges, Ruth, 1 and 2 Samuel, 1 and 2 Kings, 1 and 2 Chronicles, Ezra, Nehemiah, and Esther (12 books)

- *Poetry:* Job, Psalms, Proverbs, Ecclesiastes, and Song of Solomon (5 books)

- *The Major Prophets:* Isaiah, Jeremiah, Lamentations, Ezekiel, and Daniel (5 books)

- *The Minor Prophets:* Hosea, Joel, Amos, Obadiah, Jonah, Micah, Nahum, Habakkuk, Zephaniah, Haggai, Zechariah, and Malachi (12 books)

Ancient Jews divided the sacred Scriptures into only three sections—*the Law* (also known as *the Torah*), *the Prophets*, and *the Writings*. Today's Jewish Bible contains essentially the same content as the Protestant Old Testament but is broken into twenty-four books instead of thirty-nine.

The first two categories above (the Law and History) contain the historical framework of the entire Old Testament up to about 400 years before the birth of Christ. By reading the first seventeen books of the Bible, a person will get an excellent overview of Israel's story. Reading the other twenty-two books helps to fill in the details.

---

9. F. F. Bruce, "Israel," ed. D. R. W. Wood et al., *New Bible Dictionary* (Leicester, England; Downers Grove, IL: InterVarsity Press, 1996), 519.

It should be noted, however, that not all books—especially the last few contained in the History category—are in chronological order. Neither do the other three categories (Poetry, the Major Prophets, and the Minor Prophets) run along a rigid timeline. They all, however, fit within the time-frame of the Law and History sections.

The Law refers specifically to the giving of the *Mosaic law* and all of its tenets. This includes not only the Ten Commandments but also a sacrificial system to cover the sins of the people so that they could relate to God. Trying to understand and explain the primary purposes of the Law creates a significant point of tension between the Jewish and Christian faiths, as well as within the Christian faith itself. Jews have long believed that the obedience to the Law constitutes the primary means of *righteousness* (right standing with God). In contrast, the apostle Paul strongly contended that no human could live up to God's perfect standards (Galatians 3:24). Instead, Paul taught that the Law was a "schoolmaster" of sorts, put in place by God to point us toward the person of Jesus Christ.

Law breeds judgment, and so much of the Old Testament is riddled with punishment and retribution. Our repulsion to such activity is understandable, but we must be careful to note that the 613 commandments constituting the Old Testament law were never meant to write the end of the story. Sadly, one of the biggest mistakes people make involves trying to superimpose the Old Testament law-based mindset on the New Testament gospel. When it comes to walking with God and abiding in His grace, this is an error of epic proportions![10]

The Major Prophets are so called not because they are necessarily more important, but because the books are larger (for the most part) and have wider global implications. Accordingly, the Minor Prophets are shorter and tend to have a more limited focus.

The *Septuagint* was a Greek translation of the Hebrew Bible produced by Jewish scholars somewhere between 250 and 150 BC.[11] This Greek version of the Old Testament is sometimes identified by

---

10. For a much more detailed explanation of the essential distinction between law and grace, please refer to *The Divine Progression of Grace: Blazing a Trail to Fruitful Living* by Bob Santos
11. Geisler and Nix, *A General Introduction to the Bible*, 24.

the Roman numeral LXX (70). Legend has it that 70 (or 72) scholars individually produced identical translations over the course of 70 days. Despite questions about how it came into existence, various forms of evidence, including New Testament quotes of the Old Testament, suggest that the Septuagint was in widespread use during the time of Christ.

The *Apocrypha*—meaning "hidden" or "concealed"—are a group of ancient writings that often accompanied the recognized books of the Old Testament. These texts were at one time included in the Protestant Bible but in a separate section from the inspired books. The Apocrypha were officially added to the Catholic Bible in 1546 at the Council of Trent but later dropped from the Bible used by Protestants because the books lacked widespread support as being canonical.[12]

The Apocrypha usually include some or all of the following:

- 1 Esdras
- 2 Esdras
- Tobit
- Judith
- Additions to Esther
- Wisdom of Solomon
- Baruch
- Ecclesiasticus (Sirach)

- Letters of Jeremiah
- Prayer of Azariah and the Three Young Men
- Susanna
- Bel and the Dragon
- Prayer of Manasseh
- 1 Maccabees
- 2 Maccabees

Records show that Jewish leaders considered the Hebrew Bible to be a *closed canon* by no later than the third century BC.[13] They thought that God was finished speaking to His people apart from the Scriptures already recognized. But there was a problem with their perspective! Not only the Law, but all of the Hebrew Scriptures point toward the coming of Jesus as the Messiah—the anointed One of God. In one way or another, every Old Testament book steers us in the direction of Christ, leading us to the New Testament.

---

12. Ibid., 264-270.
13. Merrill, *An Historical Survey of the Old Testament*, 18-19.

THE NEW TESTAMENT

From a theological perspective, the New Testament stands out as the crown jewel of sacred writings; no other religious text rivals the power of the message contained within its pages. Included in its twenty-seven books are eyewitness accounts, theological instructions, and prophetic insights of various types:

- *Gospels:* Matthew, Mark, Luke, and John (4 books)

- *History:* Acts (1 book)

- *Paul's Letters (Epistles):* Romans, 1 and 2 Corinthians, Galatians, Ephesians, Philippians, Colossians, 1 and 2 Thessalonians, 1 and 2 Timothy, Titus, Philemon, and Hebrews (14 books)

- *General Epistles:* James, 1 and 2 Peter, 1, 2, and 3 John, and Jude (7 books)

- *Prophecy:* Revelation (1 book)

Many scholars believe that all of the New Testament books were written by Christ's original apostles or their close associates somewhere between AD 50 (Mark) and 96 (Revelation).[14] Being that Christ's ministry spanned from about AD 26-30, eyewitnesses to His crucifixion, resurrection, and ascension would have still been alive at the time these texts were recorded.

Matthew, Mark, and Luke are called the *Synoptic* Gospels because they provide very similar perspectives. In fact, these three records of the ministry, death, and resurrection of Christ share some common source material. Because the archaeological record is incomplete, scholars have no clear consensus on why this material came to be shared.

It's likely that the book of Acts—also written by Luke—originally was combined with the Gospel that bears Luke's name, only to be later separated so the four Gospels could be compiled together. Both Luke and Acts are replete with geographical and historical details—a large number of which have been verified through extra-Biblical sources.

---

14. *Archaeological Study Bible*, 1620, 2043.

Many of the seemingly odd names of the New Testament Epistles—
Corinthians, Galatians, Ephesians, etc.—refer to the geographic locations
to which they were sent. Corinth, Galatia, and Ephesus, for example,
were places to which the apostle Paul traveled and planted churches
during his missionary journeys. Accordingly, Paul wrote letters to
encourage, instruct, and correct the growing churches in these regions.
In time, early Christians circulated Paul's letters over wide geographic
areas.

Although we lack widespread consensus that the apostle Paul
wrote the letter to the Hebrews, the early church grouped it with Paul's
epistles. If not authored directly by Paul, it's quite possible that the Holy
Spirit inspired one of his close associates to pen this encouraging, albeit
challenging, letter.

Most of the New Testament books contain *prophetic* elements,
but the book of Revelation is prophetic in just about every sense of
the word. Most likely written by the apostle John toward the end of his
life, this mysterious work continues to captivate the attention of a wide
audience. Speculation abounds regarding how much of Revelation was
specific to the time in which it was written and how much relates to the
end of time as we know it.

Other books of that era claimed apostolic authorship and divine
inspiration, but over the years, the church gradually came to accept
only the twenty-seven books that now constitute the New Testament.
Our earliest definitive list of these books goes back to a document by
Athanasius dated to 367.[15] A process that began relatively early in the
second century finally culminated in 393 at the Synod of Hippo when
the organized church officially recognized the New Testament Canon.
Church leaders confirmed the matter four years later at the Third
Council of Carthage.[16]

The twenty-seven books chosen for the New Testament met some
challenging criteria. They had to be somehow connected with the
original apostles or Paul; their content had to be divinely inspired and

---

15. F.F. Bruce, *The New Testament Documents: Are They Reliable?* 5th Edition, (Downers Grove, IL: InterVarsity Press, 1960), 25.
16. McDowell, *The New Evidence That Demands a Verdict,* 24.

in agreement with the accepted Christian belief of the early church; and each book had to be in widespread geographic use over a long period. Consequently, the early councils did not establish the Canon but simply *confirmed* the New Testament books that the church at large had already come to recognize as God-breathed.[17]

Similar to the Apocrypha of the Old Testament, the *Pseudepigrapha* are a group of writings that were rejected from inclusion in the New Testament:

- Apocalypse of Peter
- Acts of Paul and Thecla
- Acts of Pilate
- Epistle to the Laodiceans
- Gospel of the Hebrews
- Gospel of Philip
- Gospel of Thomas

Critics often argue that books such as those listed above were left out of the New Testament for political and other manipulative reasons. Rejecting these writings from the Canon, however, had nothing to do with politics. They failed to make the cut simply because they didn't stand up to the strict tests of authenticity required by early church leaders.

> These books were written late by suspect authors who claimed to have had contact with the disciples. These works and many others never met the tests. Most include stories and material devoid of spiritual worth, no eyewitnesses and in contradiction with the sixty-six books of Scripture. A 'no-brainer' for the early church leaders.[18]

The entire Bible is now considered to be a closed canon because its content was approved by the sinless Christ or by men who personally knew Him and His teachings. Other writings, including modern ones, can help to illuminate the teachings of the Bible, but no additions can be made to the sacred Scriptures themselves.[19] Accordingly, the standard

17. Merrill C. Tenny, *New Testament Survey*, Revised by Walter M. Dunnett (Grand Rapids, MI: Erdman's, 1985; Leister, England: InterVarsity Press, 1985), 409-411.
18. Bill Donahue, *Foundations 101: How We Got Our Bible* (Downers Grove, IL: InterVarsity Press, 2000), 40.
19. We should note that the statement made by John in Revelation 22:18 was written specifically for the book of Revelation, although it is sometimes improperly quoted as referring to the entire Bible.

of Scripture is built upon the expressed intelligence of the sinless Son of God who once walked this earth.

THE VALUE GIVEN TO THE BIBLE

Throughout history, devoted followers of Christ invested their lives in the study, teaching, and transmission of the Scriptures. Without their valiant efforts, we would not have the Biblical resources—or even the Bible—that we do today. We are blessed to benefit from their countless hours spent in prayer, study, and research.

Copies of the Bible—called *manuscripts* (*MSS*)—were painstakingly produced by hand until Johannes Gutenberg invented the printing press somewhere around the year 1450. Until that time, over a span of almost 1,500 years, followers of Christ invested massive amounts of time, energy, and money to reproduce thousands of copies of the Bible.

Biblical manuscripts can be dated by a combination of factors including materials used, layout, writing style, and punctuation. Some of the earlier Greek manuscripts, for example, were written in an *uncial* script, entirely in capital letters with no spaces between words and sentences and with very little punctuation.[20] Early Hebrew had no vowels.

Somewhere around AD 1200, the Bible was separated into our modern chapters by Stephen Langton, a professor at the University of Paris who later became the Archbishop of Canterbury.[21] In 1445, Rabbi Mordecai Nathan completed a Hebrew Bible with numbered verse divisions.[22] For centuries prior, the Hebrew texts had been divided into verses marked only by spacing. In a format similar to Nathan's, Robert Estienne (Stephanus) published his 1551 Greek New Testament. Several years later, he used verse divisions in an English Bible.[23]

The invention of the first movable type mechanical printing press in the Western world proved to be revolutionary. For the first time,

---

20. Geisler and Nix, *A General Introduction to the Bible*, 352-353.
21. McDowell, *The New Evidence That Demands a Verdict*, 20.
22. Humphrey Prideaux, *The Old and New Testament Connected, in the History of the Jews, and Neighbouring Nations; from the Declension of the Kingdoms of Israel and Judah, to the Time of Christ*, Volume I (New York:Harper and Brothers: 1842), 227-228.
23. Geisler and Nix, *A General Introduction to the Bible*, 341, 451.

multiple copies of the Bible could be produced almost simultaneously. In fact, the first major book published by Johann Gutenberg and his associates was the beautiful *Mazarin Bible*—a Latin Vulgate translation that came off the presses in about 1456.[24] Producing the Bible cost Gutenberg dearly, and a related court case essentially bankrupted him. By the time he died in 1468, only a handful of people had recognized the innovative printer's immense contribution to society.

John Wycliffe—also known as "the Morning Star of the Reformation"—was incensed by the moral bankruptcy of many clergy. Seeking to make Scriptural truth available to the average person, Wycliffe spearheaded the translation of the Bible from Latin into the common English tongue. His New Testament was completed in 1380 and the Old Testament shortly before or after Wycliffe's death in 1384.[25]

Such translation efforts were often accomplished in the midst of tremendous opposition by government and religious authorities who sought to keep the common person ignorant and oppressed. Although they lived at an earlier point in history, those who sacrificed of themselves for the sacred Scriptures shared the timeless mindset of the great abolitionist Horace Greeley:

> It is impossible to enslave mentally or socially a Bible-reading people. The principles of the Bible are the groundwork of human freedom.

William Tyndale passionately believed that the Bible should be accessible to all people—a privilege not permitted by English law in Tyndale's day. Tyndale translated the New Testament into English from its original Greek and part of the Old Testament from its original Hebrew. Because of this and other "crimes against the Church," William Tyndale was strangled and burned at the stake in 1536.[26] Sadly, many Christians in our day remain unaware of the extreme price that faithful believers such as Tyndale have paid so we might have free and easy access to the Bible.

---

24. Will Durant, *The Story of Civilization: Part VI; The Reformation* (New York: Simon and Schuster, 1957), 158-159.
25. Geisler and Nix, *A General Introduction to the Bible*, 547.
26. William Byron Forbush, Editor, *Fox's Book of Martyrs* (Philadelphia: Universal Book and Publishing House, 1926), 176-184.

The seeds planted with Tyndale's blood soon sprouted and blossomed as his work became the basis for the King James Bible (KJV). Completed in 1611, this poetic translation of the sacred Scriptures has deeply touched people's lives for centuries.[27]

Today, Tyndale's dream has come to fruition. Many English translations of the Bible are readily available to the average person, and the Bible continues, by far, to be the best-selling book of all time. Also, in total or in part, the Book of books has been translated into over 2,800 of the world's languages. Countless lives have been transformed by the timeless treasures hidden within its pages!

THE COMMANDS OF SCRIPTURE

An objective framework of the Bible includes not only information about the Scriptures, but also—and more importantly—the *commands* of Scripture. We've already seen that a certain amount of the Bible is shrouded in mystery, but let's not lose sight that much of the book is rather straightforward. For example, regardless of what people do in the name of Christ, Jesus' command to love one another (John 13:34) can never be seen as optional. We are called to align ourselves with the government of God's kingdom by obeying His objective commands no matter how we feel at the given time.

Primarily because of its authoritative nature, the Bible is a controversial book. People wouldn't much care if the Scriptures presented obedience as a matter of personal discretion. *Optional* and *obedience*, however, are words that we *never* find connected to one another in the Bible. The sovereign King of the Universe has indeed given us personal freedom, but that freedom is mysteriously bound together with obedience. Our action—or inaction—carries with it long-term consequences.

CHAPTER WRAP-UP

The Bible is an amazing book! From its earliest existence, devout servants of God have invested their life-energies so that successive generations might have free access to the Word of God. William Tyndale is not

---

27. We should note that the KJV Bible is often referred to as the *Authorized Version* (*AV*) because it was authorized by the King of England—not because of a special stamp of approval from God.

the only one who paid the *ultimate* price so that we might know and understand the truth of God's saving grace. God forbid that we would ever treat His commands lightly or take the magnificent Book of books for granted.

If we are to truly know Jesus Christ—and thus reap the full benefits of a meaningful relationship with our Creator—we would do well to further establish our objective framework by examining the credibility of the Bible as the inspired, infallible, and authoritative Word of God. This we will endeavor to do in our next chapter.

6

INCREDIBLY CREDIBLE

We account the Scriptures of God to be the most sublime philosophy. I find more sure marks of authenticity in the Bible than in any profane history whatever.

—Sir Isaac Newton

Now these were more noble-minded than those in Thessalonica, for they received the word with great eagerness, examining the Scriptures daily to see whether these things were so.

Acts 17:11

For centuries, the institutional church ruled over some of the world's most influential governments; merely questioning the Bible's credibility could cost a person his or her life. Interestingly, it wasn't God who restricted the human freedom to question, but rather control-driven religious and political leaders who acted in the name of God. As the political stranglehold weakened, intelligent minds began to inquire about the inspirational nature of the Christian Scriptures.

By the 18th century, a simmering debate grew into a full-blown controversy centered in the Tübingen School in Germany. Scholars from this university formed a movement that became known as the "Higher Criticism." The general term *higher criticism* refers to a branch of literary study that investigates the origins of written texts in an effort to establish their validity. *Lower criticism*, on the other hand, works primarily within the text to reconstruct the original writing.

Because of the Bible's authoritative nature, it's only reasonable that it be thoroughly investigated by both higher and lower critics. We enter dangerous territory when mindlessly accepting religious writings that have eternal ramifications. I tend to take issue with those who proclaim the Bible to be the most important book ever written but who balk any time its credibility is called into question. We need more than someone's confident opinion if we are to put the full weight of our trust in the Christian Scriptures. Accordingly, both higher and lower criticism serve valuable roles—at least in principle—in helping to ascertain what the Bible is all about. In practice, however, the field of higher criticism often resembles a battleground more than a scientific arena.

A scholarly examination of the Bible's credibility is certainly warranted, but the Tübingen scholars went way beyond scholarship and essentially launched an all-out war on the integrity of the Scriptures. While the institutional church of the Dark Ages labored to keep the common person ignorant of Biblical truth, the Higher Criticism sought to destroy the Bible's credibility. It is one thing to search for truth with an honest heart; it's an entirely different matter to embark on a search and destroy mission. Make no mistake about it—the Bible's integrity has been assaulted viciously in recent centuries under the guise of objective scrutiny.

To destroy the credibility of the Scriptures is to cast aside divine accountability, thereby fostering human elitism. Once again, the state of the heart means everything. Embedded within human nature is an innately prideful desire to live independently from God. Consequently, humans become the highest authorities on the planet, and those with power, money, and ability begin to lift themselves above others. Thus, the absence of the Bible's influence eventually leads to social stratification and layer after layer of perverted justice.

Interestingly, the effect of the Higher Criticism has been both wonderful and terrible at the same time. While hostile critics of the Scriptures were emboldened, the long list of questions and theories proposed by the Higher Criticism also had a positive effect. When well-educated theologians called the historical reality of Christ's resurrection into question, for example, those who believed in the credibility of the Bible were compelled to respond. Digging deeper into the origins of its sacred text, they struck gold!

THE BIBLE STANDS TRUE

Advances in Christian scholarship in recent centuries have shown that believing in the validity of the Bible is by no means an act of intellectual suicide. The Bible has been scrutinized like no other historical document, but like an immovable rock battered by violent waves, it has stood the test of every storm.

> A thousand times over, the death knell of the Bible has been sounded, the funeral procession formed, the inscription cut on the tombstone, and the committal read. But somehow the corpse never stays put.
>
> No other book has been so chopped, knived, sifted, scrutinized, and vilified. What book on philosophy or religion or psychology . . . has been subject to such a mass attack as the Bible? with such venom and skepticism? with such thoroughness and erudition? upon every chapter, line and tenet?
>
> The Bible is still loved by millions, read by millions, studied by millions. It remains the most published and most read book in the world of literature. –Bernard Ramm

Voltaire, the French atheist, once proudly proclaimed, "In one hundred years the Bible will be an extinct book." A mere fifty years later the Geneva Bible Society was using Voltaire's house and printing press to publish Bibles! This same house later became the Paris headquarters for the British and Foreign Bible Society.[1] Voltaire wasn't the first person to proclaim the supposed end of the Bible, and he certainly won't be the last. The critics all die, but the Book of books still lives. And its influence continues to radically transform hearts all over our globe.

---

1. William R. Kimball, *The Book of Books* (Joplin, MO: College Press Publishing Co., 1986), 32-33.

CREDIBILITY VERSUS PROOF

Since *The TouchPoint* is primarily about connecting with God through the Bible, a thorough examination of the Bible's authenticity will not fit. Still, it's important to address the issue since any healthy relationship must be built upon a foundation of trust, and credibility is synonymous with trustworthiness. I have chosen, therefore, to condense what I believe are the most central arguments. Many more volumes have been written on this subject, so there is no shortage of material available to those who want to dig deeper.

Regardless of what plays out in the public arena, accepting and embracing the credibility of the Bible is an individual decision. No one can force us to believe anything. Furthermore, in this life, the existence of God is not a fact that can be proven. Fully embracing the inspirational and authoritative nature of the Bible is a step that requires faith. I refer, however, not to a blind faith, but rather a solid trust anchored upon both the character of God and a foundation of credible evidence.

Multiple layers of evidence bolster the credibility of our Scriptural text, but we must put everything in its associated context. Because the Bible was penned long ago in the corridors of time, we don't have access to computer hard drives or time-stamped video evidence. Instead, our understanding of Biblical times has its roots in the sister disciplines of *ancient history* and *archaeology*.

History and archaeology can both be compared to assembling a giant puzzle. As various finds are discovered, they are examined for credibility and then fit into place in an effort to complete the grand picture of history. Fitting the puzzle together involves a fluid and imperfect process requiring corroborating support and a certain amount of interpretation. Obviously, more corroboration leads to a greater measure of confidence in our historical record. As time goes on and more evidence is uncovered, our picture of the past becomes clearer and more certain. The fact that conservative scholars view both history and archaeology as welcomed friends provides a measure of credibility in itself.

OLD TESTAMENT MANUSCRIPTS

The Hebrew Bible was completed centuries before Christ, but for many years, the earliest known manuscripts—produced by the Jewish Masorete sect—had been dated to about AD 900. Questions abounded regarding the accuracy of Hebrew text that had been copied multiple times over. The discovery of the Dead Sea Scrolls (DSS) changed everything!

In 1947, a Bedouin shepherd boy named Muhammad adh-Dhib did something your typical boy would do. What followed was anything but ordinary. While trying to find a lost goat somewhere near the Dead Sea, the youngster tossed a stone into a high cave on a cliff. The sound of breaking pottery struck his inquisitive nature and led to perhaps the most significant archaeological discovery of the last century.[2]

The bone-dry air around the Dead Sea, combined with some well-sealed clay jars, had preserved hundreds of religious writings—including fragments of almost every Old Testament book (except Esther) and large portions of Leviticus, Deuteronomy, Psalms, and Isaiah. Many scholars believe that members of a Jewish sect (the Essenes) were trying to protect their religious writings from a massive assault that the Roman Empire eventually staged around AD 70. The manuscripts were found in about a dozen caves high off of the ground, and some of the scrolls dated between 200 BC and AD 68.[3]

Amongst two-millennia-old manuscripts covered with bat dung, a well-preserved Hebrew manuscript of the entire book of Isaiah was discovered. The dating of the Isaiah Scroll is especially significant because of the prophetic "suffering servant" description of Christ found in chapter fifty-three. Experts have determined that this amazingly accurate description of Christ's crucifixion was copied at least 100 years *prior to* Jesus' birth.

Furthermore, a textual analysis showed the newly discovered Isaiah Scroll to be more than *ninety-five percent* identical to one copied by Masorete scribes 1000 years later. The less than five-percent difference

2. Geisler and Nix, *A General Introduction to the Bible*, 360-365.
3. Kimball, *The Book of Books*, 169.

was mostly due to minor issues such as obvious mistakes and spelling variations.[4] The discovery of the Dead Sea Scrolls revealed the extreme care with which Jewish scribes copied their sacred Scriptures.

NEW TESTAMENT MANUSCRIPT EVIDENCE

As much as Old Testament manuscripts matter, without the New Testament, Christianity would not exist. Thankfully, intense scrutiny has helped to solidify our claim that the Bible is the inspired, infallible, and authoritative Word of God. In light of other ancient documents known to exist, the manuscript evidence for the New Testament is overwhelming!

About 5,800 whole or partial Greek manuscripts of the New Testament have been discovered to date.[5] The number is difficult to nail down because new manuscripts are being discovered every year. These are in addition to almost 20,000 later manuscripts copied in Latin and other languages. From a historical perspective, this number of ancient manuscripts is massive. No other written work of antiquity even comes close.

The sheer number of manuscripts, however, is not enough to verify the historical credibility of the New Testament; we need to know that the available manuscripts are consistent with the original writings. Not surprisingly, one criticism often made of the Bible is that we do not have *autographs* (original copies) of the Scriptures. Therefore, one of the most significant questions about the validity of the Bible involves the length of time between the original writings and the earliest copies still in existence. From a historical perspective, the time frame is negligible, but critics have a reasonable right to question whether today's New Testament text is consistent with what was originally recorded.

The New Testament is generally believed to have been written between AD 48 and 100.[6] The manuscripts most important to translation are dated about AD 325-350. A handful of copies are earlier, while the vast majority came later. Because of the fragile nature of papyrus, most

---

4. Geisler and Nix, *A General Introduction to the Bible*, 367.
5. "New Testament Textual Criticism," *Bible.org* website, https://bible.org/seriespage/1-preliminary-questions-and-answers <February 11, 2016>
6. Bruce, *The New Testament Documents*, 12-14.

of the earliest manuscripts aren't much more that fragments of the now-lost larger texts.

A person's initial reaction might be to think that a gap of more than 250 years exists between the NT autographs and the earliest credible copies, but such is certainly not the case. The earliest verified New Testament manuscript known to exist is identified as the *Rylands* manuscript; it contains a few verses from the Gospel of John dated no later than AD 130.[7] Even though the Rylands fragment is quite small, the fact that it is consistent with younger manuscript copies speaks volumes. Furthermore, if we consider that the Gospel of John was probably written between AD 90 and 100, a sense of historical credibility begins to emerge.

John walked with Jesus, serving as an eyewitness to his public ministry, crucifixion, and subsequent resurrection appearances. Sixty to seventy years later, John's recollection of the story he had spent a lifetime repeating to others publicly appears on papyrus. Now, we see a fragment of John's Gospel—dating to less than forty years after the original—that is in full agreement with the Bible we have today. Although the Rylands manuscript is but a small piece of papyrus, it plays a huge role in helping to establish the credibility and timing of the New Testament.

Scholars have dated a handful of other partial Greek manuscripts to the second and third centuries. Discoveries have also been made of Old Syriac and Old Latin manuscripts which date back to the latter half of the second century.[8] Again, the older fragments are consistent with newer copies, and again, from a historical perspective, the time gap is negligible. Considering the hostile urban (Jerusalem) environment in which much of Jesus' ministry took place, the short time gap between the original events and the earliest extant copies simply does not allow for the development of a "Christ legend" as some critics claim.

Comparing our available New Testament manuscripts to those of other ancient writings, we see that not only does the New Testament have far more existing manuscripts, but the time between the earliest

---

7. Bruce, *The New Testament Documents*, 17-18.
8. Ibid., 19.

extant manuscripts and the original writing is much closer than for the vast majority of other ancient documents known to exist.[9]

If we consider similar histories from the Biblical era—including Herodotus, Thucydides, Caesar, and Tacitus—all have less than twenty-five known manuscripts to be in existence (some are in the single digits.) Moreover, the time gap between the original writings and the copying of the earliest existing manuscripts is 1,000 years or more. The situation is only slightly better for the history recorded by Pliny Secundus, which has less than ten copies available but a time gap of "only" 750 years. Livy's history of Rome does have one partial manuscript copy that is only about 400 years later than the non-existent original, but the other twenty or so copies have a 1,000 year time gap.[10]

Moreover, the manuscript evidence for the historical credibility of the New Testament isn't just limited to copies of the New Testament itself. The early church fathers—some of whom lived late in the first and early in the second century—quoted a very large number of New Testament passages.[11] Several of these men personally knew Christ's disciples or the disciples of Christ's disciples.

According to renowned Bible scholar Norman Geisler, "if we compile the 36,289 quotations by early church Fathers of the second to the fourth centuries we can reconstruct the entire New Testament minus 11 verses."[12] This is another huge piece of evidence showing that the early church writings now part of the New Testament were in continuous use—and in a very public way—over a wide geographical area almost from the time they were penned.

What emerges from our trail of ancient manuscripts—some of which are non-Christian—is a picture of consistency that reaches back almost to the inception of the Christian faith. To think that, in the face of intense public scrutiny, Christ's followers either fabricated, or significantly altered, the New Testament text is historically unrealistic.

---

9. Greenlee, *Introduction to New Testament Criticism*, 5.
10. Geisler and Nix, *A General Introduction to the Bible*, 408.
11. Norman Geisler, *Baker Encyclopedia of Christian Apologetics* (Grand Rapids, MI: Baker Books, 1999), 529-530.
12. Ibid., 532.

WHY DON'T WE HAVE THE ORIGINALS?

The fact that we don't have autographs of the Biblical text is entirely understandable in light of ancient history. It's nearly impossible to do, but we must try to avoid transposing our contemporary cultural mindsets into ancient times. Early Christians lacked the freedom, technology, and opportunities that many of us have today. An inspired heart couldn't just walk over to the public library or log onto the internet and order the latest copy of the Bible.

To begin, papyrus—the preferred writing material at the time the Scriptures were recorded—is not very durable. The few papyrus manuscripts that survived the ravages of time were discovered in arid environments. Documents exposed to any degree of moisture would have decomposed centuries ago.

Animal skins (parchment and vellum) made a more permanent writing material, but for some reason, they were mostly neglected in favor of papyrus. It wasn't until the fourth century when Christian copyists began to realize the durability of parchment that papyrus gradually went out of vogue. Thus, some of our best manuscripts come from this period. Interestingly, mainstream copyists continued to use papyrus as they passed along the secular classics, which is probably why the historical time gaps between their creation and the earliest known copies are so large.

We should also understand that making a copy of the Bible was no weekend project. Can you imagine hand-writing a 1,000-page term paper? Not only was the work tedious and time consuming, it also required literary skills only a select group of people possessed. These factors severely limited the average person's access to God's sacred Word—especially since most people in ancient times were illiterate.

Finally, in addition to the perishable nature of papyrus, the early Christian church endured at least ten periods of intense persecution. Several Roman emperors hated Christianity, and thus, its sacred writings. Not only were copies of the Scriptures burned, those caught possessing them often paid the ultimate price. Life in New Testament times was a far cry from our age of Western education, technology, abundance, and freedom.

THE HISTORICAL CREDIBILITY OF THE NT

Because of the vast amount of historical evidence available, few (if any) classical historians have had a problem with the overall historicity of the Bible. Those who wish to invalidate the Bible as a historical document must also throw out a wide array of ancient historical documents which, having far less manuscript support than the Bible, are still relied upon as credible historical resources. John W. Montgomery, a distinguished college professor with eleven earned degrees, including theology and law, has concluded:[13]

> To be skeptical of the resultant text of the New Testament books is to allow all of classical antiquity to slip into obscurity, for no documents of the ancient period are as well attested bibliographically as the New Testament.[14]

In his excellent little book, *The New Testament Documents: Are They Reliable?*, esteemed scholar F.F. Bruce writes:

> The evidence for our New Testament writings is ever so much greater than the evidence for many writings of classical authors, the authenticity of which no-one dreams of questioning. And if the New Testament were a collection of secular writings, their authenticity would generally be regarded as beyond all doubt. It is a curious fact that historians have often been much readier to trust the New Testament records than have many theologians.[15]

Toward the end of his book, Bruce also addresses the bizarre idea that Jesus never existed:

> Some writers may toy with the fancy of a 'Christ-myth', but they do not do so on the ground of historical evidence. The historicity of Christ is as axiomatic for an unbiased historian

---

13. The fact that Montgomery is a highly educated, brilliant intellectual who has published over 250 documents doesn't necessarily establish the credibility of his statement, but it does show that professing Christians are not all mindless imbeciles, as is sometimes claimed by critics.
14. John W. Montgomery, *History and Christianity* (San Bernadino, CA: HERE'S LIFE PUBLISHERS, INC, 1983), 29.
15. Bruce, *The New Testament Documents*, 15.

as the historicity of Julius Caesar. It is not historians who propagate the 'Christ-myth' theories.[16]

My thoughts to this point have focused on the New Testament as a whole. No doubt, various books of the Bible are questioned by some scholars, but the major tenets of the Christian faith can be established from books—*Mark, Romans, 1 Corinthians,* and *Galatians*—that few scholars would even think of questioning. Furthermore, from a historical perspective, we don't need all of the books of the Bible to put critics in a quandary. For example, those who reject the Pastoral Epistles—1 Timothy, 2 Timothy, and Titus—must still account for the supernatural nature of Mark's Gospel.

According to Will Durant, the acclaimed author of a massive eleven-volume historical survey titled, *The Story of Civilization*:

> Our Gospel of Mark was apparently circulated while some of the apostles, or their immediate disciples, were still alive; it seems unlikely, therefore, that it differed substantially from their recollection and interpretation of Christ. We may conclude, with the brilliant but judicious Schweitzer, that the Gospel of Mark is in essentials "genuine history."[17]

I find Durant's comments especially interesting in that he was a classical historian and philosopher—not a Christian apologist. Durant's goal was to record a wide span of history to the best of his ability, and so his work carries a certain degree of objectivity that a critic might believe scholars such as Bruce, Geisler, and Montgomery lack.

While there is indeed a short gap between the original writings and our available information, it is historically insignificant and seems to grow smaller with each new discovery. Thus, Bruce's point, which is echoed by Montgomery and other scholars, should not be taken lightly: *theologians seem to have far more trouble accepting the historicity of the New Testament than do historians.* Why is this the case? From where I sit, the problem lies more with the critics' internal motivations than with the actual evidence.

---

16. Ibid., 119.

17. Will Durant, *The Story of Civilization: Part III; Caesar and Christ* (New York: Simon and Schuster, 1944), 556.

Frederic G. Kenyon served as the Director and Principal Librarian of the British Museum from 1909 until 1931. An expert in ancient manuscripts, Kenyon stated the following in his popular book, *Our Bible and the Ancient Manuscripts*:

> The Christian can take the whole Bible in his hand and say without fear or hesitation that he holds in it the true Word of God, handed down without essential loss from generation to generation throughout the centuries.[18]

Though these words were recorded relatively early in his career, Kenyon's years of learning, combined with additional manuscript discoveries, served only to reinforce his expert opinion of the Bible's credibility. As discoveries continue to confirm its trustworthiness, we are reminded that confidence in the Bible is far more than a blind stab in the dark.

ARCHAEOLOGICAL EVIDENCE

The discipline of *archaeology* is in many ways the study of *buried history*. Archaeologists painstakingly unearth relics and structures from the past as they attempt to reconstruct the puzzle of human history. Over the years, I've observed that conservative Christian scholars eagerly await each new historical or archaeological find relating to the Bible. Why? Each discovery serves only to *confirm* the validity of the Biblical text as we know it.

In support of their position, those involved with the Higher Criticism presented a host of arguments against the historical validity of the Bible due to missing pieces in the archaeological puzzle. Certain cities, names, and even entire people groups were nowhere to be found. However, over the past hundred years or more, many of those arguments have vaporized into oblivion as archaeologists unearthed new discoveries.

The consistency of the archaeological record causes Christian apologists to highly value research efforts in the Middle East. Most of the accounts recorded in the Bible took place within the backdrop of verifiable history. The more buried history uncovered, the more

---

18. Frederic G. Kenyon, *Our Bible and the Ancient Manuscripts*, 2nd edition (London: Eyre and Spottiswoode, 1898), 11.

confirmation we find of the Biblical record. The introduction to the *NIV Archaeological Study Bible* (yes, there is such a thing as an archaeological study Bible) contains the following statement:

> No previous generation has witnessed so high a degree of collaboration of Biblical events, persons and historical settings as we have during the past century of ongoing, successful archaeological exploration. The quantity, quality and relevancy of the artifacts and epigraphical materials impinging upon the story of the Bible from the ancient Near East have been so staggering that few have been able to incorporate them into one place, let alone link them side by side with relevant Scriptures.[19]

As a case in point, Luke the physician frequently recorded meticulous details in his Gospel and the book of Acts:

> *Now in the fifteenth year of the reign of Tiberius Caesar, when Pontius Pilate was governor of Judea, and Herod was tetrarch of Galilee, and his brother Philip was tetrarch of the region of Ituraea and Trachonitis, and Lysanias was tetrarch of Abilene, in the high priesthood of Annas and Caiaphas, the word of God came to John, the son of Zacharias, in the wilderness. Luke 3:1-2*

Tiberius Caesar, Pontius Pilate, Judea, Herod, Galilee, Philip, Ituraea, Traconitis, Lysanias, Abilene, Annas, and Caiaphas are all names and locations that have been verified through extra-Biblical archaeological research.

Only minimal effort will uncover example after example of archaeological discoveries that confirm the historical reliability of the Bible. These include not only ruins, names, and various artifacts, but also several ancient non-Christian writings that help to establish the historical relevance of Christ's life, death, and resurrection. Dr. John McRay, author of *Archaeology and the New Testament*, is only one of several eminent archaeologists to state that there has never been a verified archaeological discovery proven to contradict the Biblical record.[20]

---

19. *NIV Archaeological Study Bible*, vix
20. Lee Strobel, *The Case for Christ: A Journalist's Personal Investigation of the Evidence for Jesus* (Grand Rapids, MI: Zondervan Publishing House, 1998), 100.

THE TOUCHPOINT

One of my favorite stories centers on the person of Sir William Ramsay—a renown British archaeologist who embraced the Higher Criticism of the 1800's. Proclaiming the Bible to be nothing more than a fictitious work, Ramsay was highly critical of Luke's writings—the book of Acts in particular. This is especially significant because Luke wrote both Acts and the Gospel of Luke, which together comprise almost *one-quarter* of the New Testament.

Ramsay was commissioned in 1881 by the British Museum to research Asia Minor and the nearby Greek islands—the very territory in which the apostle Paul's missionary journeys (as recorded in Acts) took place. Ramsay thought his opportunity had finally arrived to prove Luke was a fraud and that Acts was not written until the mid-second century AD. After a period of intense study and on-site investigation, Sir William Ramsay scandalized the archaeological world by completely reversing his view and proclaiming Luke to be "an historian of the first rank."[21] Of Ramsay, F.F. Bruce writes:

> Although in his later years Ramsay was persuaded to don the mantle of a popular apologist for the trustworthiness of the New Testament records, the judgments which he publicized in this way were judgments which he had previously formed as a scientific archaeologist and student of ancient classical history and literature. He was not talking unadvisedly or playing to the religious gallery when he expressed his view that 'Luke's history is unsurpassed in respect of its trustworthiness'; this was the sober conclusion to which his researches led him, in spite of the fact that he started with a very different opinion of Luke's historical credit.[22]

By his own words, Luke claimed to have carefully investigated the events documented in his historical accounts (Luke 1:1-4). Archaeological discoveries examined by trained experts only serve to confirm the validity not only of Luke's claim, but of all that he wrote. This realization stirred Sir William Ramsay to go from being a vocal critic of the Bible to a devoted apologist of the Christian faith.

---

21. Kimball, *The Book of Books*, 104-107.
22. Bruce, *The New Testament Documents*, 90-91.

The radical change of belief by a renowned academic is by no means unique. Other honest and intelligent skeptics—C.S. Lewis, for example—have profoundly altered the course of their lives after exploring the historical and theological claims of Biblical Christianity with honest hearts. When great thinkers such as Ramsey and Lewis find themselves compelled to reverse their theological course, it's not because of closed-minded adherence to predetermined beliefs.

TRANSMISSION OF THE TEXT

Before I investigated the transmission of the Bible, I more or less pictured a lone monk making copies in the back room of a monastery. Perhaps you can relate to my former perspective. Half-famished from constant fasting (and the lack of chocolate), and with eyes drooping shut, how could this bored and lonely guy have possibly made accurate copies of the Scriptures? Even worse, perhaps he decided to alter the text to better fit his liking. Staking my entire future on the whims of a lone, frazzled monk seemed like a shaky venture at best. Little did I realize that this surprisingly popular image is terribly distorted.

Admittedly, the process of copying the New Testament documents was far from perfect. How could a person transcribe nearly 800,000 words without making some mistakes? Furthermore, the copies made during the years of persecution before Christianity was legalized were not of the same quality as those reproduced afterward when scribes were better trained. Also, we find several passages conspicuously absent from the earliest manuscripts—meaning that a copyist probably inserted his personal thoughts or possibly confused marginal notes with the Biblical text. Regarding such issues, the literary science of lower criticism has proven to be invaluable.

Picture, if you will, your typical family tree. It begins at its base with one ancient couple and then spreads into a massive number of branches, each tracing its connection back to the trunk. This type of ancestral tree, which includes a handful of distant cousins who married one another, provides a reasonable illustration of how our Bible has been transmitted through the centuries.

Various "strains" of the Hebrew Bible and the New Testament have been transmitted through a number of sources across a widespread geographical area in the form of *manuscript families*. For example, full or partial copies of the Old Testament have been transmitted through Jewish sources as both Hebrew and Greek text, through Samaritan sources, and from Christian sources of various sects and in various locations.

Although the separations between manuscript family groups aren't always clear, scholars have long sought to identify unique aspects of each family group in their work to identify the original text. Thus, those few places where a scribe or a monk tried to make changes are easily identified through comparison with other manuscript families. While the vast number of New Testament manuscripts makes the work of lower criticism all the more tedious, such abundance also helps experts more accurately determine the original content.

VARIANTS

Critics like to broadcast the fact that there are hundreds of thousands of variants in Biblical manuscript copies. What they often fail to explain is that simple spelling or grammatical errors constitute the vast majority of these differences. The number of variants found in Biblical manuscripts is high only because of the volume of writing is extremely high. The same spelling mistake on 10,000 manuscripts, for example, would constitute 10,000 variants. When multiplied by the sheer number of manuscripts written between the 2nd and 15th century, the total grows rather *quickly*.

Textual critics generally aren't concerned with such a high number of variants because a large number of manuscripts also makes it easier for scholars to identify and remove errors. If an error exists in one manuscript family but not in all of the others, for instance, scholars can easily identify where the mistake lies. For the lay person, a good study Bible will often identify the most significant passages (such as Mark 16:9-19) in question.

According to Geisler and Nix, various experts have determined that our current New Testament is over *ninety-nine percent* substantially pure. Thus, meaningful and viable variants affect less than *one percent* of the Biblical text and *no* essential doctrines of the Christian faith.[23] Make no mistake, the major tenets of the Christian faith are cemented firmly in place.

WHAT ABOUT DISCREPANCIES?

When we meticulously examine Biblical manuscripts with modern eyes, we can wrongly assume that the original writers made multiple errors, but most of the supposed "discrepancies" found in the Bible are due to differences between time and culture. Jewish history, for example, wasn't always recorded in a chronological fashion. The Jewish writers of the Bible sought to convey accurate descriptions of events with the purpose of communicating a message. Their goal was not to provide the type of linear timeline that many of us are accustomed to seeing.

The messages of both Jewish and Christian writers of the Bible centered on the interaction between God and humanity. Each event, therefore, was interpreted through the eyes of the writer. Their perceptions didn't change the historical reality of the events that took place—only the manner in which they were presented. This was normal practice for the day. Thus, if we compare the Gospels and find some disagreement in the order of events, the historical integrity of the writers need not be compromised.

In addition, minute differences in eyewitness testimonies, such as ones we see in the Synoptic Gospels, are to be expected in a court of law. They help to show that the development of these writings was a real and not contrived process. The Bible is inspired by God Himself, but He employed real humans through a very real process of writing and transmission. Even if we were to assume that minor contradictions between the Gospels existed, I feel that they would be of no consequence. According to Will Durant, who through the eyes of a historian, saw minor discrepancies in the New Testament record:

> The contradictions are of minutiae, not substance; in essentials the synoptic gospels agree remarkably well, and form a consistent portrait of Christ. In the enthusiasm of its discoveries

23. Geisler and Nix, *A General Introduction to the Bible*, 474.

the Higher Criticism has applied to the New Testament tests of authenticity so severe that by them a hundred ancient worthies–e.g. Hammurabi, David, Socrates–would fade into legend . . . That a few simple men should in one generation have invented so powerful and appealing a personality, so lofty of an ethic and so inspiring a vision of human brotherhood, would be a miracle far more incredible than any recorded in the Gospels. After two centuries of Higher Criticism the outlines of the life, character, and teaching of Christ, remain reasonably clear, and constitute the most fascinating feature in the history of Western man.[24]

The Old Testament pointed toward the coming of Jesus Christ as the Messiah, and the New Testament focused on His desire to reconcile with sinful people through the advance of His kingdom. Furthermore, central to the establishment of God's kingdom on earth were the ministry, death, and resurrection of Christ. As previously noted, credible evidence suggests that these core issues have both substance and significance in the grand scheme of human history.

CHAPTER WRAP-UP

Once again, my goal is not to prove that the Bible is the inspired Word of God, but to provide evidence of its credibility. Nor am I suggesting that easy answers can be found for every difficulty presented by the Biblical text. We're dealing with a book written centuries ago in distant lands (for most of us) and through the eyes of a foreign culture(s).

Theological conservatives, it seems, have trouble saying, "I don't know." More often than not, we try to answer every difficulty in the Bible with an air of certainty, as though the credibility of its sacred text somehow depends on our ability to defend it. Ancient history is a puzzle, and we can't expect all of the pieces to fall seamlessly into place without painstaking and time-consuming efforts toward discovery and analysis.

Still, in spite of centuries of harsh criticism, the Bible we have today stands as largely pure and historically credible. Is there a short

24. Durant, *The Story of Civilization: Part III; Caesar and Christ*, 557.

gap between the life of Christ and the time the first Gospel was written? Yes. And is there a gap between those first writings and the earliest manuscripts known to exist? Again, yes. But from a historical perspective, these issues are negligible, and the evidence for the historical credibility of the Old and New Testaments far exceeds that of other ancient documents.

All things being said, the fact that an ancient document is authentic doesn't necessarily mean that it is inspired. As important as it is for us to establish that the Bible is *incredibly credible*, we must also show that the Bible is *credibly incredible*. In the next two chapters, we'll consider some additional evidence for the authenticity of the Bible as God's inspired Word.

THE TOUCHPOINT

7

WHAT ABOUT SCIENCE?

Christians believe in the virgin birth of Jesus. Materialists believe in the virgin birth of the cosmos. Choose your miracle.

—Glen Scrivener

Then God said, "Let there be light"; and there was light.

Genesis 1:3

If I were to do a thorough analysis of the Bible in light of scientific study, I would need to pursue intensive research in several fields—archaeology, biology, cosmology, genetics, geology, paleontology, psychology, physics, and sociology, for starters. Assuming I were capable of the task, by the time I finished, changes in each field would compel me to begin all over again. Furthermore, if I compiled my research efforts into a (very large) book, the typical reader would also face formidable challenges. Materials suited for Ph.D. candidates do not make for light reading.

Of how many subjects are you thoroughly knowledgeable? Unless you're a genius—or a perpetual student—I think the number would be rather small. With most topics—especially scientific study—very few of us have the time, intelligence, or resources to delve deeply into a wide array of subjects. Let's face it; the average person possesses only a tiny fraction of all the available knowledge in our world. Consequently, we are left to trust the "experts," and the particular authorities we trust are the ones who have been presented to us in the most favorable light.

The reality is that a combination of factors makes it extremely difficult for the average person to know what to think about the scientific credibility of the Bible. More often than not, our beliefs closely correlate with whatever experts we're inclined to follow. For example, a young person reared in a traditional Christian family and schooled at home will likely study texts written by scholars who are out of step with mainstream scholarship. Consequently, serious turmoil can result if our young person attends a secular (or possibly Christian) college at which the scepter of knowledge is held by scholars who, denying the existence of a Creator, champion scientific naturalism. Conversely, someone schooled in a secular system may hold distorted views of the Bible for similar reasons.

Most of my life has been immersed in either science or theology; therefore, I am well aware of the perceived gulf between the two disciplines. And though I've had my share of conversations regarding the issue, I've also experienced minimal difficulty reconciling the two fields. Perhaps it's because conclusive scientific evidence is not as easily found as we are often led to believe.

LET'S DITCH THE POLITICS

When people attempt to influence public opinion, they generally work to create *stereotypes* with the realization that, because of limited knowledge, the general public is susceptible to manipulation. Thus, a doctorish-looking person wearing a white lab coat carries an air of credibility. (I think the sale of white lab coats would drop dramatically if pharmaceutical companies quit broadcasting drug commercials.)

A certain amount of stereotyping is unavoidable since we can't know personally the billions of people walking this earth. At the same time, we must understand that the deliberate act of stereotyping fractures our societal relationships. All too often, our public maneuvering is accompanied by condescending attitudes that belittle all who disagree with us. Consequently, the price paid is that of meaningful dialogue.

I cringe when conservative Christians paint those in the secular scientific community as godless fools. Conversely, it also pains me to see Christians who champion the credibility of the Bible stereotyped as closed-minded, stupid, and oblivious to reality. Having studied in both worlds, I've known both honest and sincere secularists as well as highly intelligent Christians.

For many centuries, scientists explored the natural world with an understanding that it was created by God with a sense of order. Highly regarded minds such as Nicholas Copernicus, Sir Francis Bacon, Johannes Kepler, Galileo Galilei, Rene Descartes, Blaise Pascal, Isaac Newton, Robert Boyle, Michael Faraday, Gregor Mendel, Max Planck, and Albert Einstein, among others, all shared a general belief in the existence of God. That's not to say that they all held orthodox Christian beliefs in a personal God, but that each one recognized the powerful link between science and theology.

The situation changed dramatically as Darwin's theory of evolution by natural selection began to take root. For the first time in history, scientists who doubted or denied God's existence felt they had a scientifically credible alternative to the idea of a created world. Suddenly, the floodgates opened, and massive shifts took place within the scientific community. Many of those in positions of power and influence began to treat science like a high-stakes basketball game in which a player boxes out all opponents in seeking to pull down a rebound. For all intents and purposes, these people of influence redefined science so that no room could be found for the influence of a Creator.

Still, in our secular academic world, large numbers of scientists continue to profess a belief in God. I've read books by proponents of intelligent design theory, listened to presentations by a high-ranking official in NASA, and been close friends with the former chair of a university chemistry department. These people are far from stupid or irrational.

At any time in history, our real problem has not been a conflict between science and theology, but political maneuvering to stifle opposing voices. Although not as much as we are often led to believe, the Medieval institutional church, at times, stifled objective scientific inquiry. Sadly, institutional science is, at times, following in Dark-Age footsteps. The way I see it, the voice with the most political clout is the one that rules at any given moment. For truth to prevail, however, reasonable minds must move beyond our political posturing and begin to look at truth objectively.

SCIENCE AND THEOLOGY

As previously explained, science and theology both should be driven by an objective quest to understand reality, and the bulk of confusion arises when we misunderstand the nature of the relationship between the two fields. Problematically, opposing sides in the science-theology debate have firmly entrenched themselves with stubborn zeal. And because the pendulum of power has swung toward scientific naturalists, their beliefs are now the order of the day in Western educational systems. But when any one topic is off the table for exploration and discussion, the pursuit is no longer objective and is, therefore, flawed. As a result, we all pay a collective price.

A big part of our problem stems from confusing the individual roles of science and theology because each provides something that the other does not. As a general rule, science addresses the question of *how* and theology *why*. Thus, the Bible does not provide a scientific explanation of how our world came into being, and science cannot answer our deeper questions about the meaning of life. Subsequently, sound scientific observation and confidence in the divine inspiration of the Scriptures need not be mutually exclusive. Do we realize how much people suffer when scientific solutions are forced upon spiritual needs?

Humanity collectively wrestles with questions about meaning and existence. When a person questions the possibility of God's existence, he or she isn't asking merely a scientific question, but one laden with underlying emotional energy. If God is good and powerful, why is there so much suffering and evil in our world? Why does injustice seem to envelope the globe? If God is all about love, why am I so unloved? Why do I hurt so bad? Why was my loved one taken in such an untimely manner? The train of emotions seemingly runs forever. And while theology may sometimes struggle to provide clear answers, these are questions that fall far beyond the scope of scientific knowledge.

Human behavior and beliefs are complicated by physical, emotional, mental, moral, and yes, spiritual dynamics. I'm not suggesting that we attempt to provide mystical answers for all of our questions, but that all of our questions cannot be answered apart from the realization that a spiritual realm exists. Consequently, when those in the academic world attempt to dismiss the existence of God as mere myth, they create a moral vacuum that produces chaos of all sorts.

I have lived in a university community for over thirty-five years—a long period of which I also served as a campus minister. Although I'm not one to champion "the good old days," recognizing the precipitous decline of student behavior has been unavoidable. Furthermore, current secular attempts to instill moral values have met with dismal failure. American culture is unraveling at breakneck speed, and no amount of scientific discovery will fix the problem.

I've also walked through situations with students who lost friends due to drug overdoses and other tragic means of death. Comforting the parents of a deceased student was even more difficult. In those pain-filled moments, science is bankrupt to provide meaningful answers. People *require* comfort, care, and hope—vital needs that academia cannot fulfill. The long and short of the matter is that people need a personal, intimate, and meaningful relationship with a loving Creator who institutional science will not allow to exist.

THE BIBLE AND SCIENCE

Skeptics tend to magnify any disparities between science and the Christian faith, but apart from the supernatural nature of miracles, science and the Bible have little conflict—except for perhaps the first several chapters of Genesis. Regarding times, people, and places, much of the Scriptural content from Abram (the latter part of Genesis 11) to the first century is verifiable. Moreover, the story of the Tower of Babel (the beginning of Genesis 11) and our world once having only one land mass is credible in light of the sizes and shapes of our continents.

None of this is to say that the Bible is without scientific difficulties. Some of our more significant challenges arise from our understanding of the creation account at the beginning of Genesis. The debate over whether the creation story is literal or allegorical is not a new one; theologians have wrestled with this topic for centuries.

In processing this potentially confusing issue, I find it helpful to remember what the Bible says about itself:

All Scripture is inspired by God and profitable for teaching, for reproof, for correction, for training in righteousness; so that the man of God may be adequate, equipped for every good work. 2 Timothy 3:16-17

Notice that the emphasis is entirely relational, and thus, moral. There was nothing scientific about it. In fact, science as we know it was virtually non-existent at the time. Applying this principle to the creation account, we recognize that the story was most likely handed down from generation to generation for the primary purpose of communicating a message. This idea is reinforced when we observe that the order of events regarding the creation of vegetation and humankind switches between Genesis One and Two. Does this mean that one of the accounts was inaccurate? Not at all. The message, not the order—and certainly not the science—is what mattered to the ancient Jewish mind.

I think Christians make a huge mistake when proclaiming, "The Bible says!" in their efforts to argue a scientific point. Instead, we should be challenging scientists to hold true to the design of objective scientific inquiry. If the God of the Bible truly exists, science and theology are complementary disciplines that should to some degree converge on the how and why of God's creation. If scientific and theological views conflict, someone's interpretation is flawed. But such flaws cannot be identified unless we objectively investigate the physical and spiritual realms in which we live.

The study of origins is particularly tenuous because there is no way to verify the validity of our theories. Any evidence uncovered must be pieced together to arrive at reasonable conclusions. This process itself is highly speculative and should be viewed as such. Science involves an *attempt* to understand our natural reality, and the line between theory and fact must be well drawn.

If a scientist cannot say, "I have a theory about our origins, but we don't know for sure," something is terribly amiss. A theory such as Darwin's on evolution—that cannot be verified or falsified by scientific testing—should never be regarded as a scientific fact. Conclusively claiming, therefore, that humanity is the product of a natural, unguided process is a scientific farce. Subsequently, the authenticity of the Bible does not hinge on whether or not our modern scientific theories mesh perfectly with a literal interpretation of the Biblical creation story.

I am by no means suggesting that we should give up the quest to understand our origins, but that definitive explanations of certain matters are few and far between. Is the earth young or old? Were the days of Genesis One literal or figurative? How do dinosaurs fit into the picture? Who were the Nephilim (Genesis 6:4)? The truth is that we cannot definitively answer these questions. Furthermore, every theory seems to have anomalies. If we turn a blind eye to certain types of evidence to promote a favored perspective, our "pursuit of truth" has been corrupted by ulterior motives.

HUMAN NATURE

I don't believe that the creation account was ever meant to be a scientific treatise. The focus of the entire Bible is on the relationship between God and humanity with early Genesis being no different. And while dialogue is necessary, I believe that our intense conflict over this issue has distracted us from other significant and vital issues.

Even though my background is in chemistry, the study of human nature—with the Bible as my text—has captivated the past twenty or more years of my life. Do you know what I've learned? Long before the fields of psychology and social science were invented, the Bible provided a spectacular depth of insight into humanity, rivaling what we have today.

The first few chapters of Genesis, in particular, lay a groundwork for human behavior that, while often overlooked, should be a primary focus. Many of our most troubling societal problems, after all, stem from human pride in its various forms. Furthermore, when Jesus lived among people, He identified the core issues of human dysfunction with laser-like precision. My continued learning in this arena only confirms that the solutions the Bible provides to the human condition are nothing short of magnificent. In no way can this Book of books be the mere fabrication of a primitive people!

OVERSTEPPING SCIENTIFIC BOUNDARIES

Does it take faith to believe that the Bible is the inspired, infallible, and authoritative Word of God? Without question. But we've already established the fact that faith is integral to a meaningful relationship with God. And while antagonists are quick to identify supposed inconsistencies in the Christian Scriptures, far greater contradictions drive scientific naturalism.

Even the most learned mind must accept the realization that there is *much, much more* that we don't know than what we do know. True science, then, involves a systematic process of discovery, research, and testing that is repeated on a continuous basis. Consequently, scientific certainty is achieved only after a rigorous process of verification. For a scientific naturalist (i.e., atheist) to claim an open and shut case for a cosmos without God, several massive leaps of faith are required. It is in this regard that the worlds of science and theology do not mix as institutional science oversteps its bounds. The "open and shut case" for scientific naturalism is riddled with gaping holes—three of which I address in the sections below.

THE EXISTENCE OF THE UNIVERSE

How much of the cosmos is visible to us? We have no way of knowing. Some astronomers claim perhaps *four percent*. If this number is accurate, around *ninety-six percent* of the universe remains out of our view— even with our most technologically-advanced telescope. Whether we're gazing into the sky on a clear evening, or studying the distant heavens with a high-powered telescope, we're quick to realize that our knowledge of all that exists is *minuscule*.

Inside our ever-expanding universe, there exist no fewer than 100 billion galaxies and possibly as many as 500 billion. Each galaxy contains hundreds of billions of stars, and each star dwarfs the size of our Earth. Again, these numbers are uncertain, but what do a few hundred billion stars matter?

Our own galaxy, the Milky Way, is about 100,000-120,000 light-years in diameter and contains 200–400 billion stars. (A light-year is the distance—5,880,000,000,000 miles—that a ray of light travels in one year at a speed of 186,282 miles/sec.) We don't know the exact number of stars because we are on one of the outer bands of the Milky Way, and it would take more time than any of us has to explore its entirety. Our nearest star—the Sun—is 93,000,000 miles away. If you decided to drive to the Sun for vacation, assuming that you didn't burn up, your non-stop trip at 100 mph would take more than 100 years. Of course, the trip would take only eight minutes traveling at the speed of light. Our next closest star—Proxima Centauri—is about 4.24 light-years (24,931,000,000,000 miles) distant.

Mind boggling. Staggering. Amazing. Awe-inspiring. Overwhelming. All are terms that could be used to describe the heavens, and each would hold true in every sense of the word. Coming to the realization that we know just a small fraction of what's out there only serves to make the reality of our cosmos all the more incredible. Moreover, practically every new scientific find, on whatever level, reveals a greater level of complexity than previously realized.

A series of discoveries during the early part of our last century led to the realization that our universe is expanding rather than remaining static. Thus, the big bang theory was conceived. All of the current evidence points toward our material world having a beginning, and if it had a beginning, then it also had a cause. There has to be a reason that we have something instead of nothing.

Not only does scientific naturalism fail to answer why an estimated 70 thousand million million million stars (or more) came into being, it can't even explain the how. Several weak theories have been floated, but they are heavy in speculation and light on true science. It is here that the influence of philosophical bias in the scientific community emerges. In spite of many objections from within its own ranks, institutional science allows absolutely no room for even the remote possibility that our massive, beautiful, and complex cosmos was created by a supernatural power. Hardly the model of objective scientific inquiry!

THE EXISTENCE OF LIFE

I remember learning about the *Miller-Urey* experiment when I was in school. The experiment was originally conducted by Stanley Miller under the supervision of Howard Urey—a Nobel Prize winner—at the University of Chicago in the early 1950s.[1] Theirs was an era of great scientific optimism as researchers exuded confidence in their ability to explain how life on this planet came to exist. Like many others, Miller and Urey pursued a model through which they believed that an electrical spark applied to the right mix of chemicals in the appropriate atmospheric environment would begin to explain the enigma of life.

The Miller-Urey experiment was historic in that it produced several amino acids—the very building blocks of life. Soon, the funding flowed, and scientists began creating all sorts of primordial soup mixes. Still, in spite of any initial success, the enthusiasm was short-lived. The atmospheric conditions utilized by Miller and Urey were called into question, but more importantly, further scientific study began to reveal that life is *far more* complex than previously realized.

Just as turning a telescope to the heavens exposes an incredibly massive universe, so too, focusing a microscope on the building blocks of life reveals a level of complexity that strikes even the most-learned mind with awe. For naturalism to hold true, an organic life form must have spontaneously formed from inorganic material at least once—and possibly multiple times. The emergence of life, however, would only be the first step. The primitive life form needed to somehow self-organize and then reproduce itself.

When I read attempts by scientists to explain either the origin of the universe or the origin of life, words such as *may, possibly,* and *speculate*

1. *JRank Science and Philosophy* website, http://science.jrank.org/pages/4344/Miller-Urey-Experiment.html <February 11, 2016>

populate their work. The idea of scientific certainty in these matters is a myth of epic proportions. More often than not, rather than furnishing viable scientific evidence, proponents of naturalism simply expand the timeline of the cosmos with the vain hope of improving the odds for the spontaneous generation of life and its unbelievably complex evolution.

Today's world of scientific research reveals a glaring absence— hardly any work is being done to explain the origins of life. It's as though the scientific community now considers the issue settled. Or is it that the task has largely been abandoned because we now feel that viable answers are beyond our grasp? In addition, modern research efforts show that dozens of unique factors contribute to a universe "finely tuned" for the specific purpose of supporting life on earth. With such a scenario, how can we possibly accept the confident conclusion that our own existence does not require the work of a Creator?

THE HIGH-LEVEL COMPLEXITY OF LIFE

While in college, I thought it might be a good idea to take a biochemistry course. Successfully completing Dr. Hartline's class was, without question, one of the more fascinating endeavors during my time in school. The professor did an excellent job opening my eyes to the magnificent biological complexity of the human body.

As the well-learned pedagogue excitedly expounded upon recent revelations involving the human body, he would invariably remind us that each new discovery opens up previously unseen dimensions of biological complexity. Though certainly not his intention, Dr. Hartline's biochem class profoundly strengthened my newfound faith in a Creator.

There's no question that life forms evolve as they adapt to the changing conditions on earth (a process known as *microevolution*). The real issue is whether *macroevolution* exists—whether random mutations can add *new* genetic material resulting in increased levels of complexity. Thus, through a naturalistic scenario, our massive cosmos mysteriously appeared, "simple" life—if there is such a thing— then spontaneously formed from inorganic material, and finally, that primitive life grew increasingly complex to astronomical levels. This includes the development of the various types of reproductive systems and organs, such as the eye, which have similar outward appearances but fundamentally different designs.

Our sense of amazement doesn't stop with the biology of organic life, however. How did living organisms jump from a primitive, single-celled existence to the formation of intelligence? Humans, in particular, are characterized by high levels of intellectual, emotional, and moral intelligence—each of which supposedly evolved through an unguided process. But our wonderful complexity is also confused by profound paradoxes. We possess the ability to reason but often act irrationally. We desire love yet sometimes we hate. We seek to do good but are frequently driven by selfish motives.

All manner of questions can be asked about human intelligence, but to me, the most mind-stretching queries relate to our moral rationales. In a purely naturalist world, the concepts of *good* and *evil* have no basis for existing. There is only survival of the fittest. And yet, moral intelligence constitutes a core dynamic of our human fabric.

In recent years, we've witnessed a simmering sense of moral outrage against corporate injustice grow to a full boil, spawning protests and even riots in our streets. And the problem isn't just that we're personally affected. We're often outraged when corporate greed exploits people (or animals) halfway around the planet.

Many of us want to vomit over the injustices that plague our world, but why the outrage? How did mere blobs of organic matter evolve to possess such an intense sense of right and wrong? When it comes to corporate greed, injustice shouldn't concern us—at least not from a naturalistic perspective. After all, life is about the survival of the fittest. How a person accumulates wealth shouldn't matter. If he or she can "out-survive" the poor saps who lack financial savvy, then so be it.

Why is it that a caring heart cringes at the thought of powerful people oppressing the powerless? Why does the hair on our necks rise at the uncovering of political corruption? Why do we tirelessly work to develop elaborate and complex legal systems? We are mysteriously wired to care about justice for the sake of justice. But why?

This line of moral reasoning also prompts me to question why evil exists and why people feel compelled to do evil deeds. Why would six young people torture and kill a mentally-challenged woman over the span of several days? And it isn't simply a matter of one sad (but true) story that transpired in our area. Open your daily paper or click on an internet news link, and you'll quickly see that evil abounds on this planet. Apart from a spiritual world, the survival of the fittest may be explained by some, but the existence of evil makes sense to none.

Science alone cannot provide adequate answers to many of life's biggest questions—or explain why those questions are even asked. In addition to the beauty, order, and complexity on every level of our existence, human attributes such as complex speech, emotion, conscience, a sense of justice, and even the desire to do evil are beyond reasonable explanation from a purely naturalistic perspective. The sheer odds of our cosmos, and subsequently, life on this minuscule celestial sphere, coming into existence apart from divine influence are staggering!

IMPROBABLE BUT POSSIBLE???

The atheist may be quick to point out that while certain scenarios are highly *improbable*, they are not statistically *impossible*. In other words, given enough time, our massive cosmos may have come into being out of nothing, life may have spontaneously formed, and primitive organisms may have naturally organized to astronomical levels of complexity. And on such speculative grounds atheism is declared intellectually superior to a belief in the existence of God? I grasp the argument, but it lacks the substance of true science. What objective, scientific explanation can be found for that which is non-existent suddenly existing—and in massive proportions nonetheless?

Given that no verifiable—or even viable—explanations can be given for the three massive improbabilities listed above, how can an atheist, with certainty, conclude that God does not exist? Speculation! Speculation! Speculation! Make no mistake about it, scientific naturalism requires several massive leaps of faith but refuses to admit the role of faith in its belief system.

For a person to confidently contend that God cannot exist is to say that he or she has complete insight into every possible dimension of our universe—including the spiritual domain. Of course, this is especially problematic for naturalists because as soon as they acknowledge that God might exist, they open the door for practically anything that defies natural law—including resurrection from the dead. What pressure all of this puts on naturalists to close themselves off from truly objective inquiry!

THE FALSE DICHOTOMY

My goal is not to attack scientific thought—or even people who doubt the existence of God—but to highlight the false dichotomy between science and faith. Far too many people, I believe, have allowed a distorted understanding of science to undermine their confidence in the Bible, and thus, their faith in God. In my opinion, the resulting unbelief has done irreparable damage to human lives.

In making such claims, I am not ignorant of the improbability of the Christian faith. How did God come to be? Can *Three* be *One*? Is it possible to be fully divine *and* fully human? Can a book written by humans be infallibly inspired by God? Did Jesus truly rise from the dead? All are reasonable questions, but by the very nature of who God is, something would be wrong if there weren't issues stretching the scope of our natural reasoning.

While we can't analytically answer all of our questions about God, we can find enough credible evidence to make faith in our Creator—and His written Word—a reasonable conclusion. Thus, I find belief in the existence of a supernatural God to be more reasonable than belief in scientific naturalism.

No matter what view of the cosmos we embrace, faith is required. But for our faith to be real, for it to have substance beyond wishful thinking, we must have the freedom to explore, discover, and dialogue. Regarding both science and theology, I stand convinced that truly objective inquiry, when allowed to run its full course, will point us toward a relationship with God. For this reason, while answers to significant mysteries may be beyond my grasp, I champion our God-given freedom to ask honest questions—even difficult ones—about both our natural and spiritual existence.

HOPE AS EVIDENCE

I am compelled to address one other form of "evidence" in support of the Bible's credibility: *hope*. To contend that hope adds credibility to Biblical claims about God's existence—or more so against the claims of atheism—may at first seem strange, but I think the idea has a degree of substance.

Hope can be defined as "looking forward to in confident expectation."[2] Implicit in this definition is the idea that we anticipate something good to come. We innately believe that when our hopes are fulfilled, life will be better than it is now.

At the core of evolutionary theory is the idea that a long, gradual series of favorable *mutations* on the cellular level will advance the growth and complexity of a species. In other words, every one of us is little more than the product of a long series of *mistakes* which happen to increase our chances of survival.

The problem is that people *require* some form of meaningful hope for a healthy existence on this earth, but scientific naturalism, at its core, is utterly *hopeless*. Pure naturalism tells us that people don't have any more intrinsic value than a blob of organic tissue, that a lion is as important as a human fetus, and that life after death is a foolish fantasy. The very best we can do, it seems, is ease the pain of a few others before we fade into nothingness. The following quote sums up the futility of naturalism well:

> If atheism is true, it is far from being good news. Learning that we're alone in the universe, that no one hears or answers our prayers, that humanity is entirely the product of random events, that we have no more intrinsic dignity than non-human and even non-animate clumps of matter, that we face certain annihilation in death, that our sufferings are ultimately

---

2. James Swanson, *Dictionary of Biblical Languages with Semantic Domains: Greek (New Testament)* (Oak Harbor: Logos Research Systems, Inc., 1997).

pointless, that our lives and loves do not at all matter in a larger sense, that those who commit horrific evils and elude human punishment get away with their crimes scot free—all of this (and much more) is utterly tragic.[3]

The famous playwright, George Bernard Shaw, began as an atheist but begrudgingly turned to *creative evolution* when the hopeless reality of Darwin's theory of natural selection became clear in his mind:

But when its whole significance dawns on you, your heart sinks into a heap of sand within you. There is a hideous fatalism about it, a ghastly and damnable reduction of beauty and intelligence, of strength and purpose, of honour and aspiration . . . To call this Natural Selection is a blasphemy, possible to many for whom Nature is nothing but a casual aggregation of inert and dead matter . . . If it be no blasphemy, but a truth of science, then the stars of heaven, the showers and dew, the winter and summer, the fire and heat, the mountains and hills, may no longer be called to exalt the Lord with us by praise: their work is to modify all things by blindly starving and murdering everything that is not lucky enough to survive the universal struggle for hogwash.[4]

Shaw didn't necessarily want to believe in God, but he couldn't make sense of an existence devoid of hope. Humanity simply does not function well without a sense of meaning, purpose, and expectation for tomorrow. As the grim reality of scientific naturalism becomes clear, a sense of futility overtakes the human heart. But when people begin to lose hope, their behavior becomes destructive. How helpful can such fatalism be to our evolutionary progression?

The expectation of a better tomorrow is not what snares people in the trap of substance abuse. Those who take their own lives aren't brimming with a sense of promise. Meaningful anticipation doesn't lead a young man to kill his family, or a fired employee his coworkers.

3. Damon Linker, "Where Are All the Honest Atheists?" *The Week* website (March 28, 2013) http://theweek.com/articles/466865/where-are-honest-atheists <February 11, 2016)>
4. George Bernard Shaw, *Back to Methusela A Metabiological Pentateuch* (New York: Brentato's, 1921) Preface xlvi.

If there's any vestige of hope in the hearts of those who do these things, it's a twisted desire for revenge or self-glorification. Having come face-to-face with the depths of human depravity, the great Russian novelist Fyodor Dostoevsky once stated, "To live without Hope is to Cease to live." How right he was.

If tangible hope is necessary for a healthy existence, and if the mind, will, and emotions are the products of an unguided natural process, why is naturalism so devoid of hope? Why would genetic mutations produce within us such a deep need for something that nature alone can never provide?

When it comes to providing truly meaningful hope in the face of suffering or unjust circumstances, naturalism is bankrupt. Is this why humanity "invented" the idea of a supernatural God? Because we naturally evolved from absolute nothing to the point where we cannot function as a race without a sense of supernatural hope?

Am I proposing that a naturalist lacks any sense of hope in this life? Not at all. Their hopes, however, are short-lived and can easily be derailed by circumstances beyond their control.

Having been created for something more, humans are instinctively drawn toward the Bible because it proclaims meaning, promise, and hope far beyond what classroom science or philosophy could ever offer. But it is a hope based on eternal reality—not wishful thinking. Thus, given its supposed shortcomings, the Christian faith simply will not die—even in light of what is often proclaimed as an "intellectually superior" atheism.[5]

I propose that we need hope not because we were unintentionally formed, but because we were created by God for value, purpose, and glory. And while our need for promise may not have the same substance as historic or scientific evidence, through it we can fit yet another piece of the Biblical puzzle into place.

We were created to revel in the reality of *everlasting* hope. As a direct result, removing the influence of the Bible from society will never, as we are often led to believe, direct us to a path of liberty. Instead,

5. I feel so strongly about the importance of hope that it is the focus of this book's final chapter.

our collective existence will become increasingly shallow, futile, and dysfunctional in a prison of meaninglessness. Furthermore, as the influence of true Biblical thinking is removed, injustice and oppression will multiply, in turn, creating an increased sense of hopelessness. Such downward societal progressions create unrest so deeply felt that the human race then begins to destroy itself through violent conflict.

CHAPTER WRAP-UP

The idea that science and faith are at odds is a false dichotomy. Both should involve objective inquiry, and if God is real, will point us in His direction. And while we face reasonable questions about the person and existence of God, atheism's unanswered questions ultimately leave the human soul feeling lost and empty. Thankfully, the Bible casts forth brilliant rays of hope and inspiration that give us *credibly incredible* promises for a better tomorrow.

In the science-theology debate, as with many others, we must be vigilant not to lose sight of the things that matter most. Whether we believe our planet to be less than 10,000 years old or more than a billion, is not an issue that impacts our eternal destinies. Faith in our eternal Creator and confidence in His infallible Word, however, are non-negotiable for our eternal well-being. Let's learn to enjoy exploring the lesser issues while firmly establishing the greater ones in our hearts and minds.

8

CREDIBLY INCREDIBLE

I became a Christian because the evidence was so compelling that Jesus really is the one-and-only Son of God who proved his divinity by rising from the dead. That meant following him was the most rational and logical step I could possibly take.

—Lee Strobel

Jesus said to them, "Truly, truly, I say to you, before Abraham was born, I am." Therefore they picked up stones to throw at Him.

John 8:58-59a

"So implausible as to elicit disbelief"—that is how one dictionary defines *incredible*.[1] Apart from being a word overused to generate hype, incredible accurately describes a lot of what's written in the Bible—especially the New Testament. So amazing are the claims and stories of Scripture that well-reasoned people sometimes have a difficult time accepting them as authentic.

Have you ever heard of the *Jefferson Bible*? A deist, the third President of the United States believed that God created the cosmos but then removed Himself from any of its doings. Jefferson appreciated the morals of Jesus, but couldn't accept that He was God incarnate or

---

1. *The American Heritage College Dictionary*, 4th Edition (Boston, New York: Houghton Mifflin Company, 2007), 703.

that He performed miracles. For Jefferson, it seemed entirely reasonable to compile the Gospels after cutting out everything hinting of the miraculous. He called his work *The Life and Morals of Jesus of Nazareth*. Evidently, Thomas Jefferson wasn't searching for a relationship with a supernatural God, but rather a form of "Jesus-flavored" humanism.

When considering Jefferson's beliefs, I can't help but think about modern mindsets. It's not uncommon for me to hear someone claim that Jesus never meant for people to worship Him as God or that the Bible has no authority in human lives. Indeed, the deistic "cut and paste" mentality seems to be making a resurgence these days, but does it correspond with reality?

Along similar lines, people often question if Jesus believed Himself to be the Divine in human flesh. After all, if the Bible is the written Word of God, its authority over humankind depends upon the authoritative deity of Jesus Christ. Did Jesus really claim to be God? If so, was the claim true, or was He simply deluded and, therefore, mentally unstable?

THE CENTRALITY OF JESUS CHRIST

The earthly life of Jesus Christ was, in every sense of the word, incredible. Born to a virgin (how often does that happen?), Jesus stepped down from the glory of heaven and lived more humbly than any human ever could. After being filled with the Holy Spirit at the time of His water baptism, Jesus entered a season of intense temptation while praying and fasting in a desolate wilderness. After this forty-day period, the "Son of Man" burst on the human scene by performing miracle after amazing miracle. He healed the sick, opened the eyes of the blind, and even brought the dead to life. This amazing man also multiplied food, calmed stormy seas, and cast out demons. And yet, all of these miraculous feats seem like a pregame warm-up compared to what came next.

After predicting that He would rise from the dead, Jesus willingly suffered and died by excruciating torture. Three days later, His supposedly lifeless body suddenly rose as a strange supernatural force rolled a massive stone from the entrance of His tomb. Forty days after that, Christ's followers gawked in amazement as their glorious leader mysteriously ascended into the heavens. Incredible! It's little wonder that rational minds such as Thomas Jefferson's would have difficulty accepting the Christian Bible in full.

Claims of the miraculous compel us to make decisions about the Bible's credibility. And because the stakes are so high, it's not surprising that some people see the need for something more than historical documentation to validate the supernatural dynamics of the Bible.

GOD'S ANOINTED ONE

For centuries, the Jews had eagerly anticipated their *Messiah* (*Christ*)—a prophet anointed by God who would ascend to the throne and restore the former glories of their once-powerful nation. The Messiah, they believed, would arise as a mighty warrior—similar to King David—to break the yoke of Roman oppression over God's chosen people.

I've already referred to the following scene that took place near the onset of Jesus' ministry. For our current purposes, it bears repeating:

And He came to Nazareth, where He had been brought up; and as was His custom, He entered the synagogue on the Sabbath, and stood up to read. And the book of the prophet Isaiah was handed to Him. And He opened the book and found the place where it was written,

"THE SPIRIT OF THE LORD IS UPON ME,

BECAUSE HE ANOINTED ME TO PREACH THE GOSPEL TO THE POOR.

HE HAS SENT ME TO PROCLAIM RELEASE TO THE CAPTIVES,

AND RECOVERY OF SIGHT TO THE BLIND,

TO SET FREE THOSE WHO ARE OPPRESSED,

TO PROCLAIM THE FAVORABLE YEAR OF THE LORD."

And He closed the book, gave it back to the attendant and sat down; and the eyes of all in the synagogue were fixed on Him. And He began to say to them, "Today this Scripture has been fulfilled in your hearing." Luke 4:16-21

The people in the synagogue that day understood that Jesus was proclaiming Himself to be the Jewish Messiah, but a huge problem soon emerged. Jesus didn't look, talk, or act like the valiant military hero they expected. Nor did He play power-mongering political games by catering to the Jewish establishment.

The fact that Jesus wasn't brash or egotistical in no way forces Him into the mold of a common human. Indeed, much of what He did and said was entirely uncommon. Still, there's no doubt that the Christ was often self-effacing and that He frequently encouraged people to keep quiet about the miracles He performed. Both behaviors, however, are easily explained.

First, the *big* problem with human nature is *pride*. Glory and significance are lifelong pursuits for all of us. As explained in chapters eight and nine of my book, *The Divine Progression of Grace*, pride is the root source of the cursed state we call *the human condition*. So much of our world's dysfunction is wrapped up in the human ego!

Jesus came to reverse the effects of our self-induced curse, and humility was one of the primary means by which He did so. Jesus Christ intentionally chose to lower Himself that He might firmly establish the dynamics of God's kingdom on earth. Today, Jesus is exalted above all others (Ephesians 1:19b-23) not only because He is inherently worthy, but also because He earned such a status by His uncommon humility (Philippians 2:3-11).

Second, Jesus' miraculous ministry drew such large crowds that it was difficult for Him and His disciples to even function (Mark 3:20, 4:1, and Luke 12:1). Imagine yourself attending a large sporting event at which God begins to use you to heal people. At first, the experience is exhilarating, but as the hours wear on, extreme weariness sets in. For almost as far as you can see, a line of needy and hopeful people anticipate your healing touch. Quickly, the word spreads, and the line turns into an overwhelming mass of human flesh. Taking time for a meal (or even stepping aside to use the bathroom) suddenly becomes a major chore. Eventually, things slow down, and you head toward home. Your heart sinks, however, as an over-the-shoulder glance reveals a huge crowd in tow. After a day or two of such intense activity, I think you too would encourage silence on the part of those you heal.

WITHOUT THE RESURRECTION . . .

As amazing as Christ's life and ministry on earth were, if one event stands out from all others through the course of human history, it would be His *resurrection* from the dead. Furthermore, if the Bible is essential to Christianity, and Jesus is the central authority of the Bible, it is the resurrection of Christ that firmly establishes His deity. Virtually everything else pales in comparison. Vastly more important than whether all facets of the four Gospels appear to agree on every detail, is the historical reality of the resurrection. Everything Christian hinges on the resurrection.

In his introduction to *The Historical Jesus: Ancient Evidence for the Life of Christ*, Dr. Gary Habermas makes the following observation:

> Of all these subjects, the resurrection is like a many-faceted diamond. Turned one way, it is the very center of the Christian Gospel. From another angle, it is the best-attested miracle-claim in Scripture (or in any other "holy book," for that matter). Turned again, it provides an evidential basis for Christian theism. Further, in the New Testament it is a bridge to almost every major doctrine in the Christian faith. . . .[2]

The historical credibility of the New Testament becomes all the more significant in light of the resurrection. If the New Testament is authentic, then the resurrection becomes a massive stumbling block for critics. (Time and space do not permit a review of the opposing arguments and alternative theories to the resurrection, but they are weak at best and downright ludicrous at worst. If you feel the need to investigate them, please don't hesitate to do so. An internet search might be a good place to start. Habermas' *The Historical Jesus* also addresses several of these theories.)

The most reasonable explanation denying the resurrection is that Christ's disciples stole His body. Accordingly, this was the story

2. Gary R. Habermas, *The Historical Jesus: Ancient Evidence for the Life of Christ* (Joplin, MO: College Press Publishing Company, 1996), 9.

proclaimed and spread by the bulk of the Jewish leadership. But if the disciples had stolen the body, why wouldn't they have "come clean" under the threat of death? Instead, the same Peter who denied Jesus the night before the crucifixion is reputed to have been crucified upside down while holding firmly to his beliefs. Even the harshest critic is compelled to admit that Jesus' disciples honestly believed that He rose from the dead and that they saw Him ascend into the heavens.

Jesus espoused high ideals of integrity that, except for Judas Iscariot, His closest followers fully embraced. Reading through the Gospels—written by the disciples or their associates—we find multiple accounts that cast the disciples themselves in a negative light. Such brutal honesty cuts against the grain of human nature. Ancient kings, for example, were known to strike anything from the historical record that might cause succeeding generations to view them unfavorably. Not so with Christ's disciples; they provided honest accounts of their experiences even at the expense of public humiliation. These men were more concerned about communicating truth than protecting images.

Even more importantly, the disciples adamantly proclaimed Christ's resurrection from the dead. Ten of the twelve original disciples—Judas Iscariot and the apostle John being the exceptions—died as martyrs contending for the historical reality of the resurrection.

In addition to the Gospel accounts, we find a very important creed recorded by the apostle Paul in his first letter to the Corinthians:

Now brothers, I want to clarify for you the gospel I proclaimed to you; you received it and have taken your stand on it. You are also saved by it, if you hold to the message I proclaimed to you— unless you believed for no purpose. For I passed on to you as most important what I also received:

that Christ died for our sins according to the Scriptures, that He was buried, that He was raised on the third day according to the Scriptures, and that He appeared to Cephas,

then to the Twelve.
Then He appeared to over 500 brothers at one time;
most of them are still alive,
but some have fallen asleep.
Then He appeared to James,
then to all the apostles.
Last of all, as to one abnormally born,
He also appeared to me.

1 Corinthians 15:1-8 (HCSB)

If we accept the standard belief that Paul wrote 1 Corinthians around AD 54-56, we can, using the Biblical record, reconstruct the apostle's life to find that he became a Christian within a decade of Christ's death and subsequent resurrection. Most likely, it was at this point that he received this early creed. Not only did Jesus' followers claim to have seen the risen Christ, and not only did they give public testimony of their experiences, belief in the sacrificial death and resurrection of Jesus Christ was integral to Christian doctrine in its *earliest* stages.

No one rises from the dead after three days. No one. Along with His virgin birth, the resurrection of Jesus Christ is *incredibly credible*; together they stand as the two most significant events known to humankind. And if we can't cut the resurrection out of the Bible, all of the other miracles belong as well.

GOD INCARNATE

A combination of factors may lead to public confusion about the identity of Jesus Christ, but there is one person who never aired a hint of uncertainty—Jesus. Not only did Jesus proclaim Himself to be the Jewish Messiah, He also made the outlandish claim of being God in human flesh—a belief that became central to the teachings of the early church. Consider just a few of the radical statements made by Jesus:

"I am the bread of life; he who comes to Me will not hunger, and he who believes in Me will never thirst." John 6:35b

"I am the Light of the world; he who follows Me will not walk in the darkness, but will have the Light of life." John 8:12b

"I am the resurrection and the life; he who believes in Me will live even if he dies." John 11:25b

"I am the way, and the truth, and the life; no one comes to the Father but through Me." John 14:6b

"I am the true vine, and My Father is the vinedresser." John 15:1

Any ordinary human making such extreme claims would be instantly branded as self-absorbed and mentally unstable, and yet, this is but a sampling of the emphatic "I am" statements made by Jesus. The Son of Joseph and Mary claimed oneness with the eternal God, generating outrage amongst the Jewish establishment. Unfortunately, much of the potency of this claim is lost in translation.

From the youngest age, Jewish children were taught about their ancestral heritage, with Moses standing as a much-revered hero. It was his strange encounter with God at the burning bush that helped mark God's identity for the Jewish people.

Then Moses said to God, "Behold, I am going to the sons of Israel, and I will say to them, 'The God of your fathers has sent me to you.' Now they may say to me, 'What is His name?' What shall I say to them?" God said to Moses, "I AM WHO I AM"; and He said, "Thus you shall say to the sons of Israel, 'I AM has sent me to you.'" Exodus 3:13-14

Can you think of a better name for God than "I am"? The Creator of the Universe was clearly revealing His self-existence. He needs nothing and no one for His survival. Indeed, all things proceed from Him.

Jesus made numerous "I am" statements—many of which were communicated forcefully by the Greek language in which the New Testament was written. In effect, Jesus was saying to the Jewish people, "I AM He who revealed Himself to Moses—the very One you have been worshiping for all of these centuries." If Jesus were not God, His words would have been blasphemous and such worship idolatrous—both of which were worthy of death under the Mosaic law.

Jewish religious leaders faced a painful choice. Accepting Jesus' claim to be the Messiah would have turned their world upside down by invalidating their lifestyles and undermining their hold on power. Instead, they accused the miracle worker of blasphemy and sought to stone Him. Make no mistake about it—Jesus believed Himself to be both the Jewish Messiah and God in human flesh. Christ's outrageous claims brought upheaval to the culture of His day and continue to wreak (much-needed) havoc on the dynamics of our human institutions.

CHRIST AS GOD

I've heard it argued that Jesus, being self-effacing, would have been appalled at the idea of His followers worshiping Him as God. The problem with this line of reasoning is that it breaks down upon further investigation of the New Testament.

> But Thomas, one of the twelve, called Didymus, was not with them when Jesus came. So the other disciples were saying to him, "We have seen the Lord!" But he said to them, "Unless I see in His hands the imprint of the nails, and put my finger into the place of the nails, and put my hand into His side, I will not believe."
>
> After eight days His disciples were again inside, and Thomas with them. Jesus came, the doors having been shut, and stood in their midst and said, "Peace be with you." Then He said to Thomas, "Reach here with your finger, and see My hands; and reach here your hand and put it into My side; and do not be unbelieving, but believing." Thomas answered and said to Him, "My Lord and my God!" Jesus said to him, "Because you have seen Me, have you believed? Blessed are they who did not see, and yet believed." John 20:24-29

If Jesus did not believe Himself to be God, He would have responded by tearing His robe in despair and convincing Thomas of His humanity. Indeed, this would have been the appropriate Jewish response, and it is exactly what Paul and Barnabas did at Lystra when the Lycaonians called them gods (see Acts 14:8-18). But instead of appealing to Jewish reason, Jesus admonished Thomas for his previous unbelief.

According to the New Testament, Jesus equated Himself with God the Father (John 10:30), the Jews recognized this claim and considered it blasphemy (John 8:58-59), and the early church leaders elevated Him to the point of worship (Hebrews 1:1-11). The age-old Christian belief in the deity of Christ began while He still walked this globe and is supported by the historical accounts of His miracles and resurrection.

Archaeologists have also discovered several ancient non-Christian documents related to the person of Jesus Christ and the common practices of the early church. One such document was penned around AD 112 by Pliny the Younger—a Roman author and administrator. Serving as the governor of Bithynia in Asia Minor, Pliny wrote to the Roman emperor Trajan for counsel regarding the Christian faith. The influence of Jesus' followers had become so profound that many pagan temples were virtually deserted, severely impacting the previously brisk trade of buying and selling sacrificial animals.

The following is a portion of Pliny's letter to the emperor explaining his concern:

> They (the Christians) were in the habit of meeting on a certain fixed day before it was light, when they sang in alternate verses a hymn to Christ, as to a god, and bound themselves by a solemn oath, not to any wicked deeds, but never to commit any fraud, theft, or adultery, never to falsify their word, nor deny a trust when they should be called upon to deliver it up; after which it was their custom to separate, and then reassemble to partake of food—but food of an ordinary and innocent kind.[3]

Within eighty years of His death and resurrection in the populous city of Jerusalem, the belief system that brazenly proclaimed the deity of Jesus Christ was having a profound impact in the greater Roman Empire. No power of humankind could stop the belief in a resurrected Christ.

Is it incredible to think of Jesus as God in human flesh and the eternal Creator of all things? Absolutely. And yet, the story is strangely credible, marked by amazing miracles and the most unlikely feat imaginable—resurrection from the dead. Such claims are supported by a wealth of evidence, which when examined with honest hearts, cannot help but stretch the limits of our collective imagination.

---

3. Habermas, *The Historical Jesus*, 199.

OLD TESTAMENT PROPHECIES

If Jesus truly rose from the dead, practically anything is possible. Christ's miracles were either the work of a strange magic or slight of hand—as contended by some Jewish authorities—or Jesus superseded the laws of nature. Incredible ideas? Yes, but also historically credible.

Supernatural events, however, did not begin when Jesus Christ took form in human flesh. The Old Testament is replete with miracles as God supernaturally moved and worked on behalf of His people. And though we have a more difficult time providing supporting evidence for Old Testament miracles as opposed to New, there remains one very powerful exception: dozens of major prophecies (and many more minor ones) identified with Jesus. All told, over 300 Old Testament predictions found their fulfillment in the person of Jesus Christ.

I once had an interesting conversation with a brilliant college student about the credibility of the Scriptures. It soon became clear that this well-reasoned young man wanted to discard the Bible, but he could not get past the mystery of Christ's fulfilling Old Testament prophecies. Ancient Hebrew prophecy was "the fly in ointment" of his atheism. He was not the first—or last—intellectual to be mystified by the Bible.

During the 1950s, an accomplished mathematician by the name of Dr. Peter Stoner gathered data to determine the mathematic probability of someone fulfilling Old Testament prophecies.[4] Stoner gained approval from The American Scientific Affiliation and the Executive Council of that same body showing that his work was free of error and bias.

Dr. Stoner calculated that the probability of one man fulfilling only eight Messianic prophecies was 1×10^{17}—that is a 1 followed by 17 zeros—reflecting only a minute possibility! To illustrate the staggering nature of these odds, Stoner went on to explain that a blindfolded person wandering around the entire state of Texas covered two feet deep in silver dollars would have a 1×10^{17} chance of picking one specifically marked silver dollar.

---

4. Kimball, *The Book of Books*, 62-69. See also: Peter Stoner, "Scientific Proof of the Accuracy of Prophecy and the Bible" on the *Science Speaks* website (Chicago: Moody Press; Science Speaks, Online Edition, © Donald Wayne Stoner C 2002, Revised Nov. 2005) http://sciencespeaks.dstoner. net/ <May 30, 2015>

Peter Stoner went on to compute the odds of one individual fulfilling larger numbers of prophecies, and they are overwhelming. Problematically, some people find Dr. Stoner's work less than convincing because Old Testament prophecy was often cryptic in nature. In many places where advocates of Christianity see clear references to Jesus, critics see only vague possibilities. Furthermore, in some places where Old Testament passages clearly point to Jesus, critics argue that He and His disciples deliberately manipulated events to give the appearance of a supernatural fulfillment.

If we accept these criticisms and allow only the "more credible" claims, the odds are *still* overwhelming. Below are listed sixteen Old Testament prophecies that were fulfilled in Jesus and over which a merely human Christ and His band of disciples would have had little to no control:

- That Christ would be born in the small town of Bethlehem (Micah 5:2 - Matthew 2:1).

- That Jesus would come out of Egypt (Hosea 11:1 - Matthew 2:15).

- That Jesus would have a ministry of miracles (Isaiah 35:5-6 - Matthew 9:35).

- That Jesus would be betrayed by a friend (Psalms 41:9 - Matthew 10:4).

- That the Christ would be betrayed for 30 pieces of silver (Zechariah 11:12 - Matthew 26:15).

- That the silver would be thrown into the temple (Zechariah 11:13 - Matthew 27:5).

- That Jesus would be rejected by His own people (Isaiah 53:3 - John 7:5, 48).

- That Jesus would be scourged and crucified (Isaiah 53:5 - Matthew 27:26).

- That Jesus would be beaten and spit upon (Isaiah 50:6 - Matthew 26:67).

- That lots would be cast for Christ's clothing (Psalms 22:18 - John 19:23-24).

- That Christ would be pierced (Psalms 22:16 and Zechariah 12:10 - Luke 23:33 and John 19:34).

- That Jesus would be crucified with evil doers (Isaiah 53:12 - Matthew 27:38).

- That onlookers would mock Jesus (Psalms 22:7-8 - Matthew 27:29).

- That none of Jesus' bones would be broken (Psalms 34:20 - John 19:33).

- That Jesus would be buried in a rich man's tomb (Isaiah 53:9 - Matthew 27:57-60).

- That Jesus would rise from the dead (Psalms 16:10 - John 20:1-29 and Acts 2:31).

Dr. Stoner calculated the odds of one man fulfilling only *sixteen* Old Testament prophecies at the astronomical number of 1 x 10^{45}![5] But in responding to the critics, we must note several things. First, the fact that the sixteen predictions listed above were recorded in the *Jewish* Scriptures, combined with the dating of the Dead Sea Scrolls, does not allow them to be added by Christians *ex post facto* (after the fact). Thus, we are dealing with ancient prophecies given long before the time of Christ and not manufactured additions to the Old Testament text. Second, these are just a handful of the dozens, if not hundreds, of Old Testament prophecies made regarding the Messiah. Third, many of these predictions are very specific. As determined by Dr. Stoner, the odds against all sixteen prophecies being fulfilled by a single person are staggering. Finally, Christ's Jewish and Roman enemies fulfilled much of what the Scriptures foretold about His betrayal and death. The *last* thing these people wanted to do was add credibility to Jesus' Messianic claims!

Do these Old Testament predictions conclusively prove that Jesus was divinely sent from heaven? Perhaps not. In spite of the

5. Kimball, *The Book of Books*, 65.

astronomical odds against Old Testament Messianic prophecies being fulfilled through the person and life of Jesus Christ, we are left with an *infinitesimal* statistical probability to the contrary. Even so, the evidence continues to mount for our incredibly credible case that Jesus was God in human flesh and that the Bible is the inspired, infallible, and authoritative expression of His intelligence. Sooner or later, honest hearts are compelled to admit that they cannot casually discard such credible claims.

REAL LIFE EXPERIENCES

Although much of what I teach is rooted and grounded in faith, my scientific background has conditioned me to look for evidence. It wasn't wishful thinking or blind ideology that compelled me to sacrifice a potentially profitable career in the field of chemistry. As I have taught from the Bible over the past twenty-five years, time and time again, I have watched God transform human lives. In fact, few things excite me more than seeing the profound influence of the Bible in the life of a person who has struggled in life.

Thus, another indicator of the Bible's inspiration is one that gets little academic attention—although perhaps it should warrant the most—the *transformation of human lives*. From ordinary folks—like Christ's original disciples—to brilliant intellectuals—such as Sir William Ramsay and C.S. Lewis—we find millions upon millions of people of all ages, backgrounds, nationalities, and races who tenaciously embrace an unlikely system of belief. The bulk of these people profess powerful and dramatic changes wrought in their lives due to the influence of the Bible. Miracles, it seems, are not limited to the past.

We find some of the most incredible evidence for the credibility of the Bible in the amazing stories of those whose lives have been radically changed by the gospel of Jesus Christ. What are we to do with these millions of people? Write them off as moronic and uneducated? Classify them as deluded or mentally ill? Any of these options might seem reasonable until you sit down for a thoughtful conversation with one of the *many* well-reasoned Christians whose faith is rooted in a genuine relationship with his or her Creator.

If you feel that the term *well-reasoned Christian* is an oxymoron, you've probably fallen prey to the intentional stereotyping of "Bible thumpers" in popular media. How many on-screen crimes are committed by self-absorbed, tightly wound, and mentally unstable religious bigots who continually quote passages from the Bible? No doubt, such people exist, but in no way do they come close to representing the entirely of evangelical Christianity.

As someone who has been involved with various aspects of Christian ministry for decades, I can personally testify to a very different experience. Undoubtedly, I've been terribly disappointed by some who have professed Christ, but I've also had the privilege of knowing many exemplary men and women of whom this world is not worthy. I consider it an honor not only to wear the label of "Christian," but also to identify with these caring individuals. Of such people, we will read more in the following chapter.

Finally, but certainly not least, in addition to the changes wrought in our lives, a vast number of Christians can personally testify to experiencing God's *supernatural presence*. We've been guided by His loving hand, we've drawn strength and courage through difficult times, we've seen unlikely answers to prayer, we've experienced His healing touch, we've tasted the sweet fruit of vital relationships, and we've been blessed by unnatural means of provision. I realize that mass belief doesn't prove anything, but such claims from typically honest people certainly warrant our attention. Either we're all overcome with delusion, or we have encountered the *real and living God*.

CHAPTER WRAP-UP

The claims of the New Testament are so incredible that it's easy to understand why a thinking mind might question them. The idea of an immensely powerful Creator who took human form only to be killed and then rise from the dead is enough to overwhelm even the most creative human brain. It's also understandable that any one form of evidence for the Bible's credibility might fail to convince a skeptic. When taken together, however, their collective corroboration puts the Bible in a class by itself. No other religious text or system of belief compares.

THE TOUCHPOINT

In the end, the Bible is either our *TouchPoint* for heavenly wisdom or it is the product of human reasoning. Through the credibly incredible evidence listed, and through the fruit of my life experience, I can't help but embrace the Bible as the inspired, infallible, and authoritative Word of God!

9

THE FAVORABLE INFLUENCE OF THE GOSPEL

O holy night! The stars are brightly shining,
It is the night of our dear Saviour's birth.
Long lay the world in sin and error pining,
Till He appear'd and the soul felt its worth.
A thrill of hope, the weary world rejoices,
For yonder breaks a new and glorious morn.

"Oh Holy Night" —adapted by John Sullivan Dwight
from Placide Cappeau

"But I say to you who hear, love your enemies, do good to those who hate you, bless those who curse you, pray for those who mistreat you."

Luke 6:27-28

I wanted to title this chapter, "The Favorable Influence of the Bible," but I just couldn't bring myself to it. Although I am obviously a huge fan of the Christian Scriptures, I won't hesitate to admit that they've been used to justify all kinds of deplorable behavior—including greed, sexism, racism, oppression, slavery, and brutality of all sorts. We are compelled, then, to more thoroughly explore and address the types of behavior that are consistent with an *accurate understanding* of New Testament doctrine.

We can all agree that the hammer is a valuable tool for building and creating. A manufacturing company can produce a hammer to be used for construction, but it has no control over how the tool is wielded. In the wrong hands, powerful instruments that are meant to build can easily be used to wreak destruction. Sadly, murder by hammer is not uncommon in our violent world, but the tool itself is in no way at fault.

Virtually everything with significant potential for good can also be used for evil. And so it is with spiritual truth. As valuable as the Bible is to shape and transform lives, its influence can also be used to bind and oppress. The sword of God's Word, when wielded by ignorant or mal-intentioned hands, will destroy—not build—human lives.

AN INSTRUMENT OF DEATH?

My first job after college was an entry-level position working in a coal laboratory. During one of our lunch breaks, I was initially pleased to discover that a co-worker and her husband participated in a home Bible study. But as we made small talk about our respective beliefs, I began to feel uneasy. Something didn't seem right. An exchange of some materials led me to realize that she was part of the white supremacist "Christian Identity" movement. In all honesty, I was somewhat unnerved as I explored their interpretations of the Bible which were opposite my own.

We should never take lightly the apostle Paul's sincere warning to his young protégé Timothy:

> Until I come, give attention to the public reading of Scripture, to exhortation and teaching . . . Take pains with these things; be absorbed in them, so that your progress will be evident to all. Pay close attention to yourself and to your teaching; persevere in these things, for as you do this you will ensure salvation both for yourself and for those who hear you. 1 Timothy 4:13-16

Paul wasn't the only one to admonish his readers along these lines. James 3:1, which was likely penned by Jesus' brother, states, "Let not many of you become teachers, my brethren, knowing that as such we will incur a stricter judgment." Those who claim to speak for God carry a significant responsibility to ensure that their influence truly reflects that of Christ.

Accurately understanding and representing the true intent of the Bible is no trite issue! If we are going to write and speak regarding matters that impact eternal destinies, we had better have a pretty good idea of what we're talking about.

Especially problematic is the fact that large numbers of Bible-believing Christians struggle to understand the relationship between law and grace—one of the core themes addressed by Paul. Those who confuse the New Testament gospel of grace with Old Testament law will produce a pseudo-Christianity that appears as God-breathed religion, but inherently conflicts with His design.

> *Not that we are adequate in ourselves to consider anything as coming from ourselves, but our adequacy is from God, who also made us adequate as servants of a new covenant, not of the letter but of the Spirit; for the letter kills, but the Spirit gives life.*
> *2 Corinthians 3:5-6*

What challenging thoughts for us to process! In effect, Paul was stating that an accurate understanding of the Bible flows from the Holy Spirit, who imparts life-filled grace. At the same time, those who are ignorant of God's grace-filled way will resort to systems of rules and regulations as means of behavior modification in their religious expressions.

The problem is not with moral laws themselves, but with the manner in which human nature responds to such laws. More often than not, moral laws are laid down for the purpose of preserving life, but contrary to their expected outcomes, our human response often leads to death (Romans 7:9-11). The Holy Bible—according to no less an authority than the apostle Paul—can actually *kill* our spiritual well-being if interpreted according to a rule-based paradigm!

We now come to realize the vast difference between actions done *in the name of Christ* as opposed to being in agreement with *the Spirit of Christ*. People can do virtually anything in the name of Jesus, so we must ask ourselves what types of behavior accurately represent that name. In particular, if our words or actions are out of step with the example and teachings of Christ, we have a serious problem.

In exercising this caution, I am in no way suggesting any inherent problem with the Scriptures themselves. The issue lies with our natural human tendencies toward law-based living combined with the careless use of the Biblical text. We must—and I repeat, *must*—seek to comprehend what the Spirit of God seeks to communicate through the Scriptures. Otherwise, our natural human reasoning will distort and corrupt our understanding of God's truth.

When I refer, then, to "The Favorable Influence of the Gospel," I have in mind the good news of God's grace as realized through the person of Jesus Christ. Such references include all that is recorded in the Bible as understood through its Spirit-intended relationship to the gospel. Getting this distinction right isn't a matter of trying to justify bad behavior on the part of professing Christians; we are addressing an issue that the Scriptures themselves emphasize.

THE GOSPEL'S REDEMPTIVE INFLUENCE

The gospel makes little sense if we fail to grasp a basic understanding of God's past interaction with humanity. The King of the Universe created the human race *in His image*—an amazing honor, for sure. However, in its desire to be like God apart from God, humanity rebelled against heaven's throne by eating the forbidden fruit from the tree of the knowledge of good and evil. All of the pain, bondage, death, and destruction in our world today have their roots in that forbidden tree.

For His part, however, God didn't create the human race to see it destroyed. Thus, He sent Jesus to pay a terrible price on a wooden cross to redeem us from sin's devastation. An appropriate New Testament definition of *redeem* would be "to cause the release or freedom of someone by a means which proves costly to the individual causing the release."[1] Had not human nature been poisoned by forbidden fruit consumption, the price paid by Jesus would have been unnecessary.

From the day that Adam and Eve ate of the death tree, God's ultimate goal has been to redeem humanity from the consequences of that rebellion (see Genesis 3:15). Much of the Old Testament points

1. Johannes P. Louw and Eugene Albert Nida, *Greek-English Lexicon of the New Testament: Based on Semantic Domains* (New York: United Bible Societies, 1996), 487.

toward an "age of redemption" that began with the birth of Jesus Christ and will end with His second coming. There will one day be an eternal judgment of all peoples, but that time is *not* now (Hebrews 9:27). Love-motivated correction is integral to our spiritual well-being, and we must, therefore, make *righteous* judgments, but these are always characterized by a redemptive dynamic. In our current age of grace, God always seeks to rescue people from sin so that the day of judgment will be a time of reward—not one of punishment.

The history of God's interaction with this planet is defined by a creation/sin/redemption pattern. God created everything good, but humanity's quest for independence brought dysfunction, destruction, and death. Our Creator then instituted a redemptive plan that found its fullness in the person of Jesus Christ. The Bible teaches that Jesus came to this earth "full of grace and truth" (John 1:14). The dynamics of grace and truth are evidenced by the fact that Christ's life on this planet centered around human restoration. He continually sought to restore people to God for the purpose of imparting freedom and life.

The Christian life never consists of a one-way relationship; our Lord expects from us the same type of wholehearted and faithful devotion that He has lovingly extended to us. Salvation from sin is free, no doubt. It's not something we can ever earn. At the same time, genuine faith comes with a significant cost as we respond to God's love and seek to fulfill His call on our lives. Because Jesus died sacrificially for humanity, those who love God will live—and sometimes die—sacrificially for Him. Such sacrifices are never a means to gain God's approval, but rather to honor Him as we seek to bless people and reconcile them to Christ.

In this age of grace, we can find at least three essential truths that move Christians to serve others sacrificially:

1. **Because God created all humans in His image, every person has intrinsic value.** Such a gospel-based mindset conflicts with our world's system which bases value on what a person has to offer through its cultural paradigms. Why do professional athletes in America command absurd amounts of money for *playing games*? They offer value for both entertainment and

glory. In contrast, those who have nothing to offer are treated as irrelevant—or worse.

One of the most powerful battles raging in our world is that of *class*. Humanity has always been elitist, but Darwin provided a "scientific" foundation for giving expression to human pride. The resulting *survival of the fittest* mentality provides further justification for some people to feel as though they are genetically superior—and therefore, deservedly elite—to others.

I remember a high school class discussion in which we were presented with a hypothetical lifeboat that had room only for a limited number of people. Two of the group would have to be cast into the sea to drown, and it was our job to determine who lived and who died. I'm not sure whose idea it was to put a classroom of developing adolescents in a position to make such life and death decisions, but the exercise had very little to do with reading, writing, and arithmetic.

I was oblivious then, but I can see now that the inherent message of our group exercise was to assign each person a *value* according to what each he or she had to offer society. We were taking our first youthful steps into the world of *eugenics* that was more or less rebirthed out of Darwin's theory of evolution. After all, wouldn't it benefit humanity to selectively breed the most superior of our race while doing what we can to remove those of the species that are genetically flawed?

Jesus Christ modeled and taught an entirely different approach! He equally valued each person regardless of ability, wealth, status, or even morality. The elite-minded hated Jesus because of the way in which He "brought them down to size." Since the day that Jesus initiated such a redemptive mindset, people moved by Christ's unconditional love have impacted our world beyond human imagination.

2. **Because of God's redemptive plan, those who love Him will seek to value and redeem others through a *ministry of reconciliation* (2 Corinthians 5:18-19).**

I can't begin to list the number of Christ-followers whose profound love for humanity leaves me in awe. I refer to people who, despite significant personal cost, unceasingly serve to help the downtrodden of society on almost every level. There's Peter, who meets the needs of the homeless in New York City; Dan and Debbie, who patiently house and serve the female victims of sex trafficking; Ron, who spends untold hours with prison inmates; and Terry, who helps those inmates reintegrate in society. I might also mention Carmen, who spends his waking hours bringing hope to drug addicts and their families; Dan and Tammy, who have adopted two special needs children from overseas; and Matt, whose organization is helping an Asian government improve the lives of autistic children.

Quite honestly, the list goes on and on. I know many more followers of Christ who spend their lives serving others, and many more who support and fund those serving on the front lines of human need. And these are just some of the people who I've personally met. Many, many more give and serve "under the radar" of human attention.

As much as pain and injustice mark our human existence, I can't imagine how much worse things would be if not for Christians who love(d) people out of a deep love for God. From its very birth, the authentic Christian church has been characterized by sacrificial benevolence.

3. **Through God's redemptive plan, each of us can find a unique purpose that goes far beyond our natural reasons for existing.** Since our Creator has thoughtfully fashioned us for these purposes, we find a deep sense of fulfillment as we live out God's design for our lives.

The apostle Paul taught that we are God's "workmanship created in Christ Jesus for good works, which God prepared beforehand so that we would walk in them" (Ephesians 2:10). The reality of this powerful statement has illuminated the hearts of millions since the days that Jesus lived among us.

Our heavenly Father has designed each of us to be unique and to touch a specific sphere of people. All of our experiences—even the negative and painful ones—will be used by Him to make us more effective in our redemptive efforts to bless human lives.

Almost from the day I surrendered myself to Christ, I have felt a deep-seated sense of purpose. And now, as the end of my season on this earth grows nearer, the passion of my calling has only intensified. Well aware that my days are numbered, I labor for the sake of the generations to follow. As much as I sometimes long to serve my own desires, I know I could never be satisfied apart from doing my heavenly Father's will.

Are there difficulties involved? Without question. Fulfilling God's plan for me has been far more difficult than I ever imagined. At the same time, this dimension of my life has proven to be immensely rewarding. In a weak moment, I might briefly regret the sacrifices made through the years, but my perspective always brightens when I consider the lives that God has graced me to touch.

Connecting with God means connecting with His heart, and connecting with His heart means fulfilling His redemptive purposes for our lives. I couldn't imagine things any other way.

CRITICISMS OF CHRISTIAN INFLUENCE

My deep love for Christ's church will not allow me to turn a blind eye to her shortcomings. Therefore, I won't try to deny the fact that many of the criticisms laid against the Christian church have just cause. More than once, I have admitted such failure to those who have been needlessly wounded by professing Christians. And the problem isn't just with the hypocrites. Even those who are motivated by God's love don't always exercise God's wisdom in their decision making.

Still, we must also realize that many of the criticisms directed against the Christian faith find substance in an unbiblical representation of Jesus. Our human images of Jesus tend to be selective. Certain aspects of His character (e.g. His loving nature) are often distorted at the expense of others (e.g. His holiness). In addition—and every bit as significant—is the fact that critics often twist truth to portray Christianity and its adherents in a negative light. In the end, Christians are expected to be more loving, but less Bible-believing. The underlying message is that we should become more like Christ by believing in Him less.

I once took a Christianity class at a secular university in which the well-meaning professor frequently highlighted the damage done by missionaries but neglected to address the evil practices of the cultures impacted. His selective instruction created a skewed and inaccurate perspective that negatively influenced the perceptions of my classmates. The cumulative impact of such an approach is quite damaging, thus, I find it necessary to address at least a few of the misconceptions that tend to keep people distant from Christ.

CHRISTIAN VIOLENCE?

Several years ago, a mentally ill man in our community killed his family and himself "in the name of God." A day or so later, I was sitting in a dentist's chair having my teeth cleaned, the hygienist expressing concern that people should never take religious faith too seriously. The content of her monologue (I couldn't say much with my teeth being scraped clean) clearly implied that wholehearted religious devotion will lead to bizarre or violent behavior.

Atheists often point toward God-sanctioned violence in the Old Testament, the Crusades of the Middle Ages, and terroristic acts by radical Muslims to support the idea that religious devotion is a primary source of conflict in our world, and that it would, therefore, be wise to eradicate religious belief from the cultural landscape of humanity. Such erroneous thinking makes it imperative that we understand the unique influence of the Christian gospel.

Under the law-based paradigm of the old covenant, God called for the complete annihilation of the Amalekites. And while the Creator of the Universe was entirely just in ordering the extermination of that wicked people group, such actions did not reflect His actual desire. How do we know? By studying and understanding the relationship between the old and new covenants. The giving of the old covenant Mosaic law marked a season of intense judgment for and by the people of God. But a law-based relationship was never God's ultimate goal. Instead, for a season, He related to the human race *on our own law-based terms* in an effort to steer us toward the superiority of Christ's paradigm of grace (Galatians 3:23-25).

For this and other reasons, Jesus Christ came to earth to reveal a fully accurate representation of the heavenly Father. Full of grace and truth, Jesus was *never* a man of the sword; His most violent act was to drive the money changers from the Jewish temple and overturn their tables. Even this was done to liberate those being oppressed by the corrupt establishment.

I'm not claiming Jesus never created conflict. A person doesn't establish an entirely new form of government (the kingdom of God) without offending and alienating those who seek to maintain their grip on power. Such strife, however, is rooted in the way people respond to the advance of God's kingdom—not in the means or methods of the kingdom itself.

> *"Do not think that I have come to bring peace to the earth; I have not come to bring peace, but a sword. For I have come to set a man against his father, and a daughter against her mother, and a daughter-in-law against her mother-in-law. And a person's enemies will be those of his own household." Matthew 10:34-36 (ESV)*

When taken in context, this passage communicates that loyalty to Christ will sometimes put a person at odds with the people he or she loves most; it is *not* a call to kill family members. Throughout His ministry, Jesus stated that His kingdom was not earthly and would advance by love—not physical violence. Furthermore, Christ's behavior was *entirely congruent* with His teaching. Even on the night He was betrayed and arrested, Jesus refused to fight—much to the dismay of His disciples who still expected Him to establish an earthly kingship via the sword.

For the next three centuries, Christ's followers were predominately *non-violent*. During this time, the church suffered through ten intense periods of persecution while seeking virtually no retribution in return.

Their pacifist leanings stand in sharp contrast to the Jewish zealots who violently battled the Roman Empire until it finally crushed their resistance somewhere around AD 132-135. According to *The Encyclopedia of Religion and War*:

> No extant Christian writings prior to Emperor Constantine's (d. 337 CE) legalization of Christianity (313) approved of Christian participation in military violence. Nor is there evidence of Christian participation in the military prior to 170.[2]

A seismic shift took place when the Roman emperor Constantine issued the Edict of Milan (AD 313), essentially legalizing the Christian faith. What was once considered a criminal movement became the officially sanctioned religion of the Roman Empire, and eventually, of other governments. And while the church was elated to be free from centuries of persecution, the politicization of Christianity brought with it many negative consequences. Not only did genuine faith begin to wane, but political efforts toward control were soon adorned with Christian trappings. And so it came to be that violent acts—some of which have been heinous in every way—were done in the name of Christ in spite of the fact that Jesus was clearly nonviolent.

Because of Christ's peaceful example, and despite the inquisitions by the institutional church during the Medieval age and following, Christians have every right to claim that violence done in Jesus' name runs contrary to what He modeled and taught. Furthermore, on no level is it accurate to consider Old Testament acts of violence as representative of Christianity. The new covenant gospel of grace—not the old covenant of law—defines our faith.

CHRISTIANITY AND ISLAM?

Having examined briefly the history of violence in relationship to Christianity, we might now consider the manner in which it is commonly compared with Islam—especially in light of the Crusades. Why must we address this issue? Because some critics see no intrinsic difference between the influence of the Bible and the influence of the

---

2. Gabriel Palmer-Fernandez, Editor, *Encyclopedia of Religion and War*, (New York: Routlledge (2004), 76

Qur'an. A few have even claimed that most wars have been religiously motivated. Such a perspective, however, is not rooted in reality.

> . . . an objective look at history reveals that those killed in the name of religion have, in fact, been a tiny fraction in the bloody history of human conflict. In their recently published book, "Encyclopedia of Wars," authors Charles Phillips and Alan Axelrod document the history of recorded warfare, and from their list of 1,763 wars only 123 have been classified to involve a religious cause, accounting for less than 7 percent of all wars and less than 2 percent of all people killed in warfare. While, for example, it is estimated that approximately one to three million people were tragically killed in the Crusades, and perhaps 3,000 in the Inquisition, nearly 35 million soldiers and civilians died in the senseless, and secular, slaughter of World War 1 alone.[3]

Even with the potential for error in the classifications given by Philips and Axelrod, the numbers speak loudly! Furthermore, of the 123 wars classified as being primarily religious in nature, 66 (about 3.75 percent of the 1,763 total) were initiated in the name of Islam.[4] *All* other religions combine for the remaining 3.25 percent. While it's difficult to clearly delineate the reasons for a war—Islam marries religion and state—the pattern of Islam's aggressive nature has been historically established.

Events of the past few decades have shown that radical Muslims can be horrifically violent, but their actions in no way characterize all Muslims. I've known several peaceful Muslims through the years who I have no problem identifying with as friends; I see them as warm, caring, and genuine people. Furthermore, I think it's quite reasonable to contend that the majority of professing Muslims in our world are peaceful and decent for the most part.

The contrast within Islam between peaceful *moderates* and violent *extremists* creates considerable confusion regarding the true nature of the religion. It certainly doesn't help that both groups quote the Qur'an

---

3. Rabbi Alan Lurie, "Is Religion the Cause of Most Wars?" *The Huffington Post* website (April 10, 2012 and updated June 10, 2012) http://www.huffingtonpost.com/rabbi-alan-lurie/is-religion-the-cause-of-_b_1400766.html <February 15, 2016>
4. Robin Schumacher, "The Myth that Religion is the #1 Cause of War," *Christian Apologetics and Research Ministry (CARM)* website, https://carm.org/religion-cause-war <February 11, 2016>

to justify their positions. Clarity on this issue is even more elusive for those with Western mindsets. Our Western way of thinking is far removed from the language, customs, and beliefs of historical Islam.

As it is with the Bible, we must consider the Qur'an through its original context. It's entirely reasonable to say that Muhammad (also known as *the Prophet*) defines the true nature of Islam the way Jesus defines the nature of Christianity. The Qur'an, in fact, is simply a compilation of messages that Muhammad claimed the angel Gabriel dictated to him.

During the early years when Muhammad recorded the Qur'an, his efforts to proselytize were mostly peaceful. As the command of his influence grew, however, he became increasingly aggressive and, unlike Jesus, conducted dozens of military campaigns, seeking to advance Islam through the sword when he saw fit. From the time that he founded Islam in about AD 610 until his death in 632, the Prophet planned sixty-five military campaigns and raids, personally leading twenty-seven of them.[5]

More than once, Muhammad ordered the execution of those refusing to convert to Islam. For example, after a twenty-five-night siege in AD 627, he ordered the beheadings of several hundred Jewish tribal members who had surrendered to him near Medina.[6] They had been given two choices: submit to Islam or die. They chose death. But there was more to Muhammad's story; he often spoke of peace and extended mercy to his enemies at unexpected times.

When post-Muhammad Muslims continued the violent aggressions of Islam, they believed they were following both the teaching and example of their most revered leader. Within only eighty years after the Prophet's death, Islamic armies had overrun the Iberian Peninsula. Not until the 732 Battle of Tours-Poitiers (in modern-day France) was the previously unchecked Muslim advance into Europe finally slowed.[7] The

---

5. Will Durant, *The Story of Civilization: Part IV; The Age of Faith* (New York: Simon and Schuster, 1950), 170.

6. A. Guillaume, *The Life of Muhammad, A Translation of Ibn Ishaq's Sirat Rasul Allah,* (Oxford: Oxford University Press), 1955, 1967, 464 (sections 689-690).

7. Martin J. Dougherty, General Editor, *100 Battles: Decisive Conflicts That Have Shaped The World* (Bath, UK: Parragon, 2012), 44-45.

military advance of Islam continued into Africa, Europe, and Asia for centuries at the cost of tens of millions of lives. Consequently, those in "Christendom" launched the Crusades—often barbarous campaigns themselves—in a fear-driven attempt to stem Islam's violent progress and to recover lands already lost.

According to Durant, "The Mohammedan Conquest of India is probably the bloodiest story in history."[8] Considering all of the conflicts we've seen on the world stage, Durant's statement is significant. Beginning as early as AD 664, and escalating around 997, Muslim invaders brutally slaughtered hundreds upon hundreds of thousands of Hindus, looting their wealth in the process.

Comparisons equating Christianity and Islam as religions advocating violence are grossly inaccurate in that Islam trends in a direction opposite that of Christianity. Christianity began entirely non-violent, but with the passage of time, many professed followers of Christ began to embrace the use of weaponry and violence. On the contrary, Islam was largely established through warfare and bloodshed, even though many of its adherents became increasingly peaceful as they developed their civilizations.

Once their conquests were advanced, Muslims coexisted with those of other religious beliefs for centuries in various parts of the world. And in many cases, professed Muslim leaders were more noble-minded and peace-loving than their counterparts who professed to be Christian. Thus, I find it irresponsible and inflammatory to claim there is no such thing as a peace-loving Muslim.

I live in a rural area marked by a significant "gun culture." Many law-abiding people not only own rifles and shotguns for hunting, but a significant number carry handguns as well. The vast majority have strong convictions regarding our Second Amendment constitutional right to bear arms. Several of my Christian friends legally carry concealed handguns, and the conversation always turns interesting when we discuss the issue from a Biblical perspective. Never has anyone said, "I'm following Christ's example by carrying a weapon." Instead,

8. Durant, *The Story of Civilization: Part I: Our Oriental Heritage*, 459.

they rationalize their convictions based on their desire to protect those they love. My point isn't that their convictions are wrong, or even that military service is unbiblical, but that a certain degree of rationalization is necessary to justify their stand. The opposite is true with Islam. Muhammad set an example of bearing the sword, and those who advocate for non-violence must labor to justify their convictions.

In recent years, numerous factors have led to the radicalization of Muslim extremists who are trying very hard to follow the beliefs of Muhammad as communicated through the Qur'an and his military aggressiveness as documented by Muslim historians. In their minds, the idea of a "peaceful Muslim" is a contradiction in terms, and so they have no problem slaughtering both non-Muslims, whom they consider to be infidels, and less-aggressive Muslims, whom they view as apostate hypocrites.

Islamic moderates don't deny Muhammad's militaristic advances, but believe he used violence only as a last resort when opposing government leaders resisted the spread of Islam. Thus, moderates tend to quote Qur'anic passages which advocate peace while the fundamentalists and radicals emphasize those with more violent tones. The percentage of radicals as opposed to moderates is always a matter of debate, and determining which group is closer to the true heart of Islam is where much of the dispute lies. Two primary issues seem to highlight this struggle.

First, by the Qur'an's own standards, later verses *abrogate* those penned prior.[9] Problematically, however, an early Muslim caliph had the Qur'an laid out according to chapter length and not chronological order. In the process, he ordered all previous copies of the Qur'an to be burned. Consequently, determining which passages should characterize modern Islam is no convenient matter.

Second, some moderates view the issue more as one of *linguistic context* rather than historical progression. Most of the problems, they contend, result from taking Classical Arabic out of context in an attempt to interpret the Qur'an through more modern dialects. Similar

---

9. The Muslim principle (or doctrine) of abrogation is based primarily on the following three verses from the Qu'ran: 2:106, 13:39, and 16:101.

arguments can be made regarding the interpretation of the Bible, so their point is well-taken. Even so, the military aggressiveness of Islam in its early centuries contradicts this perspective.

Make no mistake—both Christianity and Islam seek far-reaching, global influence. They, however, differ radically in their approaches—and not just regarding violence. Islam has a conception of grace, but unlike Biblical Christianity, it is primarily a religion of *law*. The Qur'an advocates a law-based, salvation-by-works religious code—creating an environment in which human pride thrives. In contrast, embedded in the Christian gospel are the principles of human freedom through faith and love voluntarily exercised. Islam, by its very definition—*submission*—generally rejects such principles. A one-world human government could never be Christian at heart, but it may very well be Islamic.

All in all, I respect Muslims for the sincerity of their faithful devotion to the Prophet and his teachings. I choose, however, to be a follower of Jesus. Never was there a person like Jesus who taught His disciples to love even their enemies.

DAMAGE FROM MISSIONS?

Another significant criticism of Christianity involves the damage done by Christian missionaries to native cultures. Missions, for both evangelical and humanitarian reasons, have been integral to Christian outreach since the earliest days of the church. Despite the political folly that has characterized the institutional church over the centuries, sincere and devoted believers of every era have sought to ease the pain and suffering of others while reaching them with the hope-filled message of the gospel.

After the Reformation, Protestant missions slowly gained momentum as they sought to reach the Americas and other isolated parts of the globe such as central Africa and inland China. These early endeavors began with a trickle as devoted followers of Christ, usually at great personal expense, bravely immersed themselves in dark, dangerous, and isolated environments.

Beginning in the late nineteenth century, a much larger number of missionaries—many of whom were inspired by spiritual renewal on college campuses—began traveling to the far corners of the world to invest in human lives. They built hospitals and clinics, developed educational systems, protected the powerless, and worked to eradicate poverty. For the vast majority, love—not personal gain—was the primary motivating force.

Even though basically well-intentioned, mission outreaches of this period were also plagued by misguided attempts to force Western culture on native peoples. Today, it seems absurd that wearing a suit and tie to a church service—especially in tropical climates—was once equated with authentic Christian living, but such was the mindset of the day. In addition, Christian missionaries helped, knowingly and unknowingly, to advance the imperialistic agendas of colonial governments.

Modern missionaries are well aware of these issues, and most go to great lengths to distinguish between *truth* and *culture.* Many (but certainly not all) critics of Christian missions are still living in the past—and a skewed one at that. While emphasizing the deficiencies of prior mission efforts, they fail to acknowledge that a large number of the cultures reached were violent, oppressive, and generally uncaring toward the lower classes. Throughout much of history, in fact, human life has been cheap. Wars have killed and maimed. Slavery has oppressed the innocent. Sexual abuse has produced untold pain. And human elitism has led to heinous practices such as infanticide and genocide.

Jesus set a radically different example. Appearing on the human scene, He treated commoners with the same respect and dignity He gave to "people of status." Even more significant is the fact that the Son of Man willingly died a horrific death on the cross so that *every* person—regardless of status—might have the opportunity to become a child of God and experience eternal life (John 3:16). Herein, we find what may be the most significant influence of the Christian gospel: *when the Bible is understood and taught according to God's intent, the value of human life is increasingly appreciated.* Authentic Christianity always has been, and continues to be, a voice for the powerless.

Sadly, fear, human arrogance, and the quest for control often oppose the Christian emphasis on the sanctity of all human life. More than one Christian missionary faced considerable opposition in trying to rescue and elevate the helpless. The following account from the life of Mary Slessor is not atypical:

> As the ship cast anchor off Duke Town on the slave coast of West Africa, romance quickly faded into reality. A mysterious land awaited Mary—a land governed by witchcraft and superstition, where human life was cheap, and torture by poisoning and boiling oil was the order of the day. Twins, believed to be children of the devil, were abandoned to die at birth, their mothers banished from their communities. Wives of chiefs were ceremonially strangled to provide company for their dead husbands in the world to come.[10]

A similar record from Amy Carmichael about the cultural climate of India in the early twentieth century is equally revealing:

> In 1901, the arrival of Preena, a young runaway, opened a new dimension of cross-cultural encounter. As an infant, Preena had been devoted to the gods, which meant that she would grow up in strict seclusion of the temple, and eventually assume the role of ritual prostitute. After one escape attempt, her hands were branded with hot irons. When she heard that Amy, the "child-stealing woman" was in the area, the desperate girl ran from the temple again. Over the objections of other temple women and the people of the town, Amy and her companions kept Preena. Soon other abandoned children and temple runaways found their way to Amy's bungalow.[11]

Missionaries such as Mary Slessor and Amy Carmichael displayed remarkable courage. Often, while battling personal sickness and intense feelings of loneliness, they risked their lives by confronting evil practices that had been woven into the fabrics of primitive cultures. Many societies in our world continue to show minimal concern for human

---

10. John Woodbridge, General Editor, *More Than Conquerors: Portraits of Believers from All Walks of Life* (Chicago: Moody Press, 1992), 65.
11. Ibid., 71.

life, but I can't begin to imagine how bleak the human landscape would look had Jesus never been born or had His followers never embraced His heart.

WHAT ABOUT SOCIAL JUSTICE?

Women's rights advocates often take offense to some of what the Bible teaches. Christianity, they believe, is patriarchal and oppressive. Once again, we see a skewed and inaccurate perspective that fails to take into account the cumulative influence of the gospel over the centuries.

The Bible was penned in an era vastly different from the ideals of contemporary Western culture. In His day, Jesus' treatment of women was nothing short of scandalous. The Son of God honored women in a way that puzzled even His own followers (see John 4:27). Thus, as a direct result of Christ's influence, the Bible lays the groundwork for women's rights. I seriously doubt there would be any such thing as a women's rights movement if not for the Bible's profound influence on the cultures of our world.

Still, it's no secret that the New Testament writers did little to advocate for social justice. They didn't fight against the institution of slavery or the systematic mistreatment of women; nor did they protest the oppressive policies of the Roman government. What we often fail to understand, though, was that the cultural, social, and political landscapes of the early church era essentially bore no resemblance to Western democracy. The mindsets, freedoms, and opportunities that we laud today were non-existent then.

Most governments of that age were authoritarian monarchies. Consequently, the common person had *no* voice. None. Furthermore, just about any challenge to the ruling government was either violent in itself or met with violence. Protest frequently meant death. And in the cases where revolutionaries successfully cast off yokes of oppression, the resulting regimes then oppressed in turn.

In this sense, Jesus was a radical like no other. He revolted in a non-violent manner that always emphasized a change of heart. His followers, then, sought to follow the general pattern that their Messiah had established. Their primary goal, though, was not to bring social change but to introduce people to an abiding relationship with the eternal God. As their love-motivated actions began to take root, the overall value of human life was steadily elevated.

As time went on and the faith became better established, Christian love began to find other expressions—all of which revolved around the value of people. Many of the rights and freedoms we enjoy today were gained at significant personal cost by Christians who were influenced by the gospel to make a difference in the lives of the downtrodden and oppressed.

CHAPTER WRAP-UP

Although Christian expression has undoubtedly had its low points through the centuries, the message of the gospel has exerted an influence unlike any other known to humanity. Such impact clearly reflects the creation/sin/redemption pattern found in the Bible, through which the value of every human life is held in high esteem. Jesus Christ, the Prince of Peace, died a violent death on the cross to extract the bitter roots of oppression and hatred from human hearts.

When considering the influence of the Bible, we must recognize that grasping Scriptural truth as expressed through the new covenant gospel is our goal. We don't simply seek to do things in the name of Christ, but rather to embrace fully the Spirit of Christ as well. Our world desperately needs the influence of His gospel to increase—not lessen.

10

INSPIRATION FROM HEAVEN

The Bible is shallow enough for a child not to drown, yet deep enough for an elephant to swim.

—Augustine

When He had reclined at the table with them, He took the bread and blessed it, and breaking it, He began giving it to them. Then their eyes were opened and they recognized Him.

Luke 24:30-31a

More than once, I've seen a pastor hold up a large, well-worn Bible and boldly proclaim, "This book contains all of the answers you will ever need in life!" As inspiring as such statements may seem, they are terribly inaccurate. The Bible doesn't give lists of rules for living in our technological age or answers to solve every quandary. Nor does it tell us who to marry or which job to take. If the Bible answered all of our questions, we wouldn't need a relationship with God!

The Bible is our *TouchPoint*—a powerful connecting point between God and humanity—for a dynamic relationship in which we draw upon His eternal wisdom. And because God's wisdom is so unlike our own, it takes a certain measure of insight and effort simply to navigate the Bible's pages. Learning to study the Scriptures might feel overwhelming at times, but digging deeper can be rewarding beyond description.

Many people prefer to rely on a priest or pastor to interpret the Bible and tell them what it means. It is a mistake of epic proportions to forfeit your personal relationship with God for the convenience of having someone else—who may, or may not, be right—tell you what it means and how to live. Do you want a church leader to have a relationship with God for you?

The Bible teaches us how to live, but it also does much more by providing a gateway for broken people to draw nearer to the heavenly Father who loves them beyond measure. Serious problems would result if my relationship with my wife consisted of a psychologist giving me a weekly update on what she's all about and how she wants me to treat her. Part of the adventure—and it is at times an adventure—of married life is for two very different people to learn to communicate with one another. And since the Bible is intended to guide us into a relationship with God, it's vital that we learn how to navigate its pages for ourselves. Thus, it is well worth pressing beyond any feelings of anxiety or confusion as I lay out a few basic concepts and principles that have proven invaluable to me.

THE WORD OF GOD

The Bible refers to Jesus as both the *Son of God* and the *Word of God*:

> *At the beginning God expressed himself. That personal expression, that word, was with God, and was God, and he existed with God from the beginning. All creation took place through him, and none took place without him. In him appeared life and this life was the light of mankind. The light still shines in the darkness and the darkness has never put it out. John 1:1-5 (PHILLIPS)*

Two Greek words—*logos* and *rhema*—are most often translated as "word." *Logos*—the one most prevalent in the New Testament—is used in John 1:1-2. It essentially describes speech as an expression of intelligence.[1] (*Rhema* is often interpreted as "the spoken word of God."[2] However, the distinction between *logos* and *rhema* is not always clear.)

1. Spiros Zodhiates, *The Complete Word Study Dictionary: New Testament* (Chattanooga, TN: AMG Publishers, 2000
2. Johan Lust, Erik Eynikel, and Katrin Hauspie, *A Greek-English Lexicon of the Septuagint: Revised Edition* (Deutsche Bibelgesellschaft: Stuttgart, 2003).

Jesus is the embodiment of truth and all that is written in the Bible flows from His intelligence. If we define *Biblical truth* as "spiritual reality revealed," we begin to see that Jesus—God in human form—was the perfectly accurate expression of heaven's reality on earth. In Jesus, the natural and supernatural expressions of God's intelligence converged like never before.

One of the most profound things about Jesus as the Word of God is that He can relate to people on any intellectual level. It doesn't take a Ph.D. candidate to know God and draw upon His wisdom, but a high-level intellectual will be as captivated by our Creator's unfathomable intelligence as will the most simpleminded among us. Again, the barrier isn't the measure of a person's intellectual ability, but rather his or her pride in that ability. Once more, we are reminded of the vital need for humility if we are to gain accurate spiritual insight.

THE HOLY SPIRIT AS OUR TEACHER

At least several of Christ's original twelve disciples were mostly uneducated, and yet, eleven of them helped to change the course of this world without ever completing a college degree (or routing an enemy platoon). Of course, they walked with Jesus in the flesh, but consider what the Son of God told them just before He went to the cross:

> *"These things I have spoken to you while abiding with you. But the Helper, the Holy Spirit, whom the Father will send in My name, He will teach you all things, and bring to your remembrance all that I said to you." John 14:25-26*

> *"But I tell you the truth, it is to your advantage that I go away; for if I do not go away, the Helper will not come to you; but if I go, I will send Him to you." John 16:7*

Some of us might think that John 16:7 applies to the original twelve disciples only. We would be mistaken.

> *AND HE CAME AND PREACHED PEACE TO YOU WHO WERE FAR AWAY, AND PEACE TO THOSE WHO WERE NEAR; for through Him we both [Jews and Gentiles] have our access in one Spirit to the Father. Ephesians 2:17-18*

THE TOUCHPOINT

When Jesus lived among us as the Word of God incarnate, He took every conceivable opportunity to teach others. Whether speaking to large crowds or small groups of disciples, Jesus provoked people to pursue an understanding of His divine ways. But as awesome as it was for the Son of God to live and breathe in the midst of humanity, His effectiveness was limited because He had confined Himself to a physical body. It's somewhat difficult to accept, but Christ's ascension into heaven was for our benefit. The establishment of the new covenant through the Messiah's blood vastly improves our lot, because through the Holy Spirit—the third person of the Trinity—God's truth can be communicated without physical limitation.

How amazing to think that the Holy Spirit comes to dwell within the heart of every individual born from above through faith in Jesus Christ (Ephesians 1:13). Each Christian then becomes a *living temple* in which the very presence of God dwells (1 Corinthians 6:19). Because of the Spirit's nearness, *all* Christians—regardless of social status or geographic location—have direct access to heaven's wisdom. A non-Jewish (Gentile) writer living near Pittsburgh, Pennsylvania, is now as privileged to learn from God as is a Messianic Jew dwelling in Jerusalem.

In 1 Corinthians 2:16, the apostle Paul wrote, "we have the mind of Christ." His point was that if the Holy Spirit is a member of the three-person Trinity, it stands to reason that He knows everything the Father knows. Moreover, if the Holy Spirit dwells within a person's heart, so abides the eternal wisdom of God. Mind boggling!

> *"But when He, the Spirit of truth, comes, He will guide you into all the truth; for He will not speak on His own initiative, but whatever He hears, He will speak; and He will disclose to you what is to come. He will glorify Me, for He will take of Mine and will disclose it to you. All things that the Father has are Mine; therefore I said that He takes of Mine and will disclose it to you."*
> John 16:13-15

Having the mind of Christ does not mean that we automatically know all that God knows. We are, however, given the opportunity to learn directly from God Himself. And as much as I value sound Biblical scholarship, I take delight in the idea that I can, on my own, open the Bible at any time and call upon our Creator for wisdom, insight, and inspiration. The Divine Teacher of Heaven dwells within my own heart. It doesn't get any more personal than that!

OUR PRIMARY TEACHER

The Scriptures were *inspired* by God (2 Timothy 3:16), meaning they were *God-breathed*. Understanding the Bible isn't about us trying, by human ability, to figure out what it says. God Himself is able to give each of us an understanding of what He seeks to communicate. *Anyone* who has the Spirit of God (i.e. every Christian) can receive insight and revelation of our Creator's ways.

> *"Yet I know that the touch of his Spirit never leaves you, and you don't really need a human teacher. You know that his Spirit teaches you about all things, always telling you the truth and never telling you a lie. So, as he has taught you, live continually in him." 1 John 2:27 (PHILLIPS)*

Talk about reason for excitement! Minuscule, imperfect me can learn directly from the God who created our entire cosmos. A vast number of Christians will testify that they've experienced times when a familiar passage of Scripture suddenly "jumped off the page" and came to life. The Holy Spirit is at work, and He loves teaching us His ways.

Is 1 John 2:27 saying that we don't need pastors, teachers, and Bible scholars? Not exactly. Scripture itself speaks otherwise (see Ephesians 4:11-13). If we take John's statement in its New Testament context, we can see that grasping God's wisdom comes by fully embracing the Holy Spirit as our Master Teacher. Most certainly, He will speak through people He has gifted to preach, teach, and write, but we are to see *Him* as the *primary source* of our understanding.

Comprehending the Holy Spirit's role in teaching me God's ways has led to one of the most exciting dimensions of my Christian experience. When I look to Him for understanding, He uses virtually every experience to teach and shape me. He may begin speaking through a personal failure on my part, expound on the message through my pastor's sermon, and then confirm it through a conversation with my non-Christian neighbor. Almost nothing is off of the table when it comes to the Holy Spirit teaching us His ways, but the secret lies in posturing ourselves to learn.

GOD SPEAKS TO PEOPLE?

The idea of God speaking to humans may seem bizarre to some of us, but communication is integral to any healthy relationship. Identifying Jesus as the Word of God strongly implies God's desire to communicate His reality to us, and the presence of the Holy Spirit in our hearts provides the most intimate way for God to speak and reveal His truth.

Some Christians teach that God speaks to people *only* through the Bible, but the Scriptures themselves provide no grounds for such a claim. The Holy Spirit is a person—not an inanimate supernatural force to be manipulated for good or evil. And if He is a person, He is able to speak and communicate with us in multiple ways. Story after Biblical story tells of God communicating with His people through dreams, visions, inner leadings, angels, and even audible voices. Limiting God to speak only through the Scriptures allows Him only a limited relationship with His people.

In my campus ministry days, I had the privilege of working with a young woman named Meghan. Meghan almost didn't make it to college; she had come within seconds of committing suicide several years prior. Only God's grace spared her from following through.

Though having a general belief in God, a series of unpleasant and unfortunate factors, including a rough home environment, led Meghan to have a rather dismal outlook on life. On one particularly difficult day in the ninth grade, a negative comment from a teacher made her feel completely worthless. Meghan's personal account of the story is as follows:

> The following period, I went into the bathroom with a mirror from my compact. After breaking it, I began to slit my wrists. As I did so, I heard a very clear and distinct voice in my head say, "Meghan, what are you doing?" That shook me out of my

mood, and I had a friend take me to the nurse. I believe that was the voice of God that day. Since then, despite how bad things get, I remember that day, and suicide is not an option.

Meghan has continued to deal with significant ups and downs, but God is now her rock of stability through troubled times. Furthermore, through the Lord's loving grace, she has learned to look outward in seeking to bless others. Meghan is alive and helping others today because our heavenly Father loves us too much to confine Himself to the parameters of our human theology. Our relationship is not with the printed words on a page but with the living Word of God who speaks to His children whenever and however He pleases.

Still, as a caution, we should understand that even though God is not limited to speaking to us through the Bible, the Scriptures must be integral to our efforts to commune with our Creator. As explained below, without the objective truth of the Bible, natural human desires can be easily confused with the Holy Spirit's leading.

COLLECTIVE LEARNING

When Paul wrote of having "the mind of Christ" in 1 Corinthians 2:16, there was a sense of *plurality* in his statement. To have the mind of Christ isn't just an individual endeavor, but a collective one. Jesus alone had a perfect connection with the Holy Spirit. The rest of us must still deal with the corrupting influences of our fleshly bodies. Until our human frames are supernaturally transformed at the return of Christ, none of us will have perfect insight and understanding. For this and other reasons, it is essential that we build healthy connections with the greater body of Christ.

Group dynamics can prove invaluable as we humbly exchange thoughts and hash out our perspectives. By diligently applying ourselves to the learning process, and aligning our lives with God's design, the corporate mind of Christ will become increasingly evident. Of course, group discussions about theological issues can also present significant challenges, but as a whole, the time and energy expended are well worth the price. The value of eternal life dwarfs all else in comparison.

Paul's words to Timothy, his protégé, carry as much weight for us as they did for the young pastor almost 2000 years ago:

> *Until I come, devote yourself to the public reading of Scripture, to exhortation, to teaching. Do not neglect the gift you have, which was given you by prophecy when the council of elders laid their hands on you. Practice these things, immerse yourself in them, so that all may see your progress. Keep a close watch on yourself and on the teaching. Persist in this, for by so doing you will save both yourself and your hearers. 1 Timothy 4:13-16 (ESV)*

The same apostle Paul, who informed the Corinthian church that they had the mind of Christ, also admonished Timothy to put more than incidental effort into his pursuit of truth. If my mechanic says, "The front end of your car is out of alignment," I'll consider scheduling an appointment in the next week or two to resolve the problem. But if he says, "Your brake lines are rusting through," I'll address the issue *right now*. God's ways should never be addressed casually. Inaccurate—or merely incomplete—instruction has ruined the lives of many.

Sometimes, falsehood is taught as truth, and sometimes, truth is simply presented selectively. There was a time when "faith teaching" was very prominent in the American church as several key leaders called people to rise up and believe God in ways they had never considered. In principle, the faith teaching met a significant need for a generation of doubters, but in some circles, wisdom was desperately lacking. Failure to adequately address the dangers of selfish motives led people to "believe God" to fulfill all manner of self-serving desires. The somber result was rotten spiritual fruit corrupting many a professed follower of Christ.

In this world, we will always live with a tension between an amazing opportunity to learn of God's ways and a fearful sense of responsibility as we influence others (James 3:1). I'm not suggesting that a person must have a seminary degree to comprehend the primary doctrines of the Bible, but that we need to apply some very important principles when seeking to understand the Scriptures.

An understanding of God's ways doesn't come naturally, and humans who aren't susceptible to deception simply don't exist. A person needs only to plant the seed of a prideful or selfish thought, and an entire harvest of false teaching can result. Furthermore, the Bible is a big book full of mystery, and more than one cultish leader has used it to control and manipulate others. Sadly, false prophets are never in short supply. A lone charismatic personality can ensnare a whole bunch of well-meaning people (see Matthew 7:15-20 and Acts 20:28-31). A leader without accountability is a disaster in the making.

The unfortunate reality of false prophets leaves us in a somewhat delicate situation. On one hand, we set ourselves up for trouble when we refuse to submit to God-given authority (Proverbs 17:11; Romans 13:1-7; and Hebrews 13:17). I've seen more than one person go down a pain-filled road because he or she refused to submit to any type of leadership authority. We all need a measure of accountability. Even leaders need other leaders who can call them into account and speak truth into their lives.

At the same time, our submission to human authorities is not absolute. If earthly authorities compel us to sin against God, we must conscientiously object—regardless of the personal cost. I also suggest taking considerable care in finding spiritual leaders who live humbly and in a non-controlling manner. No matter how gifted he or she may be, a self-aggrandizing, controlling leader is a disaster in the making!

MESHING THE SUBJECTIVE AND OBJECTIVE

The pursuit of wisdom is an imperfect process because we are all flawed in one way or another. Still, because God is gracious and wants us to know Him, even imperfect people can learn of His ways. Debi and I have had our share of failures and regrets, but the Lord has still blessed our marriage, our parenting, and our ministry efforts as we have sought Him for wisdom. Our confidence is in Him—not our elusive personal perfection.

One learning key involves recognizing the importance of both *subjective inspiration* and *objective information* in our efforts to comprehend the truths of Scripture. Looking to the Holy Spirit as our primary Teacher requires an objective framework through which to filter all we believe He is teaching us. Without such a structure, we can easily twist the written Word of God toward our own personal ends. Our objective framework includes not only Scripture itself but also extra-Biblical resources such as Bible dictionaries.

We once had an out-of-town visitor who spent a couple of months in our community because of job requirements. We welcomed him to attend the small group study that met in our home, but the guy became agitated when we mentioned the idea of using a book other than the Bible for the content of our study. "The Bible is the only book I'll ever read!" was the message he brandished like a badge of honor. We were somewhat relieved that he didn't stay in town for very long.

The Holy Spirit is to be our primary Teacher and the Bible our *TouchPoint* for wisdom, but that doesn't mean we should ignore the extra-Biblical resources that provide insight into ancient languages and cultures. Furthermore, it's both arrogant and foolish to think that we don't need input and instruction from other believers who have walked with God and labored hard to learn His ways. Again, *we* as the people of God, have the mind of Christ as we learn and grow together.

It's likely that even the apostle Paul used extra-Biblical materials in his study of the Old Testament Scriptures (2 Timothy 4:13). In addition, both Old and New Testament writers made references to non-canonical writings (e.g. Joshua 10:13; 2 Chronicles 9:29; and Jude 1:14-15). These men esteemed the Scriptures as sacred and authoritative, but nonetheless, they didn't limit their learning to what we now recognize as the inspired Word of God.

Today, we have a vast number of excellent resources (many of which can be had at little or no cost) available to help us navigate the pages of the ancient book called the Bible. Online resources, computer programs, concordances, Bible dictionaries, and commentaries can all be tremendous assets to our Bible study efforts.

I'm not suggesting that we raise these resources to the level of Scripture, or even that we gullibly accept all that they teach. Scholarly resources may effectively facilitate the transfer of truth, but they can also convey error. If a highly esteemed leader communicates an idea, or if a viewpoint gets desirable results, widespread acceptance can follow with few questions asked. Certainly, we must take care when using extra-Biblical resources, but still, I think it's a huge mistake to ignore them. The key, I believe, is to continually pursue an understanding of truth. As we grasp the core elements of the Christian faith and how they fit together, we're better able to discern between truth and error.

VITAL QUESTIONS

As we read and study a particular passage of the Bible, we want to answer three primary questions as best we can. The goal with each successive question is to establish a foundation for spiritual truth that we can then personalize when appropriate.

1. What was this passage communicating to the original audience?

2. What is the universal truth we can draw from this passage?

3. What is this passage saying to me?

Each passage of the Bible was written to a specific audience that lived a long time ago. The use of extra-Biblical resources helps us to understand the histories and cultures of those audiences. At the same time, the Bible is full of universal truths that apply to all people of all eras. Finally, God seeks to touch and teach each of us individually through His timeless Word. The following section from Paul's letter to the Colossians provides an excellent example of these principles:

> *Slaves, in all things obey those who are your masters on earth, not with external service, as those who merely please men, but with sincerity of heart, fearing the Lord. Whatever you do, do your work heartily, as for the Lord rather than for men, knowing that from the Lord you will receive the reward of the inheritance. It is the Lord Christ whom you serve. Colossians 3:22-24*

Some people might be inclined to use this passage as an attempt to justify slavery, but that is not the intent of the original message. Slavery was, unfortunately, integral to the fabric of Roman life, and the early church was in no position to challenge the practice. Instead, Paul sought to encourage enslaved Christians by providing an eternal perspective of their situation.

The universal message of Colossians 3:22-24 is that our primary service in life is not to man but God. Regardless of what humans think or how they treat us, we work for God and should do so wholeheartedly. The Lord is never ignorant of His faithful servants' devotion and will reward them in due season.

Finally, many of us can find personal inspiration through this passage. My first job out of college was rather tumultuous. I worked very hard, but my boss always seemed to ignore me while applauding others. This was despite the fact that he frequently utilized my lab skills for projects which most of my coworkers were unqualified. When others received their designated lab tech promotions, the boss posted letters congratulating them for their hard work. But when my buddy and I received promotions, our letters thanked *everyone else* for helping us along!

I learned, during that season, that it didn't matter what anyone else did or didn't do at work. My service was to God and God alone. Day in and day out, I gave it my all—not to gain the boss's approval but to honor the Lord that I serve. Over the course of two years, my supervisor never really acknowledged my value in the workplace, but my God was faithful to provide a far better position when the timing proved right. That early influence of the Scriptures left an imprint on my life that produced sweet fruit for many years to come.

I am well aware that this chapter is full of warnings, but experience has taught me more than I want to know about human nature. As a general rule, we humans are self-centered and tend to twist the Bible toward our own ends. It's not uncommon for people to put personal spins on Bible passages they find meaningful without attempting to discover what God was trying to communicate to the original audience. Such habits may be very helpful in times of need but also dangerous if applied haphazardly.

Colossians 3:22-24, as our case in point, was never meant to provide justification for selfishly enslaving others. Asking questions about a passage's original intent and universal truths helps us to realize that God's purposes transcend our individual lives. Then, as we begin to grasp the essence of what He is seeking to communicate, can we safely make specific applications to ourselves.

Undoubtedly, effort is required to gain an accurate understanding of the Scriptures, and sometimes that work is not fun. Difficult questions nag at us, Biblical resources aren't always easy to navigate, and scholars frequently contradict one another. Often, we have to dig carefully through a lot of "dirt" to find gems of wisdom, but that doesn't make the treasure any less worth pursuing.

I'm always reading a book (or two—or three). Most are non-fiction, and most focus on some element of spirituality. Some works send my heart soaring while others make a good melatonin substitute for sleepless nights. Furthermore, I may not understand everything I read in a book. Sometimes, I'll painstakingly labor through a 300-page volume and come away with only one or two truths that I find significant, but how valuable those truths prove to be! I'm not suggesting that you have to follow my pattern in order to walk with God, but you do need to posture yourself as a lifetime learner.

A GOD WITH FEATHERS AND WINGS?

"Do you believe the Bible should be taken literally?" is one of my "favorite" questions. More often than not, the query is employed in an attempt to disqualify the authority of the Scriptures. If we say *yes*, we're accused of being legalistic (law-driven) fundamentalists who leave no room for literary expression. But if we say *no*, we open the door to treating the entire Bible as an allegorical work subject to human interpretation and with no substantive authority.

Elements of the Bible are undoubtedly literal, but it also contains hundreds of illustrations, figures of speech, and other literary devices which are intended to increase the effectiveness of its message. For example, part of Psalm 91:4 reads, "And under His wings you may seek refuge. . . ." Is God a huge winged creature? Not at all. The imagery is a *zoomorphism* in which God is given animal-like characteristics for the purpose of communicating a message—one of security and protection in this particular case.

As recorded in the first part of John 10, Jesus spoke of sheep, a sheepfold, a door to the sheepfold, and a shepherd. Verse six clearly communicates His methodology:

> *This figure of speech Jesus spoke to them, but they did not understand what those things were which He had been saying to them. John 10:6 (emphasis added)*

Jesus was a master teacher and communicator who frequently used rhetorical devices in the common tongue to drive home His message. He also spoke from a perspective that was entirely foreign to human thinking. Even the most well-intentioned learner can be quickly confused by failing to take these things into account.

God's Word is truth, but not everything in the Bible is to be taken literally. At the same time, no passage of Scripture involves a matter of personal interpretation (2 Peter 1:20-21). God seeks to communicate with His people through the Scriptures, and we play a vital role as we humble our hearts and search for insight, wisdom, and revelation.

Identifying which passages are literal and which involve figures of speech involves some degree of effort. As a general rule, we assume a passage is to be taken at face value unless given good reason to believe otherwise. We also look to the scholarly work of others who have studied Biblical languages, as well as the Holy Spirit, who is able to lead us into all truth. Yes, this learning process can at times be frustrating, but it's also immensely rewarding as God's reality comes into focus.

During my high school years, I developed a strong affinity for chemistry (how strange is that?) and an equally strong distaste for biology. Why? At that level, I saw chemistry as a realm of mysterious concepts just waiting to be understood. My biology class, on the other hand, required memorizing long lists of kingdoms, phyla, and orders. Low-level biology left my inquisitive mind mired in boredom. At least one of my close friends felt differently as he preferred to cram long lists into his head rather than stretch his brain to learn concepts.

Some people prefer to see the Bible as a literal rule book for life. Others, however, are enamored by an exciting "treasure map" overflowing with mysterious truths to be revealed and concepts to be understood. To guard against thieves, treasure maps are often filled with cryptic language. A figure of speech doesn't fit well in a rule book but is perfectly at home on a map protecting hidden treasure. For the person who wants to know God and understand His ways, the Bible is the gateway to an endless cache of eternal riches.

CHAPTER WRAP-UP

The Holy Spirit is to be our primary Teacher of spiritual truth. When we faithfully tune our hearts to God's wisdom, the Spirit of God instructs us from every direction. It's normal to wrestle with passages, but we must do so in faith, trusting Him to illuminate His truth and guide our paths (James 1:5-8). And though understanding the Bible may sometimes feel beyond our grasp, patient and persistent effort will uncover hidden gems that will spare us many a pain while enriching and transforming our lives.

THE TOUCHPOINT

11

UNDERSTANDING THE BIBLE

No one statement wrested from its context is a sufficient warrant for actions that plainly controvert other commands. How excellent a thing it would be if the whole Church of Christ had learned that no law of life may be based upon an isolated text. Every false teacher who has divided the Church, has had, "it is written" on which to hang his doctrine.

—G. Campbell Morgan

Be diligent to present yourself approved to God as a workman who does not need to be ashamed, accurately handling the word of truth.

2 Timothy 2:15

Debi and I live in a small town with a state university of nearly 15,000 and a borough population that's about the same—very much a college community. Those who pursue careers in higher education often do so with a desire to invest in others, and their quest to better humanity can't help but spill over into various levels of community involvement through which many people benefit. At the same time, some of our college students reflect the typical college student stereotypes. Loud parties are not uncommon, keeping the love-hate relationship between the campus and community always interesting.

Just across the township line on the east end of town is a nice little street that ends in a wooded area. I've often thought it would be a great place to live, but the properties were pricey. No small number of people want to live on the edge of a community where they have the benefits of town and country all rolled together.

Things began to change a few years back when college rental apartments moved into that little corner of our community. Not long after we heard reports about large parties, houses in the area began to pop up on the real estate market. Only this time, the owners were struggling to get decent prices for their properties. The once-serene street no longer had its country draw and was now deemed an unsuitable family location.

In dealing with real estate, we are told that the primary issue is *location, location, location.* Communication is very similar; meaning always revolves around *context, context, context.* When it comes to accurately understanding a conveyed message, the neighboring context helps to establish the meaning of the content.

Just about all of us are familiar with the thirty-second political ads showing a sour-looking candidate immersed in a gray background. A few out-of-context statements help portray an image of a politician devoid of compassion and out of touch with reality. As much as we all hate these deceptive ads, they continue to run for one reason: they succeed at imparting negative perceptions of candidates. When removed from its original context, practically any statement can be distorted—as is constantly evidenced by the overwhelming number of these ads.

CONTEXT IS KING

If we want to understand the true intent of the Bible, context must be "king." There's no way around it. A verse taken out of context can be twisted every which way to produce virtually any desired meaning. When we allow human reasoning and desires to corrupt God's holy communication, we enter dangerous territory. Thus, extra-Biblical resources play an invaluable role as they help us understand the languages, geography, and cultures of peoples far different from us.

The four contextual questions below prove invaluable as we seek to plumb the depths of the Bible for God's transformational truth:

1. **What is the *linguistic* context?** Language matters because it is used to communicate meaning. If the nuances of a language—figures of speech, verb tenses, etc.—are incorrectly applied, the original intent can be easily distorted. Making this especially challenging is the fact that most of the New Testament was written in Greek but with a Hebrew mindset. I don't know about you, but I didn't grow up speaking Biblical Hebrew or Greek. We are compelled, therefore, to rely on the hard work of devoted scholars to assist us in this area.

   I explained in chapter five that grammar can also present a stumbling point. Ancient Hebrew had no vowels and no punctuation. The original Greek writings of the New Testament probably lacked punctuation while employing a sentence structure quite different from modern English (think of Yoda from *Star Wars*). The formal Greek text often used ALL CAPITAL LETTERS, while personal correspondence—such a letter by the apostle Paul—was written in a sort of cursive hand. Furthermore, many older Greek manuscripts had NOSPACESBETWEENWORDS.

   The simple placement of a comma can change the meaning of a passage. It's much preferable to sit down to dinner and say, "Let's eat, Grandma!" as opposed to, "Let's eat Grandma!" People who lived in Biblical times were fully accustomed to the nuances of their particular styles of communication. We, for our part, are far removed from that time and culture, so vigilance is necessary.

   Modern Bible study resources have become increasingly user-friendly, enabling the average person to dig deeper into the original meanings.[1] In particular, I have always enjoyed word studies in which I use a Bible dictionary and a concordance to explore the original meaning(s) of a word while discovering how it applies throughout the text. This practice has helped me see

---

1. For laypeople interested in the nuances of Bible translation, an edition of the New English Translation (NET) Bible contains 60,932 translator notes.

that the Bible is more like a tapestry of interwoven threads than a collection of isolated writings.

Words can have multiple definitions, though, so an element of caution is advisable. The fact that a word has a particular meaning does not give us free reign to apply that connotation to every passage in which the word is used. The context—especially with the Hebrew language—often helps to establish the specific nuances of the word.

2. **What is the *historical* context?** Knowing something about the times in which the Scriptures were penned can be invaluable to the learning process. During the lifetime of Jesus, for example, Israel was full of chaos and intrigue. Christ's commandment to love one's enemies becomes all the more meaningful when a person begins to recognize the seething hatred between the Jewish people and their Roman oppressors. Jesus wasn't simply presenting nice ideas to help His disciples fall asleep more quickly at night; His words struck at the very heart of Jewish pride and identity.

As a newly married couple, Debi and I lived above a bar. Our landlords were great, but life sometimes got interesting. One evening, a bruised (from a fight with her drunken boyfriend) and intoxicated girl came with a friend to our door in search of help. We drove them to the hospital and, in the process, met an acquaintance of Debi's boss. The next day at work, Debi was complemented for being a "Good Samaritan."

When Jesus told the story of the good Samaritan, the connotation was radically different (Luke 10:25-37). To the Jewish mind of Jesus' day, the term "good Samaritan" was self-contradictory. Jews and Samaritans despised each other, and so, to His audience, good Samaritans were nonexistent. Christ's parable is much weightier with this context in mind. Try to imagine Jesus talking to a group of fundamentalist Christians about an atheist homosexual activist helping an injured person, and you might get a better sense of the story's original impact.

3. **What is the *cultural* context?** The Bible contains information from a different era and from cultures that differed vastly from those of our modern Western world. As much as we want the Bible to be all about us, it isn't. If we attempt to interpret Scriptural concepts solely through our own cultural perspectives, we'll soon be cruising down deception lane.

    For example, a *covenantal* worldview was integral to the cultural landscape throughout the 1,500 years in which the Bible was written. God has always interacted with humanity through sacred covenant relationships. Jewish life—and that of many other ancient cultures—was lived out in a covenant context.

    To our detriment, the concept of covenant is mostly foreign to Western culture. Consequently, people living in nations such as the United States face some huge challenges in seeking to accurately understand the Bible. Making Christianity culturally relevant has its limits. There comes a time when we must educate people to the Bible, rather than attempting to explain everything in a culturally relevant manner.

    Simply teaching on the topic of covenant can create significant discomfort for people who have divorced, so we should exercise gentleness and care while seeking to minimize the condemnation that so often accompanies such discussions. But the issue must be addressed nonetheless. If we don't understand covenants and their roles in Biblical history, there's a lot about God that won't make sense to us.

    As a case in point, human sexuality has always been a topic of controversy, but it constitutes a major point of contention in Christian circles today. And the consequences are far-reaching! A huge part of the problem is that we often attempt to frame our understanding of love and sexuality apart from the covenantal context of the Bible.

    If a person truly wants to understand what the New Testament communicates about human sexuality, he or she should consult some extra-Biblical resources that show how Judeo-Christian attitudes toward sexuality and covenant relationships were shaped by Old Testament commands, the words of Jesus, and then the teachings of the apostles. Resources such as Alfred Edersheim's, *The Life and Times of Jesus the Messiah*, prove invaluable for these purposes:

> At the same time it must be borne in mind, that marriage conveyed to the Jews much higher thoughts than merely those of festivity or merriment. The pious fasted before it, confessing their sins. It was regarded almost as a Sacrament. Entrance into the married state was thought to carry forgiveness of sins. It almost seems as if the relationship of Husband and Bride between Jehovah and His people, so frequently insisted upon, not only in the Bible, but in Rabbinic writings, had always been standing out [in] the background. Thus the bridal pair on the marriage-day symbolised the union of God with Israel.[2]

Edersheim went on to note that even funerals gave way to marriage processions.[3] Grasping the fervor of this Jewish cultural mindset—shaped in large part by the writings of the Old Testament—helps to illuminate the intensity with which the apostle Paul addressed the issue of sexual immorality in his letters. And while we never want to utilize resources such as Edersheim's in lieu of Scripture, they do provide much-needed background for what we read in the Bible.

Our discussion of culture brings us to another vital matter regarding Biblical interpretation: in establishing the cultural contexts in which the Bible was written, we must work to discern between *culture* and *command*. Distinguishing between culture and command is a challenge that the church has wrestled with for centuries. Ignorance in this arena has led to—and continues to produce—confusion, conflict, oppression, and all sorts of undesirable behavior.

---

2. Alfred Edersheim, *The Life and Times of Jesus the Messiah, Complete and Unabridged in One Volume* (Peabody, MA: Hendrickson Publishers, 1993), 244.
3. Ibid.

From a Biblical perspective, commands are authoritative. Originating in heaven, we have no right to alter them. Cultures, on the other hand, find their roots in human preference and diversity. A command calls us to obey God. Culture is negotiable, staying highly fluid as human desires and opportunities continue to change.

More than 200 times the Bible commands God's people to rejoice and praise His name. The Psalms also mention worshiping God with various instruments such as the harp, lyre, organ, and flute. To praise and worship God is clearly a Scriptural command. The exact instruments we use, however, are cultural. The command never changes, but our ability to produce musical expressions evolves over time. We can see how the difference between culture and command has huge implications for our local church worship services.

Whether we use organs as opposed to full worship bands, or whether we sing hymns versus contemporary songs, are cultural issues. More than anything else, they are a matter of human preference. And that's okay! Sadly, some of the biggest (and most unnecessary) conflicts in the church have been the result of cultural confusion over music.

I'll take things a step further and contend that the older generations should be willing to yield their cultural music preferences to attract the younger generations. If more seniors had the vision of investing in young people, fewer churches would be closing their doors.

The *altar call* and *sinner's prayer* are two other significant examples of this principle. Their use reflects a relatively modern phenomenon, but they are often treated as Biblical commands. Many of us have come to view them as *Biblical practices* when they are actually *practices employed by some who follow the teachings of the Bible*. The difference can be significant— especially if these cultural methods are used in ways that lose sight of the covenantal nature of our faith.

We can make a similar distinction between *sacraments* (*sacred practices*) and *symbols*. Christianity has two primary sacraments—*Baptism* and *Communion*—that are covenant-related and integral to our faith. As a general rule, these sacraments should be considered necessary and non-negotiable.

A *cross*, however, is a symbol. And while the cross of Christ must always be central to our theology (1 Corinthians 2:2), using a cross as a symbol of our faith is a cultural practice never addressed by the Scriptures. To some who are unfamiliar with the Christian faith, the idea of prominently displaying a symbol of torture and death might seem quite bizarre. Regardless of our personal perspectives, when we argue and fight over whether to display a cross in a church, not only do we lose sight of what truly matters, we also violate the purposes for which Jesus suffered and died on the cross. Of His death, there was nothing symbolic.

Since God has given to every Christian the ministry of *reconciliation* (2 Corinthians 5:18-20), our goal is to help draw others to His truth, as much as we are able, in culturally relevant ways. We can accomplish this seemingly monumental task only by learning to distinguish God's eternal truth from the cultural context in which the Scriptures were written. Admittedly, such separations aren't always easy because the Jewish culture of New Testament times was itself deeply influenced by the Hebrew Scriptures.

Finally, I would be remiss if I didn't at least briefly mention the ongoing struggle over the role of women in the church. The heart of the conflict lies not with the validity of the Scriptures, but with our attempts to separate Biblical commands from cultural practices. The issue is too involved to thoroughly explore here, but I will say that, due to the era in which it was penned, the New Testament lacks definitive clarity on this issue. Therefore, it is essential that we extend grace to one another in a matter of such significance.

4. **What is the *Biblical* context?** Practically every passage of Scripture is influenced by its neighboring text and by the Bible as a whole. Ignoring this element of context leaves us perilously subject to speculation and the weight of personal opinions.

The practice of *proof-texting* involves using a short portion of Scripture to support an argument while ignoring the original intent of that passage. Yanking a verse out of its Biblical context is easy; anybody can do it! I've seen speakers and writers make huge doctrinal errors by pulling a verse or passage out of context to support a particular point. In many cases, their ideas sound reasonable—they're using the Word of God for support, aren't they?—until the actual context of the original passage is taken into account.

On my office shelf sits a pretty little plaque, engraved with delicate flowers, that quotes part of John 13:27 from the KJV: "That Thou Doest, Do Quickly." The message seems inspirational, but a look at the entire verse tells a very different story: "After the morsel, Satan then entered into him. Therefore Jesus said to him, 'What you do, do quickly.'" Jesus was talking to Judas who was about to betray Him! I keep that plaque to remind me that context matters.

The issue of *judging* provides another relevant example. I can't begin to list how many times I've heard someone say, "You're judging me, and the Bible says that we aren't supposed to judge!" Did Jesus teach that we aren't to judge? Undoubtedly. But few people realize that He also taught that we *are* to judge.

"Do not judge so that you will not be judged." Matthew 7:1

"Do not judge according to appearance, but judge with righteous judgment." John 7:24

Was Jesus confused? Did He contradict Himself? Not at all. We simply need to understand each of these comments in its Scriptural context. Consider the first statement in light of the greater passage:

"Do not judge so that you will not be judged. For in the way you judge, you will be judged; and by your standard of measure, it will be measured to you. Why do you look at the speck that is in your brother's eye, but do not notice the log that is in your own eye? Or how can you say to your brother, 'Let me take the speck out of your eye,' and behold, the log is in your own eye? You hypocrite, first take the log out of your own eye, and then you will see clearly to take the speck out of your brother's eye." Matthew 7:1-5

By grasping the fuller context of Matthew 7:1, we can see that Jesus was speaking specifically to hypocrites who were in the habit of making *unrighteous* judgments. Judgments are a necessity of life, and judging in the form of discernment is always a good idea. Hypocritically judging others, however, is an entirely different matter. We can see, then, that Matthew 7:1 and John 7:24 are totally congruent. Only by taking Matthew 7:1 out of context do people mistakenly conclude that all forms of judgment are bad.

This example also helps us recognize that not only is the immediate context important, a verse or passage should also be examined within the greater context of the entire Bible. By considering Matthew 7:1-5 in light of Galatians 6:1, we can see that righteous judgments are not only appropriate, they are encouraged.

Brethren, even if anyone is caught in any trespass, you who are spiritual, restore such a one in a spirit of gentleness; each one looking to yourself, so that you too will not be tempted. Galatians 6:1

The process of correction requires that we make *righteous* judgments. Motivated by gentle love, with an attitude of humility, and the goal of restoration, we are called to speak into the lives of others who are making sinful choices. But all too often, people pull Matthew 7:1 out of the larger Biblical context while trying to brush off correction so they can justify self-willed behavior. (Darn, there goes my excuse for doing whatever I want!)

Much of my life revolves around teaching and writing, so I understand how cumbersome quoting large sections of Scripture can become. Thus, I've concluded that it's okay to pull out and utilize short passages of Scripture as long as we stay true to their Biblical context. Over time, as we apply ourselves to the pursuit of Biblical truth, the ability to recognize the Scriptural context of a passage becomes all the more natural.

OTHER THOUGHTS ABOUT CONTEXT

The tendency to isolate concepts from one another is endemic to Western culture. Mostly through repeated use of visual media, we have been conditioned to separate ideas from their greater whole. Consequently, I have found it common for Christians to understand isolated concepts while failing to recognize how they intricately connect to one another.

Entire church denominations have been built upon a single concept at the expense of others. Their faithful adherence to that particular tenet of faith then becomes the standard by which they judge all others. Meanwhile, another denomination may be doing the same thing by isolating and emphasizing a different concept. Distinctives can play an important role in our individual expressions of the Christian faith, but they shouldn't serve as marks of validation over and against others.

All of Biblical truth is interrelated. So when it comes to processing truth, magnification almost always leads to distortion. (Remember the earlier caution regarding word studies?) A relevant example involves a modern-day attempt to define God by a human understanding of *love*. All too often we ignore the fact that God's love cannot be understood apart from His justice, and justice cannot be established apart from a foundation of moral truth.

Analytically separating and outlining truth has significant value as a teaching tool, but its effectiveness is also limited by the fact that truth does not always come in neat packages tied up with colorful bows. And while recognizing the interconnectedness of Scriptural concepts may cause a bit of confusion, piecing together the bigger picture opens our eyes in amazing ways.

We might make a similar statement regarding systems of doctrine. Undoubtedly, our theological constructs help to create a valuable framework for understanding Biblical truth, but they can also cause huge problems when we try to conform the Scriptures—and thus God—to our human systems of belief. We shouldn't bend the Scriptures to fit our theology; we must adjust our theology to fit the Scriptures.

Trying to define the relationship between God's sovereignty and human free will is another issue that has created considerable conflict over the years. The problem is that the Bible supports *both* perspectives to varying degrees. When we focus on one to the exclusion of the other, not only do we distort the larger picture, we also try to force upon various passages meanings that simply do not fit. As uncomfortable as it may feel to live with a tension between the two poles, doing so is probably the option that most accurately reflects our grand reality.

I want the courage to acknowledge that God's truth is bigger than all of us combined. I don't need a clearly defined analytical explanation for every facet of truth, but I do need to learn to live with the tension between two seemingly contradictory concepts such as God's sovereignty and our human free will. As much as I want to understand *everything* with crystal clarity, there are times when I have to admit that I simply don't know. Please, let's allow the Scriptures to speak for themselves rather than trying to force them into our preconceived belief systems. Christianity does not involve the promotion of an ideology or systematic theology as much as the pursuit of a divine, unseen reality.

If I could identify one notable exception to the principles of context, it would be the way New Testament writers sometimes quoted the Old Testament—and especially OT prophecy. The Holy Spirit enabled those who penned the New Testament to recognize the often-cryptic nature of Old Testament foretelling, and so their illumination of such passages need not conform to our principles of interpretation. In the end, God has the freedom to veil truth in whatever form He desires, but we don't have the freedom to twist Scripture to promote personal opinions.

THREE MORE TIPS

Three other issues of context are worthy of at least a brief mention. First, whenever possible, we want to *interpret Scripture with Scripture.* As recorded in John 1:29, when John the Baptist saw Jesus, he proclaimed, "Behold, the Lamb of God who takes away the sin of the world!" If not for the sacrificial practices outlined in the Old Testament, John's statement would make little sense.

Leviticus is one of the most difficult books of the Bible for people to process, and yet, its description of the Jewish sacrificial system supports the idea that John recognized Jesus as the "sacrificial lamb" that would cleanse the sins of the Jewish people. As difficult as this idea of a blood sacrifice may be for our modern minds to process, a key verse in Leviticus provides significant insight:

"For the life of the flesh is in the blood, and I have given it to you on the altar to make atonement for your souls; for it is the blood by reason of the life that makes atonement." Leviticus 17:11

Adam and Eve's original sin in Eden brought spiritual death to their descendants by separating humanity from God. For the relationship to be restored, the barrier of sin had to be somehow eradicated. It is in this light that we are incapable of redeeming ourselves through good works.

For whatever reason, the ancients understood what God was communicating through this passage: the life found in blood is the only viable means to erase the blight of sin's death. God provided a short-term answer to our dilemma through the blood of innocent animals. Animal blood, however, could only temporarily cover—not fully cleanse—the death-ridden stains of human sins. By voluntarily shedding His blood as a perfect and innocent sacrifice for our sins, Jesus became the eternal Lamb of God who restored the once-severed relationship between God and humanity. Understanding John's "Lamb of God" declaration, then, is best accomplished in light of the entire Bible.

Second, another important application of Biblical context involves *emphasis.* We sometimes make the mistake of magnifying things that are given minimal attention in the New Testament while virtually ignoring concepts or issues that the Scriptures emphasize. I can't begin to tell you how much I have learned by studying subjects such as *covenant, fruitfulness, glory, hardness of heart,* and *law* that the Bible repeatedly emphasizes but are given relatively little attention in our Western practice of the Christian faith.

Finally, *where* we find something in the Bible is also significant. Everything that Jesus said was important, but it would make sense that His last words before going to the cross (or His ascension) carry particular weight. By studying the last words of Jesus, Paul, or any other New Testament personality, we can gain valuable insight into the things that mattered a great deal (e.g. the kingdom of God) to the early church.

THE NEW TESTAMENT IN LIGHT OF THE OLD

The difference between the Old and New Testaments presents a significant struggle for many who seek to understand the Bible. One of the keys to unlocking the mystery lies with the concept of *typology*. We can define a physical *type* in the Old Testament as "a prophetic symbol that foreshadows or illuminates a spiritual truth contained in the New Testament." As a whole, physical people and illustrations from the Old help us understand the spiritual truths of the New in a way that would be virtually impossible if the New Testament stood alone.

The story of the exodus, for example, paints a portrait of our New Testament salvation. We might compare Pharaoh to the Devil, Moses to Jesus, and life in Egypt to being bound in sin. Such types abound in the Old Testament and work to establish an essential base for understanding: *the Old prepares us for, and helps to illuminate, the New.*

The use of typology in Hebrew Scripture leads us to a marked distinction between the Old and New Testaments. The Old Testament emphasis was primarily on *physical* (*temporal*) things while the New Testament focuses more on *spiritual* (*eternal*) matters. God's blessings in the Old were mostly material; the New emphasizes eternal, spiritual riches. Armies fought and conquered in the Old; warfare in the New is primarily spiritual. The physical nation of Israel was a constant focus in the Old; the kingdom of God gains all of the attention in the New.

I do not claim that spiritual matters were unimportant in the Old or that physical issues are irrelevant in the New. Old Testament believers still had a sense of "other-worldliness" while Jesus healed physical bodies and provided for material needs. It's all a matter of *emphasis* (see Matthew 6:24-33; Romans 14:17; and Ephesians 1:3).

The distinction between the Old and the New matters a great deal—especially when it comes to our perspective of material prosperity. In the Old, God's blessings over men such as Job, Abraham, and Solomon were highlighted by an overabundance of earthly possessions. But Jesus introduced a radically new concept as He marked heaven's blessings by spiritual qualities and virtues. The apostle Paul is an excellent case in point. In so many ways, Paul's life was a dismal material failure, but an overwhelmingly spiritual success. I contend we fall into serious and idolatrous error when we blindly try to apply the Old Testament emphasis on material prosperity to new covenant Christianity.

I'm no advocate for a poverty-based lifestyle. In other words, I want to do well financially. I live in a decent house, and when possible, I prefer to drive a vehicle that doesn't break down every other day. I also understand that God gifts some people with an innate business sense to earn money. At the same time, I cannot deny the penetrating words of both Jesus (Matthew 6:19-24) and Paul (1 Timothy 6:3-12) cautioning about the dangers of material prosperity and the importance of laying hold of that which is eternal. The key, I believe, is always to keep our physical prosperity subservient to a greater spiritual reality.

The Old Testament is the inspired Word of God as much as the New, but the Old was written with one primary purpose in mind: to prepare the way for our new covenant in Christ (John 5:39). Based on life experience, I believe that the failure to recognize the different emphases between the two can lead to all sorts of theological confusion.

LAW AND GRACE

The Old Testament is dominated by the *Mosaic law*, whereas the *gospel of grace* characterizes New Testament theology. Those who fail to make this distinction begin to see the entire Bible as a book of moral rules when it is intended to be a book of enduring relationship (John 17:3). While there is no one key to spiritual vitality, understanding the difference between living by law and living by grace will have more of an impact on a person's life than practically any other concept.[4]

From a New Testament perspective, living by law involves *self-justification*—trying to find acceptance (i.e. righteousness) with God by working to measure up to various standards. Some people refer to this as a "salvation by works" mindset. It aligns closely with those who believe they can go to heaven simply by being "good" people. The problem is that heaven is a perfect place, and none of us is good enough to meet such standards of perfection. And if our sin and pride aren't somehow neutralized, humanity would corrupt heaven just as it has our planet. The gospel of grace is God's loving answer to this dilemma:

> *For by grace you have been saved through faith; and that not of yourselves, it is the gift of God; not as a result of works, so that no one may boast. Ephesians 2:8-9*

Through faith in the person of Jesus Christ—including His sacrificial death and subsequent resurrection from the dead—even the worst among us can draw upon God's multi-faceted grace. This grace takes three primary expressions in the life of a believer. First, it covers us with an unmerited favor in the eyes of God that none of us deserves. Second, grace empowers us to live in victory over the power of sin. And third, God equips and strengthens us through grace to help and bless others in ways that far exceed our natural abilities.

The new covenant gospel of grace is uniquely different from every other human system of belief. I don't argue that most religions share some common beliefs, but the New Testament emphasis on God's grace makes Christianity entirely unique. Other religious codes are somehow driven by self-effort, which only fuels the fires of human pride. But through the gospel of grace, we are made acceptable to God (justified) by the perfection of Christ through the cleansing of His sacrificial blood. The weight of our salvation from sin, then, lies *outside* of ourselves. In this reality, true freedom is realized.

---

4. As mentioned previously, a much more detailed explanation the old covenant paradigm of law can be found in my book, *The Divine Progression of Grace: Blazing a Trail to Fruitful Living.*

What is our response to God's saving grace? Not to seek acceptance with God (which the Christian already has), but simply to love Him in return for His goodness. We live by a new law, then, the *law of love* which governs our actions. Am I claiming the Mosaic law to be now worthless? Not at all. We can never be accepted by God by trying to meet the standards of the law, but the moral elements do help us gauge—like a thermometer—how well we are aligning with His design. The Mosaic law, however, cannot serve as a "thermostat" to increase our spiritual temperature.

Does the law-grace issue really matter all that much? Absolutely! Grasping the difference between the two, and how they relate to one another, will mark the line between spiritual life and spiritual death.

It's difficult for some of us to think that reading the Bible can be detrimental to a person, but attempting to live by the letter of the law to gain God's approval will kill our spiritual vitality. With a correct understanding of grace, however, the Bible becomes a source of amazing life.

> *Not that we are adequate in ourselves to consider anything as coming from ourselves, but our adequacy is from God, who also made us adequate as servants of a new covenant, not of the letter but of the Spirit; for the letter kills, but the Spirit gives life.* 2 Corinthians 3:5-6

> *Just as in the entire world this gospel is bearing fruit and growing, so it has also been bearing fruit and growing among you from the first day you heard it and understood the grace of God in truth.* Colossians 1:6b (NET)

We can understand the new covenant only through the context of a grace paradigm. When we get it right, human lives will be powerfully transformed! But if we get it wrong, dysfunction will reign even in our "Christian" environments.

In his second letter to the Corinthians, Paul paints the Mosaic law as a ministry of death and condemnation in contrast to the New Covenant ministry of the Holy Spirit through righteousness and reconciliation (2 Corinthians 3:7-9 and 5:18-19). For the Christian, the true ministry of righteousness is that of reconciliation and not condemnation. The difference between living by grace as opposed to law is an essential reality we must all grasp!

CHAPTER WRAP-UP

The Bible is an amazing book; through its pages, the Creator of the Universe speaks to transform human lives. At times, the very idea of understanding the Bible can seem overwhelming. Understanding a few key concepts, however, can minimize our confusion. First, a primary key to understanding the Book of books is to realize that context is king. Second, grasping the unique purposes of the Old and New Testaments will help bring further clarification. Finally, recognizing the extreme importance of the gospel of grace—as opposed to law-based systems of belief—will open our eyes to an amazing paradigm for life that stretches the limits of our natural thought processes.

12

CRACKING THE BOOK

After reading the doctrines of Plato, Socrates or Aristotle, we feel the specific difference between their words and Christ's is the difference between an inquiry and a revelation.

—Joseph Parker

One thing I have asked from the Lord, that I shall seek:
That I may dwell in the house of the Lord all the days of my life,
To behold the beauty of the Lord
And to meditate in His temple.

Psalms 27:4

On a typical morning—if such a thing exists—I'll climb out of bed and eventually make my way to the kitchen. Some mornings, I'll fry an omelet complete with cheese, greens, and whatever meat I can find in the fridge. On other days, it's a protein shake (chocolate, of course) or a bowl of yogurt with a handful of nuts and frozen blueberries. In either case, I'll then sit at the dining room table and begin my daily Bible reading while I'm eating. There's nothing quite like feeding the body and the soul at the same time!

After breakfast, I'll push in my chair, clean up my mess (like a good husband), and then move to the couch to continue my reading. Sometimes, I'll read a few chapters. On some occasions, it might only be a few verses. From there, I'll focus on praying or trying to memorize a few verses. The format often varies, and distractions are not uncommon; I'm not nearly as disciplined as I'd like to be.

My typical morning routine may differ considerably from yours. At this stage of life, I don't have young children underfoot, and I don't have a deadline for arriving at work as I once did. Writing requires a lot of thought, and morning seems to be the time I think best, so a quiet house provides an excellent environment for contemplation. Still, even though the specifics of my daily routine have changed over time, starting my day with the Bible has been a way of life since my earliest days as a Christian.

I feel bad about using the word *routine* to discuss my devotional habits; I'd much prefer to focus on drama and excitement. I'd like to say that if you just crack open your Bible in the morning, the heavens will part as brilliant rays of light burst forth. I'd like to tell you that if you just take the time to read a chapter or two of Scripture, your day will never get off to a bad start when you punch the clock at work. But I can't claim any of these things—at least not with honesty. The truth is that sometimes your Bible reading will catapult you to the heavens, and sometimes, it will feel rather dull and routine to where you question the value of your efforts. Overall, however, the cumulative process of incremental growth matters more than the ups and downs of any particular day.

WHY WE NEGLECT GOD

Time is a huge issue for many of us. I get that. With family, work, and other responsibilities, carving out time to read and study the Bible can seem near impossible. Furthermore, we're inundated with information and confronted by an almost-constant need to make decisions regarding a wide array of options in practically every facet of life. Consequently, information overload and decision fatigue are very real issues for many of us. It's no wonder that at the end of the day we just want to plop in front of a TV screen and "veg out." Winding down the day with a little mindless comic relief or carefully-scripted drama comes ever so easily. All too often, the idea of reading the Bible ends up being little more than an afterthought as we fall into bed worn out and exhausted.

I don't question that our lives are overflowing with things to do and decisions to make, but in all honesty, I think being too busy to read the Bible is mostly an excuse. Rather, our subconscious feelings and underlying beliefs hinder us from drawing nearer to our Creator. The internal motivation—or lack thereof—for opening the Bible may seem like a minor issue, but it can have a huge influence on our long-term relationship with God.

There are multiple reasons we fail to seek God, but I'll highlight only three. First, people who don't have a devotional life generally don't think they need a devotional life. Why do I spend at least a little time in the Bible every day? Sure, I enjoy it, but I also know that I can't live without the sustenance of God's eternal Word.

When the Devil tempted Jesus to turn stones into bread during His forty-day fast, the Son of God responded by quoting Deuteronomy 8:3:

> *"The scripture says 'Man shall not live by bread alone, but by every word that proceeds from the mouth of God.'" Matthew 4:4b (PHILLIPS)*

Why do we eat food? Both for pleasure and survival. And in this case, our physical reality mirrors the spiritual. Regardless of our reasoning, if we don't draw near to our heavenly Father and feed on the spiritual sustenance He provides, our spiritual selves will grow weak, impotent, and susceptible to all sorts of "spiritual diseases."

I worked with some very interesting people at my first lab job after graduating from college. We frequently engaged in animated discussions about religion and spirituality as we performed our duties. For my part, I was often viewed as somewhat of an oddball because of my devotion to God. On one particular occasion, a fellow employee, Ted, accused me of using religion as a crutch. My reply? "I don't need a crutch; I need a wheelchair!" I don't think that was the response Ted expected.

I've never been very good at this thing called *life*. I've never been big enough, fast enough, or strong enough. And although I did well in school, my intellect fell short in helping me overcome my personal struggles. Still, not until after becoming a Christian did I realize that in addition to wanting to know God, I also needed (and continue to need) Him desperately. Strong people often subconsciously believe that their self-efforts are sufficient to meet heavenly requirements. Deep down, they don't feel they need God and, thus, the Bible. The world's humanistic mantra—"Believe in yourself!"—provides enough self-confidence for their day-to-day existence—at least until times of crises force them to consider a Higher Power.

A second reason for avoiding time with God is almost opposite the first: we believe that we're miserable failures unworthy of His presence. Perhaps the primary problem is a horrific track record, or maybe we can't get past a recurring sin. Regardless of the source, guilt, shame, and condemnation form huge barriers that keep us distant from God's presence. And more often than not, such negative feelings about ourselves seamlessly knit with a skewed perspective of the heavenly Father. (What miserable wretch wants to come into the presence of someone they view as an exacting and heavy-handed perfectionist?) The grim reality is that *not one* of us is worthy of God's favor. In fact, it's only through the awareness of our sinfulness that we become serious about our desperate need to look to Jesus Christ as our Savior.

Do you recall what I wrote in the last chapter about the importance of understanding law and grace for a healthy relationship with God? Well, here's where it matters. Walking with God *never* depends upon any measure of worthiness on our part, but rather the unmerited favor of God's grace received through faith in the sacrificial death and subsequent resurrection of Jesus Christ. When the revelation of God's amazing grace begins to dawn in our hearts, we learn to abide in His presence and are forever changed. On the contrary, if we live under a law-based mindset, guilt and condemnation will keep us forever distant from the One who loves us most passionately.

These aren't truths that we'll learn about on a daily news feed, TV talk show, or rerun of a favorite sitcom. If we want to know God, understand His ways, and live in the nearness of His presence, the Bible is indispensable. Such a pursuit has nothing to do with obligation and everything to do with love.

Finally, deep-seated feelings of disappointment may also hinder us from seeking God. Our stories may vary, but the feelings are essentially the same. Maybe a heartfelt prayer went unanswered, or a once-trusted friend committed an act of betrayal. It's also possible that a "marriage made in heaven" turned into a travesty from hell. Or maybe life feels like little more than a miserable existence, and the Lord of the Universe doesn't seem to care. "And if God doesn't care about our well-being," we reason, "why bother to seek Him?"

Our reasons for failing to open the Bible may vary, but the overall result is always the same. God either becomes—or remains—distant, we subject ourselves to unhealthy spiritual influences, and the true vitality of life eludes us. And more often than not, our problems are exacerbated by the ignorance of God's character and the manner in which He interacts with people.

I can't speak to the specifics of any person's situation, but I can testify to God's impeccable character. No matter where you've been, what you've done, or what you've gone through, He loves you. And not only does He love you, He always wants to draw you nearer. Wallowing in disappointment never helps, nor does avoiding His presence. Only by faithfully seeking our Savior can any of us finally step out of the muck into a blessed existence. Instead of quitting, if you allow God to finish your story, *disappointment* will be the *last* word to describe your emotions.

MAKING ROOM

In spite of our busy schedules and low income during our college years, Debi and I somehow managed to go on dates and spend time together. Later in life, when I came across a hunting or fishing item that I really wanted to buy, I usually found a way to make it happen. When a person has a deep-seated desire, he or she seeks creative ways to see it fulfilled. Consequently, our pursuit of God starts not with opening the Bible, but with examining our motives to assess where we are in life and what we value.

If you've read this far, I can only assume that you put a relatively high premium on connecting with God and understanding His ways.

After all, there are plenty of other things to occupy your time. Examining our basic desires, however, is only the first step. Once we evaluate the things that drive us, an appropriate next step is to examine, with an objective mindset, how we fill our days. Generally speaking, young (or retired) people with fewer responsibilities will have more free time. And by making wise decisions about employment, family, and living arrangements, they can help set the stage for a future built around a vital, life-giving relationship with their Savior.

When Debi and I considered marriage, we surrendered our relationship to God to ensure it fit His plans and purposes. When I searched for a job or was offered a promotion, I always contemplated the implications to my spiritual life and family relationships. And when we considered buying a house, we painstakingly worked to find one requiring minimal maintenance (if there is such a house!) and debt. Without question, we felt pulled by our natural and worldly desires for more, but we always sought to carve out an existence built around God and family rather than worldly status or possessions. Looking back over our quality of life during the past thirty or so years, I think we could have handled a few things better, but our overall strategy worked great.

Those already inundated with the responsibilities of life will have a more difficult time changing the flow of their daily routines, and I don't recommend divorcing a spouse or abandoning children to spend more time reading the Bible. The employment world has also changed with people working multiple jobs or stuck in situations that demand more than they feel they can give. Change may be in order, but circumstances don't always offer viable options. Regardless of any current situation, it's always best to keep debt to an absolute minimum—or if possible—avoid it entirely. Debt and high standards of living can make career changes all the more difficult.

Every person's situation is unique, so there is no uniform solution to apply to all. One of us may painstakingly carve time out of his daily routine to draw near to his Savior while another decides that radical changes are necessary for her spiritual vitality. God will guide those who seek His wisdom and yield to the leadings of His Spirit.

Whatever you do, the goals are always a closer relationship with God, a deeper understanding of His ways, and a greater impact on the world around us. We're not trying to be perfect Christians or fulfill obligations to avoid guilt. The heart of new covenant living is motivated by a deep-seated love that flourishes in an atmosphere of freedom.

All of us will, at one time or another, fall short in our efforts, and so learning how to process failure is an essential skill that enables us to make "emotional room" for God. Too often, well-meaning people will commit some sort of sin and then avoid reading the Bible because of their guilt. Actually, steering clear of the Scriptures is one of the *worst* things we can do. It makes no sense to avoid our greatest source of help when we are in need of help.

If you feel as though you've failed God, confess your shortcoming(s), ask forgiveness if you feel the need, believe He has forgiven you, and then get back into the Word (see Hebrews 4:14-16, 10:19-25; and 1 John 1:9). Allowing the pain-ridden rot of guilt and condemnation to cloud our emotions will always squeeze God to the perimeter of our lives. Jesus died on the cross so that we wouldn't have to wallow in our shame; let's not allow the extreme price that He paid to be in vain.

CHOOSING A BIBLE TRANSLATION

Some people are adamant in claiming the King James Bible to be the only valid English version available, but I think it's a huge mistake to force Early Modern English on people 400 years removed from that era. Understanding the Bible can be challenging enough; trying to grasp its truths through an older linguistic style makes things all the more difficult. I highly recommend that you choose a version of the Bible well-suited to your individual reading ability.[1]

Doing a little research into modern Bible translations, we find that teams of highly educated academics often combined their efforts to produce works that are both readable and true to the original

---

1. The following link to the Search for Me Ministries, Inc. website provides helpful information for choosing a Bible translation and Bible study materials: http://searchforme.info/bible-study-resources/

meaning. And while some people may be bothered by the large number of translations available, I think it works to our benefit.

With today's technology, a person can pull up a verse on the internet and easily compare a half-dozen or more versions. Some Bible software programs even provide graphs showing how closely passages in various translations compare to one another. The cumulative result is that outliers are identified, and a consensus of the most accurate meaning is formed.

Your best Bible version will balance accuracy and readability. I tend to prefer the New American Standard Bible (NASB) because that's what I started with, and its level of accuracy is highly regarded. Some people, however, find even the updated (1996) NASB to be somewhat "stiff" when it comes to readability. That's okay. The New King James Version (NKJV) maintains the poetic nature of the KJV, and versions such as the Holman Christian Standard Bible (HCSB) and the English Standard Version (ESV) have become increasingly popular. Of course, there's always the New English Translation (NET) Bible with its 60,932 translation notes!

I suggest that, if possible, you find a website on which you can compare multiple Bible translations to see which fits best for you. However, before you settle on a particular version of the Bible, research its credibility while looking into the credentials of the translating team. Information about the translators can often be found in comparison charts or on the website of a version's sponsoring organization.

Some modern versions of the Bible are *paraphrases* produced by lone individuals who did their best to record the Scriptures in contemporary language. These works, which include the Living Bible (LB) and the Message (MSG), among others, may provide additional insight and inspiration for some passages, but they are poor choices for everyday use. While multiple translators do not guarantee accuracy in translation, a lone translator certainly increases the potential for error.

The New World Translation (NWT) by the Jehovah's Witnesses is highly suspect because it shows evidence of being manipulated to fit the doctrines of the Jehovah Witnesses. Furthermore, nothing is known about the qualifications of the translating team. A quick online search will produce the names of about forty scholars who worked on the original New American Standard translation and almost twenty more who contributed to the updated version. Further effort would establish their academic qualifications for undertaking such a work. The list of NWT translators, however, has always been kept secret, and so we know nothing of their qualifications.

The goal of a Bible translator should always be to convey, accurately and objectively, with maximum readability, the original meaning of the text into another language. While the work is often tedious and difficult, an open effort with multiple translators expertly educated in the Hebrew, Aramaic, and Greek languages helps to ensure both accuracy and objectivity.

READING THE BIBLE

Sometimes we avoid reading the Bible simply because we don't get it; no matter how hard we try, it doesn't seem to make sense. Long-term feelings of "spiritual stupidity" are enough to keep anyone from opening the Bible's pages. However, there is a way for each of us to connect with God through the Scriptures; we just need to find the methods that work best for us as individuals. I see no problem with doing some research and experimenting with different versions, as well as various approaches to reading the Bible.

Each of us can pursue our connection with God through the Bible on several different levels. For those who are extremely busy, some creative solutions may be necessary. Mothers with young children seem to face the most significant challenges with getting into God's written Word. Reading during nap times, perusing short passages, and posting memorization verses around the house can all be helpful.

No matter which approach(es) we choose to take, one of our biggest obstacles is human pride. Assuming that we can, by our own intelligence, understand the dynamics of spiritual truth, will keep us blind to a deeper understanding of God's ways. Therefore, it's always wise to begin reading with a simple faith-filled prayer for God to open our eyes and illuminate our hearts to His truth. I find a huge difference in the quality of my Bible reading times when I humble myself and pray for wisdom as opposed to when I don't.

It's also helpful to develop a *realistic* plan for daily Bible reading. I've seen a lot of people "burst out of the gate" in zealous pursuit of God only to fade into oblivion as they repeatedly fail to meet their unattainable standards. I ran the mile for our high school track team. I wasn't very good, but neither was our team, so I fit in well. Once, the coach asked me to run the mile relay. It seemed like a great idea—especially since I'd be running only a quarter of my usual distance. Grabbing the baton from my teammate before me, I took off like a bullet, leaving my opponent gasping in a cloud of dust—or so I hoped. But by the time I entered the first turn, the error of my ways began to dawn. Soon, I was out of breath and struggling just to finish a single lap around the oval. We didn't even come close to winning the race, but we would have done much better if I had approached my leg of the relay more like I handled a typical long-distance race. Be sure to exercise wisdom by setting sustainable goals for Bible reading and building from there.

For those just beginning to read the Bible, starting with the New Testament is probably the best option. The Gospels of Matthew, Mark, and Luke are very similar, so I recommend beginning with Luke and reading forward from there. For those who are ready to delve into the Old Testament, I find it helpful to simultaneously read the New Testament. Genesis and early Exodus can be fascinating, but the latter part of Exodus and the entire book of Leviticus have shipwrecked many a well-intentioned Bible reader. By reading the New and Old together, we can avoid getting lost and bogged down in the sections that tend to lose our attention. Structured reading plans are also readily available through various apps and online sources.

Even though I do the bulk of my reading in the New Testament, I try not to neglect the Old as its content can be quite rich. I also think it's a good idea to read the entire Bible through every so often to develop and maintain a healthy perspective of the big picture. It's much more difficult to piece together a scenic puzzle if you don't have an overall grasp of the entire landscape.

Bible reading is best accomplished when we're awake and alert and with minimal distractions. Mornings seem best for most people. I've found that if I don't read in the morning, it's all too easy for me to let my Bible reading slide later in the day. However, some people gain much more by reading before bed, and so I don't see a problem with going that route if that's what works best. Shift work can make life all the more complicated, so again, I suggest experimenting to discover the best approach on an individual level. Of course, there's nothing to say that a person can't read multiple times throughout the day.

In our technological age, one of our bigger struggles often involves our smartphones and tablets—the very tools some people effectively utilize to help with their Bible reading efforts. Many of us are addicted to our smartphones and feel that we need to respond to every beep, buzz, or gobble (I have some unique friends).

To make matters worse, as soon as we begin reading or praying, our minds often fill with tasks that cry for our attention. (Isn't it nice to know that you're not the only one who struggles with these tendencies?) Such distractions may not be healthy, but we can take comfort in knowing that they are normal.

Concerning emails and texts, I do my best to silence or ignore the notifications. Developing the discipline to push distractions aside requires some effort, but it can be healthy on multiple levels. Most of the time, only a (rare) true emergency requires a response.

When it comes to tasks that pop into my mind, I've found it best to write them down so they don't clutter my thoughts. A note-taking app on my smartphone serves me well for this purpose. After a few minutes, the mental flow of tasks will diminish, and I'll be free to focus my attention elsewhere.

Distractions of all sorts hinder the growth of a healthy spiritual life, and so we are wise to address the issue. At the same time, there's no official "Christian" way of dealing with the things that divert our attention from seeking God. Feel free to find an approach that works best for you.

LISTENING TO THE BIBLE

For one reason or another, some people can only read the Bible for very short periods, or perhaps, not at all. In these cases, listening to an audio version might be an excellent alternative. Listening may also be a good way to augment your reading. While this approach may not be the most effective for the average learner, it's certainly preferable over no exposure to the Scriptures. In addition, some people may glean more from listening to the Bible than from reading it.

It goes without saying that we should take care when listening to the Bible while driving. Those unable to simultaneously focus on both the road and the Scriptures would be better off finding an alternative solution. The inspiration of God's Word doesn't give us the freedom to supersede the natural laws that require us to pay attention while driving!

MEMORIZING SCRIPTURE

We all have our issues in life—many of which are the products of unhealthy thought patterns. Our natural tendencies, combined with lifelong habits, often keep us bound in the prison of sinful living. Real change happens only as we *renew our minds* with God's Word.

> *Therefore I urge you, brethren, by the mercies of God, to present your bodies a living and holy sacrifice, acceptable to God, which is your spiritual service of worship. And do not be conformed to this world, but be transformed by the renewing of your mind, so that you may prove what the will of God is, that which is good and acceptable and perfect. Romans 12:1-2*

I've found it especially helpful to memorize promises of God that meet the points of our greatest needs and weaknesses. For example, many Christians tempted to worry often rely heavily on Philippians 4:6-7:

> *Be anxious for nothing, but in everything by prayer and supplication with thanksgiving let your requests be made known to God. And the peace of God, which surpasses all comprehension, will guard your hearts and your minds in Christ Jesus. Philippians 4:6-7*

By reciting this passage to ourselves, we not only draw upon the strength of God's Word but also remind our hearts that thankfulness is a powerful expression of faith. I don't recommend limiting our memorization to personal needs, but it's certainly not a bad starting point.

Consistently using one primary translation of the Bible helps with the memorization process. Not only do we avoid the potential confusion involved with memorizing from different versions, repeatedly reading a passage in the same translation will help it "stick" in our hearts and minds.

For years, people have used small memorization cards that can be carried in a wallet or a purse. Today, memorization apps are now readily available for smartphones and tablets, and I've found them to be quite helpful. For people such as me who struggle to memorize God's Word, every little bit helps.

PRAYING, CONFESSING, AND SINGING

The Bible tells us that, "Faith comes from hearing, and hearing by the word of Christ" (Romans 10:17). Confessing the Word and praying the Scriptures back to God can be very powerful! Not only does it help our prayers align with God's will, our faith is bolstered and spiritual power released. Some of the prayers penned by the apostle Paul (e.g. Ephesians 1:15-23, 3:14-21; and Philippians 1:9-11) provide an excellent starting place. We don't confess God's Word as a sort of "magic wand" to manipulate our circumstances, but rather to express faith and bring ourselves into better alignment with His eternal truth.

I'm a musical disaster, and so I've never seriously considered singing the Scriptures. Those who are more gifted in this area—and even those who aren't—may find great comfort and benefit in lifting Scriptural verses to God in this way. After all, many of our contemporary worship songs are essentially adaptations of the Psalms.

MEDITATING ON THE SCRIPTURES

Biblical meditation differs significantly from that of Eastern religious practices which tend to emphasize the importance of emptying oneself. Our intent is not simply to empty ourselves, but to fill our hearts and minds with truth. Of course, we seek to put aside mental clutter but for the purpose of filling our hearts and minds with life-giving sustenance from heaven.

In Biblical Hebrew, *meditate* essentially means "to mutter."[2] We're talking about slowly "chewing on" and "digesting" the Scriptures. Personally, I've found that truth identified or revealed to me directly by God through meditation has more "staying power" than when I hear it from others. Each truth gained becomes another important block in the foundation of my understanding.

> *How blessed is the man who does not walk in the counsel of the wicked,*
> *Nor stand in the path of sinners,*
> *Nor sit in the seat of scoffers!*
> *But his delight is in the law of the LORD,*
> *And in His law he meditates day and night.*
> *He will be like a tree firmly planted by streams of water,*
> *Which yields its fruit in its season*
> *And its leaf does not wither;*
> *And in whatever he does, he prospers.*
> *Psalms 1:1-3*

Meditation is the discipline that comes most readily to me. I am a thinker by nature, and so I simply need to direct my thoughts to Biblical truth. On some days, I'll read only a short passage of Scripture, which I then chew on for much of the day. The one drawback for me, though, is that because meditation comes so naturally, I find memorization to be a difficult discipline. Perhaps it goes back to my chemistry versus biology issues in high school!

Meditating on God's Word only works when we rely upon the Holy Spirit to open our eyes to His truth. Once again, praying for insight and revelation is essential. Fasting (as explained in chapter three) is another practice that catalyzes the effectiveness of meditation. If you've never

---

2. James Swanson, *Dictionary of Biblical Languages with Semantic Domains: Hebrew (Old Testament)* (Oak Harbor: Logos Research Systems, Inc., 1997).

done so, you might want to consider skipping a meal and spending the time crying out to God for insight and revelation. Then prayerfully pick a passage of Scripture to meditate on for a couple of days. The results can be amazing! More often than not, what we get out of God's Word depends on the amount of effort we invest in seeking a deeper understanding.

STUDYING THE BIBLE

Bible study differs from mediation in that we deliberately carve out time to sit down with the Bible and any of a wide array of extra-Biblical resources. No person or book should ever replace the role of the Holy Spirit to reveal and illuminate God's ways, but we are foolish to ignore the tremendous value of the scholarly works others have labored hard to produce. We all rely on scholarship to one degree or another. Even those who choose to read the Bible and nothing else are relying on the academic work of the translators.

We can utilize multiple methods to study the Bible, and numerous books have been written on the subject.[3] Two methods have proven especially helpful for me. *Exegetical* Bible study involves taking a passage (or book) of Scripture and "pulling it apart" line by line. The primary goal is to comprehend the original intent of the passage, and in the process, we use extra-Biblical resources to help establish the linguistic, historical, and cultural contexts. We also read the surrounding passages and follow the cross-references (found in certain study Bibles) to help establish the greater Biblical context. Exegetical study methods are used effectively by many pastors and can help to make studying the Bible a revolutionary experience.

I've already highlighted the value of word studies. With laser-like focus, we can examine the nuances of a particular concept. Exclusively focusing on word studies and themes can be problematic, however, in that we tend to avoid dealing with topics that we find unpleasant. Sometimes, the thing we need most is the one we want to deal with the least, so it's wise to use multiple approaches to studying the Bible.

---

3. A book such as *Bible Study Methods: Twelve Ways You Can Unlock God's Word,* by Rick Warren provides a good starting place to learn more about studying the Bible.

ATTENDING CHURCH SERVICES

Sadly, the words *church* and *sermon* seem to have been given bad connotations in some circles. Even so, corporate gatherings have been a part of the Christian experience since its earliest times. It's difficult to put in words, but when the *life of God* is made manifest in a community environment, inspiration becomes the order of the day. God is undoubtedly willing to touch a lone individual, but there are also ways that He moves *only* as His people come together in response to His Scriptural commands.

All of us can benefit from hearing well-prepared, Biblically-based messages. I have listened to thousands of sermons in my life. And though I remember very few individual messages, collectively they have contributed to my spiritual growth while supplying insight, encouragement, and hope during difficult times. More times than I can count, God has used a pastor's sermon to provide a timely word to meet my present need.

PARTICIPATING IN GROUP BIBLE STUDIES

I must admit that as much as I value weekend church services, small group Bible studies resonate with me the most. While a larger service offers corporate dynamics for worship that a small group can't, the give-and-take of a small group study invigorates my soul like few other activities. When done well, a small group study provides one of the most effective learning environments imaginable. Few methods can compare to in-depth teaching combined with lively discussion of Scriptural principles in a safe, relational environment. It is through the loving and honest interaction of small group Bible studies that God's living Word touches some of the deepest areas of our being.

If you've never participated in a small group study, you might want to give the idea serious consideration. As it is with attending church services, one of the keys to small group Bible study is consistency. I've led quite a few groups over the years, and one pattern is quite clear: those who attend the most faithfully are the ones who grow the most. And while I realize that modern family and work schedules can make consistency nearly impossible at times, we always want to do the very best that we can.

NOTE TAKING AND JOURNALING

It's been wisely said that *repetition is the mother of learning*. Thus, we benefit most when we record and review what God is teaching us. The process can involve simply taking notes during a message or going more in-depth by recording the insights God gives through personal reading and study of the Bible. Periodic review of these notes then reinforces the truths that transform our hearts.

TEACHING THE BIBLE

The idea may sound really scary to some people, but one of the best ways to learn is to teach. I still remember the first time I spoke at one of our campus ministry meetings a year or two after becoming a Christian. It was a nerve-wracking experience, but immensely rewarding nonetheless. I learned so much in my preparations that I spoke for over an hour. Thankfully, my audience was very gracious (at least they seemed to be).

One of the most effective ways to grasp a concept is to teach it to others. When I lead a Bible study, I will often ask the group participants if they understand what I am communicating. More often than not, they will nod their heads in agreement. Sometimes, I'll then ask them to explain what I just taught. I always know we need to rehash things when a speechless person looks at me with an expression similar to that of a deer staring into car headlights on a particularly dark night. If we can't explain a concept to others, it's likely we don't understand it ourselves.

One of the beautiful things about being part of a healthy group of Christians is that relatively young believers can be given opportunities to teach with the oversight and support of those who are more mature. The central idea of discipleship is not to make people dependent on their leaders, but to invest in them so that they can reach their fullest potential. I realize that not everyone has the gifting to teach on a routine basis, but we never really find that out until we provide opportunities for them to discover the gifts God has entrusted to them.

CHAPTER WRAP-UP

The Bible is our *TouchPoint* for life as it provides a vital point of connection between God and humanity. No other book in existence can compare to its depth of insight and profound ability to transform human lives. If you find yourself avoiding the Scriptures, try searching your heart to see if you can identify the reason(s).

What we get out of the Bible depends on the effort we put into mining its truths. The Bible will do us no good if it sits on a shelf (or in a digital device) collecting dust. Both by personal and corporate pursuits, all of us benefit by incorporating the Word of God into the core dynamics of our lives. The cumulative effects far transcend all this world has to offer!

13

KNOWING GOD

While it is good that we seek to know the Holy One, it is probably not so good to presume that we ever complete the task.

—Dietrich Bonhoeffer

"This is eternal life, that they may know You, the only true God, and Jesus Christ whom You have sent."

John 17:3

Have you ever been in the presence of a "perfect" person? There are, of course, those nearly intolerable people who *act* as though they are perfect. No one can meet their standards; nor is any meaningful dialogue possible because they always consider their opinions superior to all others. But there are also those individuals who—unlike me—excel in virtually every area of life to the point that they appear to approach perfection. Being in the presence of either type of superiority has the unfortunate effect of magnifying our own flaws.

Years ago, a young woman from our church married a former professional football (NFL) player. Debi and I had known Kathy fairly well, so we were invited to the wedding along with several others from our fellowship. The ceremony was beautiful, as was the reception that was held in a high-end Pittsburgh venue. I have to confess, I have never seen so many seemingly perfect people in one place.

Other than the ten to twelve ordinary folks from our church and some of the couple's family members, most of those in attendance seemed to be connected to the NFL. Every male was incredibly handsome and muscular and every female slender and gorgeous. At one point, a friend and I stood in a line behind a guy who was wearing a Super Bowl ring. In the world of sports, they don't come much more successful.

Now, don't get me wrong. Not one of them acted arrogant or aloof. Sure, they each exuded an air of confidence, but not even the most glamorous among them treated us like peons. Still, that was how we all felt—dumpy, imperfect, and insignificant. Thankfully, our table of commoners had enough humor to make light of the issue over dinner, so the experience wasn't so bad in the end.

I also have vivid high school memories of some fellow students (there weren't many of such caliber) who seemed to be morally perfect. On one occasion, an unfortunate substitute teacher was given the challenge of overseeing our class. Most of us were somewhat intelligent, but also mischievous—a really troublesome combination for a replacement teacher to manage.

As a person would act out, the substitute would make him (or her) stand and face one of the four classroom walls. We were so bad that not more than one or two of our classmates were still in their seats by the end of the period. And we hated them for it! Why? Their moral "perfection" clearly and painfully exposed our rottenness. Rather than accept that we were flawed and needed to change, our natural reaction was to rail against them for being "goody two-shoes"—an old term to deride those who came across as unreasonably virtuous. And while our descriptive language may have changed through the years, our mindsets have not.

These two stories provide a mere hint of the challenges faced by sinful, imperfect humans in trying to relate to the flawless Creator of our universe. In every way, God is morally pure, holy, and just. Furthermore, heaven knows no corruption; it is a perfect, peace-filled environment unlike anything known to planet Earth. The only imperfections ever found in heaven are the scars borne by Jesus Christ, and those scars represent the wounds of perfect love.

GOD'S INGENIOUS PLAN

It's nothing short of impossible for imperfect humans to dwell in the eternal presence of our perfect Creator. I am confident that at least two phenomena would take place if God opened wide heaven's gates to anyone who wished to enter. First, we would be overwhelmed by the magnified misery of our sinfulness. The experience might be compared to that of a person emerging from years spent in a dark cave into the brilliance of a sunny, cloudless day.

Second, if we were somehow able to remain in the community of heaven, our selfish pride would eventually have the same corrupting influence that it has had on earth. I don't believe it would take long for the streets of paradise to run red with blood, human violence taking its never-ending toll. Every form of wickedness known to humanity will be transplanted into heaven unless pride is disarmed, and we are transformed from being inherently self-centered creatures. Otherwise, the entire human race is without any meaningful and realistic hope.

Even though humanity is collectively at fault, one of the bigger issues that causes us to doubt God's goodness is that of human suffering. The reality of human pain is always easier to process from a distance, while coming face-to-face with deep suffering tends to stir emotional doubts that lead us to deny the existence of a God, who is both all-powerful and all-loving. To think, for example, that a newborn infant dying of a genetic deformity would somehow accomplish the purposes of a loving God can create a huge difficulty for the reasoning mind.

Can it be? Is it really possible that our magnificent cosmos is ruled by an omnipotent and benevolent God who deeply values and loves every human ever born? And if God is truly the genius that creation would indicate, He must have an exceptional plan for humanity. Behind that plan, there must also be reasonable and intelligent purposes for all that He does. Furthermore, the painful reality of the human condition must somehow be accounted for in the grand scheme of God's design.

I readily concede that we can never fully comprehend every aspect of God's good plan, and I cringe when well-meaning Christians give trite answers in response to deep emotional trauma. At the same time, I contend that we can at least grasp the overall picture of God's design and also experience His goodness through even the worst of times. Keeping these things in mind, let's consider a very brief overview of the mindsets associated with God's plan for the human race as presented in the Christian Bible.

THE TERROR AND BEAUTY OF LOVE

Death and suffering exist not because God turns a blind eye, but because He created humanity *in His own image* with the capacity to love (Genesis 1:26-27). But by its very nature, love demands freedom. Subsequently, the ability for us to fully love is rooted in the freedom to also act selfishly. Unfortunately for us, we can't experience the beauty of someone's choice to love without also experiencing the terror of the choice not to love. And terror is what we've certainly faced. Thus, God did not create evil, but He did create the potential for evil to exist on our planet by graciously giving us the free capacity to love.

Do you see it? Contrary to popular belief, rather than nullifying His existence, pain and suffering *validate* God's goodness. Love is good, and because God so highly valued the human race, He granted us the privilege to share love's freedom. In the process of this design, He also chose to embrace personally the pain that human freedom would breed.

Has anyone paid a steeper price for our freedom than the God who created us? It hurts to care, and our Creator cared so much that He gave His only begotten Son to die a horrific death so we might know true life (John 3:16). And not only did Jesus endure the excruciating physical pain of crucifixion, the full weight of human sin crushed down upon His shoulders as He also experienced the pain of all human suffering (see Isaiah 53). Furthermore, even though Jesus stepped down from His eternal throne to make provision for our every need, through brokenhearted love, He is constantly confronted with our individual and global sufferings day in and day out. Such is the beauty and terror of love.

Why would God risk so much? What caused Him to pay such a terrible price? The anticipation of an intimate, loving relationship with each of us. In other words, the heavenly Father felt that sharing eternity with you and me was worth the collective price we would all pay for the freedom to love. In recognizing His desire, we realize that ours is not a world spinning out of control, but one in which a loving hand is patiently steering all things toward a powerful end.

On my personal journey, I have slowly but progressively gone from feeling abandoned by God to seeing His loving faithfulness all around me. The human condition, I have learned, is not due to any failure on the Lord's part. No, the real problem is rooted in our selfish and stubborn human pride.

It is pride that keeps God at arm's length in the face of human pain and suffering. And pride is why the powerful unjustly exploit those who are vulnerable. If there is any disbelief to be had, it should be over our human stubbornness more than anything else. Pride is the mountainous obstacle that rejects God's love and blots out our hope.

Do you find fault with God's reasoning? Why not raise your hands to heaven and totally surrender your life to your Creator? After all, if we each allowed God to "program" us for selfless good, we'd no longer have a care about evil. I suspect that virtually every person on the planet would—at least initially—balk at such a request. How we cherish the freedom to love in both its beauty and its terror!

WHAT DOES GOD WANT?

We humans expend a lot of energy deciding and pursuing what we want out of life, but do we ever take time to ponder what God wants? And apart from the Bible, how would we even begin to understand God's desires? Our only reasonable recourse would be to superimpose our mindsets on His, and that approach doesn't work especially well.

Those seeking to discover God's desires might begin by recognizing the importance of *covenant* relationships throughout the Bible. We can define a *covenant* as "an especially sacred and binding relationship," and it is through a progressive series of covenants that God has historically drawn near to His people. In spite of our sinful and pride-filled choices, our Creator has, throughout the course of human history, taken repeated steps in our direction. The focus always seems to come back to *His relationship with us.*

Early Genesis emphasizes God's relationship with His newly-formed human creatures. In many ways, humanity is viewed as the *crown jewel* of His creation. God walked with Adam and Eve in the garden of Eden, but human rebellion then severed that relationship. The entire progression of the Bible is wrapped up in our Creator's efforts to restore the intimacy that has since been lost.

It was God who sought out Abram (Abraham) and called Him from an idolatrous environment. Heaven's King took the initiative by speaking to Moses from the burning bush. Upon delivering the people of Israel from bondage in Egypt, God then chose to dwell in a tent so He could be in the midst of His chosen people. Only reluctantly did the Lord allow the nation of Israel to build a stone temple for His manifest presence, but even the magnificent splendor of such a dwelling failed to satisfy His thirst for relational intimacy with those whom He loved.

In the most amazing act of selflessness ever imagined, Jesus stepped out of paradise and took on human flesh to suffer and die so that He might erase the separation between God and humanity. And as if such an extreme sacrifice wasn't enough, also high on Christ's agenda was something that often goes unnoticed—Jesus wanted to know us *experientially.*

Admittedly, this is a difficult concept to process, for in principle, God possesses all knowledge. But when Jesus took on human form, He also took on a human perspective. For the first time, God experientially knew weakness. And not only did the Christ subject Himself to our physical limitations, He willingly took upon His shoulders all of the physical and emotional pain of humanity.

All of this means that there isn't anything you'll ever go through that God doesn't understand. He's nothing like a brooding and cruel drill sergeant who screams at a struggling recruit to get his act together. No, the Son of God is also the Son of Man who truly relates to our individual struggles. That's how much God wants to know us. Amazing! Still, there's even more to the story.

THE TEMPLE OF GOD

In the Jewish temple, a thick cloth veil separated the presence of God (in the *Holy of Holies*) from the people. The Jewish high priest (a male) alone was permitted to enter the Holy of Holies and only one time a year—on the Day of Atonement. *The Holy Place*, which lay immediately outside the veil, was accessed on a daily basis but only by Jewish priests (again males). Next, came the Court of (Jewish) Men, then the Court of (Jewish) Women, and finally, far from the center of God's manifest presence, the Court of the Gentiles.

The imagery of the temple design conveyed a powerful message: *access to God was limited only to the elite few.* This design wasn't so much an expression of God's desire as the consequence of law-based, sinful thinking on our part. The commoners—and especially the non-Jew—had no right to access God's presence. In fact, a fifty-four-inch-high stone wall separating the court of women and the court of the Gentiles proudly displayed the following inscription at various intervals:

> No foreigner is allowed to enter within the balustrade surrounding the sanctuary and court enclosed. Whoever is caught will be personally responsible for his ensuing death.[1]

Herein, we find the grim reality of attempting to build a relationship with God through law-based requirements. But when Jesus died on the cross, the thick veil of the temple was torn in two (Matthew 27:51). Furthermore, the apostle Paul wrote in his letter to the Ephesians that the "barrier of the dividing wall" between Jew and Gentile has been torn down through the cross of Jesus Christ:

> *For He Himself is our peace, who made both groups into one and broke down the barrier of the dividing wall, by abolishing in His flesh the enmity, which is the Law of commandments contained in ordinances, so that in Himself He might make the two into one new man, thus establishing peace, and might reconcile them both in one body to God through the cross, by it having put to death the enmity. Ephesians 2:14-16*

---

1. *The Archaeologicial Study Bible: An Illustrated Walk Through Biblical History and Culture* (Grand Rapids, MI: Zondervan, 2005), 1917.

This passage conveys at least three powerful truths. First, all people, regardless of race, nationality, or gender, now have *direct* access to God's presence. Second, because Christ's sacrificial blood has the power to cleanse and remove the barrier of sin, the Holy Spirit can draw near to humanity. Third, the exalted edifice of elitism has been demolished; *all* men and women are equal before God. In God's dynamic, people may serve different functions, but separations of value based on gender, race, or class are non-existent. This mindset was evidenced in the early church as even slaves could become leaders.

On the Day of Pentecost (see Acts 2), the church was birthed as the Holy Spirit filled God's people. In mystery beyond mystery, people—both individually and corporately—became the temple of "living stones" in which God's presence dwells (see 1 Corinthians 3:16, 6:19; and 1 Peter 2:4-5). What does God want? To be with us! To be in us!

THE AWESOME BEAUTY OF FAITH

One of the encouraging things about the Bible is that we can discover how the story ends. Revelation 21 and 22 confirm that our Creator's ultimate goal is to be with the people He loves—in a state of perfection, for all time, and without barrier. There's only one problem that we dare not overlook: not everybody gets in—but for very good reason.

God's true genius is revealed in His plan of salvation through faith in the sacrificial death and resurrection of Jesus Christ. To begin, intimacy requires trust. Those who have experienced the heartache of betrayal understand well the need to build trust before baring one's soul. Few things are as painful as exposing our intimate places and having our hearts crushed by callous disregard. If we want a relationship with God, it is necessary that we trust Him in even the most vulnerable areas of our lives.

The strategic importance of faith in Christ runs deeper still. As already explained, if God were simply to absolve our sins and grant us all unbridled entrance into paradise, the hell of violence, abuse, and oppression that we experience on earth would follow, nipping at our heels. As has happened on our pain-ridden planet, all that is good would be tainted by corruption and ruin.

Enter the gospel of Jesus Christ! The word *gospel* literally means "good news."[2] Even though the human race blatantly disregarded God's clear command to avoid the forbidden fruit, He set in place a brilliant plan to disarm the power of human pride. But for such a well-conceived plan to be fully realized, all humans must be placed on equal footing. Herein lies the offensive nature of the Christian gospel.

Each of us is born into this world naked. All that we have—or don't have—is due to parental influence. Regardless of what happens through the course of our lives, we'll all leave this earth in the same way we came into it—empty-handed. Elitism lies not in one's birth or death, but in the fleeting period that lies between. Even at that, the idea of human elitism is nothing more than a myth.

> *Men of low degree are only vanity and men of rank are a lie;*
> *In the balances they go up;*
> *They are together lighter than breath.*
> *Psalms 62:9*

The gospel of Jesus Christ strikes at the heart of the human ego by vaporizing the myth of elitism and bringing us all into equality. In the eyes of eternity, no person is superior over another because of gender, race, nationality, wealth, performance, or moral purity.

> *But the Scripture has shut up everyone under sin, so that the promise by faith in Jesus Christ might be given to those who believe.*
>
> *But before faith came, we were kept in custody under the law, being shut up to the faith which was later to be revealed. Therefore the Law has become our tutor to lead us to Christ, so that we may be justified by faith. But now that faith has come, we are no longer under a tutor. For you are all sons of God through faith in Christ Jesus. For all of you who were baptized into Christ have clothed yourselves with Christ. There is neither Jew nor Greek, there is neither slave nor free man, there is neither male nor female; for you are all one in Christ Jesus. And if you belong*

---

2. Robert L. Thomas, *New American Standard Hebrew-Aramaic and Greek Dictionaries: Updated Edition* (Anaheim: Foundation Publications, Inc., 1998).

to Christ, then you are Abraham's descendants, heirs according to promise. Galatians 3:22-29

Law-based living, you see, is all about *measuring up to standards.* Elitism has its roots in the idea that one person—or group of people—can meet certain standards better than the less gifted. Of course, human standards are somewhat fickle; they change with the times and opinions of those who hold and manipulate power. The fashion industry is a classic example. Small groups of influential people sit in conference rooms determining what the general populace should purchase and wear for the next six months. Those who fail to meet their ever-changing standards quickly become the targets of ridicule. (Admittedly, I gave up my leisure suit long ago, but I do plan to keep my cargo shorts.)

Our loving Creator will have none of this type of thinking. Through the law of Moses (including the Ten Commandments), God has shown that all men and women fall hopelessly short of heaven's perfect standards. His purpose in doing so was never to condemn, but to steer. With the goal of reconciled relationships always in mind, God used our failure in light of the Mosaic law to point us toward the new covenant gospel of salvation by faith. This gospel removes the burden of sinless perfection from us and places it squarely on the shoulders of Jesus Christ.

We can't be good enough—or do enough—to redeem ourselves from the sins of our past. We can only choose to trust God through faith in Christ. In doing so, we enter into an unlikely fellowship with our Creator. This relationship centers on a *divine exchange* in which God takes our sins and gives us His righteousness.

He made Him who knew no sin to be sin on our behalf, so that we might become the righteousness of God in Him. 2 Corinthians 5:21

Wow! Through faith in the sacrificial death and resurrection of Christ, not only are our sins cleansed, we are also clothed with His robe of righteous perfection (Isaiah 61:10). Our decaying sinfulness no longer alienates God, and He begins to look upon us with the same favor that He holds toward Jesus.

Only as we begin to understand the wisdom of salvation by faith does its sheer brilliance dawn in our hearts. God's goal is always to redeem people, but because human pride is so pervasive, the source of that redemption must lie *outside* of ourselves. The wisdom of such an approach makes the new covenant in Christ unique compared to all other (law-based) belief systems.

Through the multiple dimensions of God's amazing grace, we are both favored by God and empowered to live according to His will. And because our high position in Christ is established by faith, none of us has grounds for self-glorification. The best a drowning person can do is reach out and grab a life preserver, but once safely on board the boat, he or she has nothing in which to boast. Imagine a near-drowning victim pridefully boasting, "Sure, I disobeyed the warning signs and got sucked into the rip current, but I'm still amazing because I reached out and grabbed a life preserver!" Never will that happen.

The fact that not everyone will be allowed entrance through heaven's gates is a painful reality that cannot be avoided. The issue isn't one of fairness, but of wisdom. For paradise to remain a place of eternal bliss, it must be "quarantined" from human pride, but unlike those subject to infectious diseases such as Ebola, we have a choice in the matter. Using salvation by faith in Jesus Christ as the "antidote," heaven's entrants are inoculated forever against the ravages of human pride and elitism. The perfect and free society we think God should have established on this planet we call Earth will then last forever in heaven.[3]

THE NEW COVENANT OF GRACE

In the garden of Eden, God warned Adam and Eve that they would die if they ate the fruit of the forbidden tree. Physical death did not come instantly for Adam and Eve, but a torrent of death was unleashed into our world nonetheless. Spiritual death is by far the worst. The human spirit, which once freely communed with its Creator, was suddenly separated from its source of life and vitality. No longer could humanity walk intimately with the King of the Universe. Thankfully for us, God's grace is amazing beyond the imagination.

---

3. Christians may not be entirely free from pride on earth, but the situation will be quite different in heaven.

For sinful and seemingly insignificant people to form an intimate bond with the holy and magnificent Creator of the Universe is a challenging concept to fathom. The difficulty of reconciling this reality tends to increase as we draw closer to God. Seeing Him more clearly can't help but expose the pervasive selfishness in our own hearts. If not for the unmerited favor of grace, a hopeless lot we would be.

Understanding the dynamics of human sinfulness in light of God's perfection leads us to recognize the pure genius of the new covenant gospel of grace. Long before Adam and Eve ate of the forbidden fruit of the tree of knowledge of good and evil, the all-knowing Creator of the Universe devised a plan to create a perfect society that would be free from evil, immersed in peace, and characterized by selfless love freely given.

Too often, though, grace is presented like a sugary treat on a carnival midway. Our entire focus seems to be on receiving God's unmerited favor so that we can one day go to heaven. Not only is this approach mostly irrelevant to our daily lives, it falls desperately short of the gospel's compelling beauty. The Bible's message isn't just about a future destiny; God wants us to walk with Him *now*, in our present age.

When a person is born again (or born from above), the Holy Spirit fuses with his or her human spirit and brings it to life (John 3:3). In a very real way, a new dimension of sensory perception is awakened with the spiritual abilities to "see" and "hear." Subsequently, not only is God as near as can possibly be, we can also know Him on the most intimate level.

The new covenant provides us with a new and unique way of relating to our Creator. By drawing near to God through Christ's merits rather than our own, we are free from the compulsive need to measure up to religious standards to gain God's approval. Under law, we try, by our own strength to appease God from a distance. But with grace, He dwells *in* us and works *through* us.

The freedom provided by grace isn't expressed through anarchy, but through *devotion*. In other words, Christians live differently from the rest of the world because of their deep and abiding love for God.

And when our lives are aligned by faith according to God's design, we are given the power to live in dominion over sin (Romans 5:17).

The Christian life is the expression of a personal relationship with God brought to fruition. Any relationship involves a learning curve as we seek to understand and communicate with one another, but the challenge is even more significant as imperfect, naturally-minded humans try to understand and align with God's spiritual mind. As much as entering the new covenant comes at God's expense, and as much as He has repeatedly taken the initiative to draw us near, we must still expend effort if we are to learn and grow in His ways.

WHAT DOES GOD EXPECT OF ME?

It's sometimes difficult to grasp through the complexity of theology and the craziness of our human existence, but a vital relationship with God is marked by *simplicity*. All healthy relationships are based on the same general characteristics—of which *trust (faith)*, *love*, and *wisdom* are three of the essentials.

Even a casual reading of the Bible will reveal the importance of *faith* to the Christian life. It is a theme that runs from the beginning of Genesis through the end of Revelation. When Jesus interacted with broken people, He continually emphasized the importance of faith. Why does faith matter so much? Again, because it is necessary for relational intimacy. Think for a moment about your personal relationships. How much do you open yourself up to people you don't trust?

We may seek comfort, fulfillment, and security in all things human, but such mentalities work against us in the long run. The central importance of faith is a vital reality that our loving Lord will not allow us to brush aside. Those who want to know God deeply cannot help but embrace a life that is dependent on Him and characterized by trust. If we fail to grasp the beauty, necessity, and centrality of faith, Christianity will make little sense.

It's also obvious that *love* is integral to healthy relationships, but the love so highly touted in the Bible is nothing like the self-seeking sort celebrated in contemporary music and film.

"This is My commandment, that you love one another, just as I have loved you. Greater love has no one than this, that one lay down his life for his friends. You are My friends if you do what I command you. No longer do I call you slaves, for the slave does not know what his master is doing; but I have called you friends, for all things that I have heard from My Father I have made known to you. You did not choose Me but I chose you, and appointed you that you would go and bear fruit, and that your fruit would remain, so that whatever you ask of the Father in My name He may give to you. This I command you, that you love one another." John 15:12-17

Amazingly, God doesn't just call us to love Him with all of our hearts; He also expects us to devote ourselves to others. The call to love others makes more sense if we understand that God has the same perfect love for every human. None of us is loved more than another; nor will His love increase or decrease based on our actions. But only as we actively love others is God's love fully realized. Faith isn't genuine until it translates into action.

The third primary component in a relationship with God is *wisdom*. The bottom line is that life in this world can be confusing, and we don't always know what faith and love look like in any given situation. We also need wisdom to understand when God speaks and what He is communicating.

Some people make the massive error of equating God's voice with the human conscience. We don't know with certainty, but I can build a strong case that the internal moral law we each possess stems from the fruit of the tree of the knowledge of good and evil. We each have an innate—though not always accurate—awareness of right and wrong. And while conscience has its benefits, we are gravely mistaken to attribute its voice of condemnation to our loving Father (Romans 8:1).

Truly spiritual wisdom opens our eyes to God's ways and enables us to align our lives accordingly. In this, the Bible is a gift replete with treasure. The Scriptures not only provide nuggets of invaluable wisdom for daily living, they also steer us on paths of magnificent discovery.

As humans, we are confronted by a massive dilemma. The universe surrounding us points to an immensely powerful and incredibly intelligent Creator, but nature provides us with painfully little information about how that Creator thinks or interacts with the material world. If not for God's gracious gift of the Bible to humanity, our "knowledge" of Him would be nothing more than human opinion. But because He breathed life into written words, we can develop a reasonably accurate understanding of who God is, how to relate to Him, and what He expects from us. This knowledge, developed through incremental steps taken in God's direction, enables us to align our lives according to His design.

THE KINGDOM OF GOD

Humanity itself is beset by contradiction. We are marvelously made, yet plagued by sickness and disease. We seek love and peace, but manage to kill large numbers of our own kind. Our hearts long for significance, meaning, and justice, yet they elude us. Each of us has ingrained within us a moral law, but we lack the power to meet its demands. Supposed answers such as wealth, popularity, and success promise to meet our innate needs, but somehow leave us feeling empty in the end. Surely, there must be more, something—or someone—beyond ourselves. If not, our concept of life is but a sad travesty.

This world has problems, that's for sure. Poverty, corruption, and hatred have held sway far too long. Such corporate problems merely reflect the vast number of individual struggles we face with issues such as materialism, pride, and bitterness. The solution to our ongoing dysfunction, however, lies not in creating our own reality, but in laying hold of His.

When Jesus' disciples asked Him how to pray, He responded with what we now call *The Lord's Prayer*:

"When you pray, say:
'Father, hallowed be Your name.
Your kingdom come.
Give us each day our daily bread.

And forgive us our sins,
For we ourselves also forgive everyone who is indebted to us.
And lead us not into temptation."' Luke 11:2-4

The kingdom of God represents heaven's perfect society governing the hearts of God's people. It is His reality destined to fill planet Earth (Daniel 2:44). Entirely unlike any government known to humanity, it is a social structure characterized by love, peace, and wholeness experienced through an almost mystical measure of freedom. Can you envision a culture with no sickness, no crime, and not even a condescending thought? All are signatures of God's kingdom as it advances through human lives, wrought through the amazingly simple laws of faith and love.

The dynamics of God's kingdom flow from the loving and faithful nature of its eternally-ruling King. But as appealing as the kingdom may seem, its advance is virtually impossible apart from the Bible. Our natural human ways are so vastly different from God's spiritual reality that we can never experience His fullness without first knowing and aligning ourselves with His ways (remember Isaiah 55:6-9?). Perhaps this is why the kingdom of God is such a dominant theme in the teachings of Christ and His early followers.

The Bible—and especially the New Testament—is also *The TouchPoint* to God's kingdom over which Jesus Christ reigns as the King of kings and Lord of lords. A lifetime of Bible reading marks a lifetime of discovery as we come to know the nature and character of our Lord, the simple expectations He places on our lives, and yes, even our flawed desires that hinder the kingdom's advance.

THE NAMES OF GOD

The Bible is our starting point for discovering God's character, and there are multiple avenues we can pursue to gain a better grasp of who He is. Studying the *attributes* of God, for example, can be powerfully illuminating.[4] Another option is to study the Old Testament *names* by which God reveals Himself to His people.

---

4. I really like *The Knowledge of the Holy: The Attributes of God*, by A.W. Tozer for this purpose.

Those who take the time to study the names of God as given throughout the Old Testament will find their lives greatly enriched and in very personal ways. In many situations, God revealed new dimensions of Himself in response to times of intense human need. A few examples are:

- Jehovah Jireh - The Lord our provider - Genesis 22:8-14

- Jehovah Ropheka - The Lord our healer - Exodus 15:25-26

- Jehovah Shalom - The Lord our peace - Judges 6:22-24

- Jehovah Tsidkeenu - The Lord our righteousness - Jeremiah 23:5-6

Throughout the history of His interaction with humanity, our Creator has taken deliberate steps to reveal a better understanding of Himself. And while we can never grasp the entirety of God's being, He has provided abundant insight into the richness of His amazing character.

CHAPTER WRAP-UP

Whether we study the personal teachings of Jesus Christ, a deeper understanding of His gospel of grace, or the names of God as found in Scripture, each measure of effort will further open our eyes to His unseen reality. None of us ever fully arrives this side of eternity, but each incremental step toward our Creator will captivate our hearts and transform the fabric of our lives.

Much more could be said about knowing the King of the Universe, but it's not for me to write your story; that's between you and God. Our loving Lord passionately desires to draw you nearer to Himself. It is for that reason, and that reason alone, that heaven paid such a steep price for human redemption. If you haven't embraced Jesus by faith and made a full surrender to His Lordship, what's holding you back? Whatever such a decision might cost you, the price paid pales in comparison to intimately and eternally knowing our Savior and Lord. Eternity begins today. Please don't foolishly leave it for tomorrow.

THE TOUCHPOINT

14

THE TOUCHPOINT OF EVERLASTING HOPE

Never be afraid to trust an unknown future to a known God.

—Corrie Ten Boom

For whatever was written in earlier times was written for our instruction, so that through perseverance and the encouragement of the Scriptures we might have hope.

Romans 15:4

Some people are early risers. Not me. Morning seems to be the time I do my best sleeping. That's not especially good news for someone who enjoys the outdoors. Nature is at its very best in those early, pristine hours when the sun breaks over the horizon. If only we could find a way to make the sun rise later in the day!

One cold December morning, in spite of my desire to stay snuggled under warm blankets, I reach over and shut off my annoying 4:45 alarm and stumble out of bed. Not long after, I'm standing in my friend's tree stand hunting for deer. Towering twenty feet above the ground on a wooden platform perched on a high hill, I watch in awe as the newborn day emerges from darkness. The brilliant rays of sunshine illuminating the frosty field grasses. The light fog drifting over the valleys. The dazzling sparkle of sunlight reflecting off melting ice crystals. What an awesome case of sensory overload!

Soaking in the wonders of nature, I momentarily forget about putting meat in my freezer as my thoughts steer toward the Creator of the majesty surrounding me. While lamenting that I don't have more opportunity to soak in the beauty of nature, a thought suddenly strikes me. Of all God's created beauty in the universe, human eyes see only a fraction. And yet, the beauty is always there.

Images from the Hubble telescope have revealed the wonder and beauty of deep space that is always present even when our human presence (or technology) isn't. How quickly the realization dawns that the created order doesn't revolve around us. Our vast cosmos continues to get along nicely regardless of our knowledge or influence—and perhaps, *better* without us.

Whether we rocket into the far reaches of space, dive to the ocean depths, or simply hike into the mountains, the more we explore nature, the more its profound beauty breathes a sense of awe into our hearts. In a similar vein, the more we, by faith, search for God, the more we experience His magnificence. Like exploring a universe without end, each fresh discovery not only opens our eyes to the wonders of a previously unseen world, it also fills us with overwhelming wonder at how much more lies beyond.

KNOWING GOD BREEDS HOPE

Fathoming the depths of God has a fascinating effect on the human psyche as a growing sense of hope begins to flood our souls. In fact, another powerful Biblical theme is that of *promise*. Only closed eyes and small minds remain deficient of the expectation for a better tomorrow. When hope fades into darkness, humanity sinks into a pit of deep trouble. Any real meaning in life, I've discovered, is impossible apart from a sense of anticipation for the good to come. Remove the hope of a better tomorrow from a generation of young people and hedonism will soon follow. After all, if today is all we have, why shouldn't we extract every ounce of pleasure before we die?

I've also learned that hope can be found on two primary levels: the *temporal* and the *eternal*. And while most of us fix our hopes on things that are tangible to our natural senses—a new car, a better job, a successful relationship—the Bible serves as a *TouchPoint* to an eternal hope far exceeding even the best of this world's offerings.

Apart from hope, the human race cannot prosper. But the type of hope for which the human soul thirsts involves more than the desire for a nice house, a prestigious job, or a thousand social media friends. As spiritual beings, we long to fully realize a depth of hope that transcends our natural human existence. In this vein, the Bible leads us on a truly meaningful trail that finds its desired end in the person of Jesus Christ. Our hope lies not in the Bible itself, but in the God who has provided His written Word as a connecting point so that we might know *Him* and begin to fathom the depths of His glory.

HOPE BEYOND OURSELVES

I grew up in a government-run housing project and hated it. I should have been grateful for a decent roof over my head, but for multiple reasons, I found myself longing for a better existence. My dream was to escape that God-forsaken (at least in my mind) place and establish a meaningful existence in the ever-promising middle-class America.

A college degree became my goal. After that, I planned to pursue a profitable career, marry a fantastic woman, have kids, and live comfortably ever after. Do you know what happened? My plan worked—at least at first. I graduated with a degree in chemistry and married an amazing person, and together, we birthed two wonderful children. But as I began to settle into my individualized version of the American dream, some unexplainable dynamic didn't seem quite right.

As much as I appreciated life in middle-class America, my heart longed for something more. I had a great family, a well-paying job, and a small but nice home. Friends were close, and our church provided a platform for Christian service. On top of that, hunting, fishing, and gardening opportunities abound in western Pennsylvania. All of this goes without mentioning the nearly-always-competitive Pittsburgh sports teams. Still, I wasn't satisfied with a temporal existence; I needed to know, experience, and share more of God's reality. Jesus had ruined the American dream for me, and I am so glad that He did.

"What's wrong with the American dream?" a person might ask. While I still think it's great to desire a healthy family life, I grew to realize that the "Dream" is all about *consumption*. Driven by an intrinsically selfish desire to accumulate more stuff, life in the U.S. is too often characterized by what we can get more than what we can give. But money and material goods are intended to be tools that we use to advance God's kingdom purposes in and through us. Only as our material resources serve these purposes can our lives be truly blessed and our hearts satisfied. When Jesus said, "It is more blessed to give than to receive," He knew what He was talking about (see Acts 20:35)!

King Solomon was able to achieve the type of materialistic dreams that so many of us hope to realize. But notice the self-centered emphasis in the following passage from Ecclesiastes, and then consider how *unfulfilled* Solomon became:

I explored with my mind how to stimulate my body with wine while my mind was guiding me wisely, and how to take hold of folly, until I could see what good there is for the sons of men to do under heaven the few years of their lives. I enlarged my works: I built houses for myself, I planted vineyards for myself; I made gardens and parks for myself and I planted in them all kinds of fruit trees; I made ponds of water for myself from which to irrigate a forest of growing trees. I bought male and female slaves and I had homeborn slaves. Also I possessed flocks and herds larger than all who preceded me in Jerusalem. Also, I collected for myself silver and gold and the treasure of kings and provinces. I provided for myself male and female singers and the pleasures of men—many concubines.

Then I became great and increased more than all who preceded me in Jerusalem. My wisdom also stood by me. All that my eyes desired I did not refuse them. I did not withhold my heart from any pleasure, for my heart was pleased because of all my labor and this was my reward for all my labor. Thus I considered all my activities which my hands had done and the labor which I had exerted, and behold all was vanity and striving after wind and there was no profit under the sun. Ecclesiastes 2:3-11

It's not uncommon for people to have full houses and empty hearts. Substantive hope lies beyond the confines of our physical senses; it is something "extra-human." If our hope comes only from within our natural sphere, it will never fully satisfy the deepest longings of our hearts. In this, the Bible plays a crucial role as it points us toward a sense of anticipation far transcending the offerings of this natural world.

HOPE AS A PERSON

Hope, I discovered, is not an impersonal concept. Real and lasting hope is embodied in the person of Jesus Christ. Why? As already explained, natural things can never fully quench spiritual thirst. Furthermore, earthly hopes are always subject to forces beyond our control. As much as we want to think we control our own destinies, life in these human bodies is painfully fragile.

My plans for college worked out well, but any number of things could have derailed them. My funding could have been cut. Sickness could have overtaken me. An unfair professor might have pushed me to drop out—especially midway through my first semester when I almost quit because of some poor grades. After graduation, the sagging economy limited my career opportunities. And later, when I finally landed a well-paying job, I watched in angst as corporate leaders jilted some of my coworkers. What I had long suspected was at last confirmed: our "use it up and throw it away society" views people as expendable resources. Let's face it—our earthly hopes are tenuous at best.

In contrast, Jesus is not subject to human desires, opinions, or economies. He stands above and beyond anything physical. Jesus Christ, therefore, offers a *living hope*.

> *Blessed be the God and Father of our Lord Jesus Christ, who according to His great mercy has caused us to be born again to a **living hope** through the resurrection of Jesus Christ from the dead, to obtain an inheritance which is imperishable and undefiled and will not fade away, reserved in heaven for you, who are protected by the power of God through faith for a salvation ready to be revealed in the last time. 1 Peter 1:3-5 (emphasis added)*

If there is one word I could use to characterize our hope in Jesus, it would be *resurrection*. Even death could not hold Jesus down. And if the power of the grave is subject to the eternal Son of God, no natural force or act of human will can ever extinguish the everlasting hope we find in Him.

The hope we hold in the person of Jesus Christ is expressed in written form through His eternal Word. But without the reality of God's truth impressed on our hearts through the Bible, our perspectives dim and our hearts grow weary during difficult times. When we fail to draw near to God through His Word, hope is all too easily lost.

Not everyone has the type of opportunity I had for improved circumstances. Injustice, a lack of ability, and any number of circumstances beyond our control can limit our opportunities for success. At the same time, our hope in Christ transcends the world of our natural senses. Regardless of what transpires in our earthly existence, we can experience the untold blessings that come through abiding in God's presence. Personally knowing the all-sufficient Creator of the Universe will give us the strength and courage to persist regardless of what this world throws at us.

HOPE TO PROVIDE SIGNIFICANCE

One of the deepest longings of the human heart is for *significance*. We all need to know that we're loved, valued, and appreciated. Due to my childhood circumstances, I lacked the sense of worth that my psyche needed. Consequently, I found myself on a never-ending quest to prove that I was significant. A degree in chemistry wasn't just about a better life; I also needed to show the world that I was somebody worthy of their admiration.

Although this quest for significance consumed my thoughts and actions, I'm not sure that many others cared. Even when I managed to impress a handful of people, I quickly discovered that human glory fades faster than the sinking sun on a summer's eve. The blazing fire of today's triumph will soon be rendered into the smoldering memory of tomorrow's ashes.

As I pressed into the Scriptures, I began to understand that the gospel isn't just about sin and forgiveness; it is an identity message. If all of the sin, destruction, and death in this world came from an identity issue ("you will be like God" - Genesis 3:5), then at its core, the solution to the human condition is intricately tied to who we see—or want—ourselves to be. The good news is that our hope lies not in our performance, but in our connectedness with the living God through faith in Jesus Christ.

The awe-inspiring message of the gospel tells me that even when I was at my absolute worst, the eternal King of the Universe offered not only forgiveness but also the right to become His child (John 1:12). Being called God's son or daughter may not seem like much in our world of celebrity adoration, but when the King's glory is fully revealed, every person ever born will drool at the thought of joining His cherished family and becoming spiritual royalty.

When it comes to my vocation, I must prove myself. I need to work hard at speaking and writing with meaning and clarity. But when it comes to my personal identity, I don't need to prove anything to anybody. My "work" is simply to believe. Everything else will follow in its time. Talk about freedom and hope! Any one of us can be a person of significance without the exhausting effort that self-validation requires.

HOPE TO EASE OUR BURDENS

It's nearly impossible to measure quantitatively the hope we find through a Biblically-based relationship with God, but the influence is profound nonetheless. The gospel enables us to process reality in a healthy and productive way. I don't know about you, but I need a lot of help in this area. The realities of life on this planet don't always contribute to my happiness.

How do you feel about staying on top of current events? I'm often conflicted. I want to know what's happening, so I can help make a difference, but the sheer amount of information that floods our brains is nothing short of overwhelming. To make things worse, modern technology gives us almost immediate access to a vast array of negative issues.

Not long ago, I turned on the nightly news. Considering commercial breaks, I suppose that a typical thirty-minute broadcast would contain about twenty minutes of actual news. On that particular evening, I didn't even need the full twenty minutes to begin feeling depressed. Even the customary "happy moment" at the end of the broadcast did little to temper the stark reality of life on this globe.

On any typical evening, we'll hear about natural disasters, city riots, brutal murders, and government corruption—all leading to tremendous pain and suffering. Choose practically any arena of life—health, food, sexuality, the environment, business, government, religion, etc.—and you will find an abundance of disturbing issues to drag you down. It's no wonder that depression and anxiety are so prevalent in our technologically-advanced societies.

Problematically, the burdens of life aren't limited to our news feeds. We may struggle with deep concern for a wayward loved one. Financial difficulties can put a huge damper on our ability to enjoy life. Health problems turn even simple tasks into major chores. And of course, there is always the future. None of us knows what tomorrow will bring, and we're often powerless to make things go the way we want. Accordingly, most of us seek to control our lives and circumstances, while failing to realize the heavy toll the resulting burdens exact. In our quest to become mini-gods, we forfeit the joy of living.

Those who, by faith, align themselves with God's design begin to understand that "the government rests on His shoulders" (Isaiah 9:6). Not only does Jesus promise us hope for tomorrow, He also provides the opportunity to roll the weight of our cares upon His more-than-capable shoulders. It may be difficult to grasp, but our loved ones mean more to God than they do to us. Furthermore, I never cease to be amazed at the attention my Lord gives to some of the smaller details in my life. While He's deeply concerned about things like warfare and poverty, He still mysteriously manages to ensure that I catch an anticipated phone call or receive a desired package. In all honesty, I sometimes struggle to understand how all of these things work, but His love shines through regardless.

When we live by faith, nothing can keep God from faithfully bearing the burdens that would otherwise overrun our hearts and minds. The burdens of life can drag us down, and though trusting God to lift them may not come easily, our loving Lord has gifted us with the Bible as a means to lay hold of His faithful promises. Without the Word of God pointing toward our living hope in Christ, we're left with the last three minutes of the nightly news broadcast to momentarily brighten our dark worlds.

HOPE TO MAKE A DIFFERENCE

Somewhere along life's path, I discovered that not all apathy is due to laziness. Some people have simply resigned themselves to the reasoned "reality" that the problems and tragedies of this world are beyond their influence. A combination of factors has instilled within them a sense that, being powerless to make a difference, seeking comfort and pleasure is the next best option.

The world of politics is an arena that promises us the opportunity to make an impact while often failing to deliver. How many of us have actively campaigned for a candidate only to learn that he or she is part of the same broken establishment of human hierarchy? The cumulative effect is often one of hopeless resignation. More than one young person has jumped on the "change" bandwagon only to climb down—or be thrown off—battered and disillusioned. Their subconscious mantra then becomes, "We can't make a difference, so let's live for ourselves."

Because we care about the future of our nation, we never want to surrender our rights to influence the political process. Still, over time, we may begin to wonder whether even taking a few minutes out of our day to vote is worth the hassle. In a similar way, many of our religious environments are characterized by a sort of spiritual hierarchy. The power to produce change lies with those who are gifted, educated, wealthy, or "super-spiritual"—or so we think. The best we feel we can do is add a few meager crumbs to the offering plate in response to near-constant prodding. How little we understand about the nature of God!

Nowhere is our living hope more powerful than through the presence of the Holy Spirit dwelling within the hearts of God's people.

It doesn't matter where we've been or what we've done, who we aren't or what we don't have, God wants to use each of us in a meaningful way. And in God's economy, His purposes always involve making a viable difference in human lives. Furthermore, if our sovereign Lord created each of us with a purpose, He will, by His grace, empower us to fulfill the objectives involved.

Some readers may think that such ideas sound too good to be true—that they are beyond hope or have nothing to offer. Consider that a lie. If there's anything that will hinder us from making an impact in our world, it will be our own small-minded thinking that limits God from working in and through our lives.

Coming to understand our potential in Christ is yet another reason that we need the influence of the Bible. God's Word won't try to sell us an unrealistic dream. Nor will it tell us that we can do anything we set our minds to. Instead, the Scriptures teach that we were created for a meaningful relationship with God and with significant purposes for living. Accordingly, the Holy Spirit will empower God's people to do everything our heavenly Father calls us to do.

HOPE FOR THE LAST DAY

Recently, while reading the sixth chapter of John, I was struck by Jesus' emphasis on "the last day." He seemed to be instilling within His disciples a firm hope for the final tomorrow.

> *"For this is the will of My Father, that everyone who beholds the Son and believes in Him will have eternal life, and I Myself will raise him up **on the last day.**" John 6:40 (emphasis added)*

I find this emphasis significant for several reasons. We all long to see a wide array of earthly hopes—some of which may be realized eventually—fulfilled. The bottom line, though, is that life isn't about our dreams, desires, and wants. God isn't a sort of heavenly Santa Claus, who exists to make us happy. Only as we live for Him are we truly blessed in ways seen and unseen. Furthermore, there will be times when unjust actions or unforeseeable circumstances steal the potential for our dreams to be fulfilled.

Human nature itself presents one of our biggest hindrances to experiencing God's blessings. Three "anti-virtues" are deeply ingrained in our human fabric—*selfishness, the desire for control,* and *self-glorification.* Anyone who seeks to spur favorable changes in this world must also overcome these sinful tendencies in his or her own heart. On either front, the battle is fierce!

Fulfilling God's plans and purposes for our lives comes with a price. On a personal level, there are many things that I value about my calling in life, but it has also cost me. I've had to surrender freedoms that others cherish. Sacrifice seems to be a daily reality and financial security an elusive quest. When these things begin to weigh on me—and they sometimes do—I find comfort in looking forward to that "last day." When I finally see the revealing of His kingdom with untarnished focus, I'll know that any price paid was small and well-spent.

When we're passive or ignorant, injustice prevails, but when we get informed and take up worthy causes, our hearts can easily become burdened and our emotions wounded. Those who fail to fix their hope on Christ Jesus will enter a jaded and bitter twilight. If, however, we rest secure in the confidence of a final triumph, we'll not only persevere, we'll overcome with flying colors.

Our struggles are never wasted when we love and trust our Savior. In this life, our Lord promises to work every situation toward a greater good. And when our time on earth has run its course, we will experience, beyond our greatest imaginations, the fulfillment of an everlasting hope in Christ. Today, we may struggle, but tomorrow we will see Him face to face.

CORPORATE HOPE

The church suffers considerable criticism for being hard and judgmental. No doubt, some of the unfavorable commentaries are justified. At the same time, these negative characterizations frequently stem from seeing the bad fruit of legalistic environments. And—I must be adamant—not all churches are legalistic. Fellowships in which the grace of God is understood and realized contain some of the most hope-filled environments on the planet.

Despite the problems associated with human relationships, the corporate interaction of God's people can be amazingly uplifting. I speak from experience. More than once, I've emotionally limped into a church service only to walk out with a spring in my step. Sometimes, it's the music. Sometimes, it's the message. Sometimes, it's a prayer. Sometimes, it's a word of encouragement from a friend. Sometimes, it's the evidence of a life being touched. And sometimes, it's "simply" the presence of God made manifest as His children gather in unified worship.

I'll be the first to admit that we must exercise wisdom when choosing a local fellowship, but I also believe it's a huge mistake to avoid church involvement entirely. As personal as the Christian faith may be, it can be lived out fully only in a relational environment. We won't find nearly as much cynicism and dysfunction in a grace-rich, Christ-centered church as we will among those doing their own spiritual thing.

The truth is that God often reveals Himself to people through people. Our Lord undoubtedly meets with us as individuals, but as a whole, the New Testament encourages a community mindset. According to God's design, individual faith and love are lived out and expressed in a corporate environment. Only together can we maintain tender, faith-filled hearts as we lift up and encourage one another in the midst of an ever-darkening world. Only together can we experience the fullness of His everlasting hope.

HOPE EXPRESSED

My mother, who faced considerable adversity during her life, often turned to the Psalms for hope and encouragement. Penned under a paradigm of law, these spiritual songs were at times violent and edgy as their writers expressed anguish amid cries for justice. But regardless of each unique situation, the underlying message of the Psalms is one of hope. No matter how dark things got, no matter how much injustice seemed to triumph, and no matter how distant God appeared to be, the Psalmist's complaints turned to hopeful anticipation as they pried their focus from unfavorable circumstances and riveted their attention on the faithful character of their Creator.

Although in a somewhat different form, this same basic sense of anticipation characterized much of the New Testament church. The early church grew in hopeful expectation against all odds. Assaulted by not only the mighty Roman Empire, but also by many of their own Jewish leaders, they celebrated God's presence. Almost mystically, their message won the hearts of Gentiles while radically opposing the idolatry and sexual immorality of pagan cultures. In spite of experiencing the bitter pills of cultural contempt and religious persecution, a sense of everlasting hope fueled the earliest followers of Christ. Such encouragement was experienced through the shared Word, songs of praise, mutual encouragement, and the manifest presence of God.

Considering all of the abuse hurled at the Bible for being supposedly cruel and oppressive, I am fascinated by the depth of hope and meaning that it provides. The Bible overflows with words of life, but the full power of those words is realized only through the person of Jesus Christ. Because of who He is, what He has done, and where He stands, we can each know and experience an everlasting hope. The written promises we find recorded in the Bible serve as gateways to our living hope in Christ.

Time and time again, the Bible commands us to rejoice, to praise, and to thank God. (Terribly oppressive, isn't it?) As we actively take such steps, our hearts are aligned with the joy-filled environment of eternal paradise. The result is that we then begin to experience a manifestation of God's presence as heaven's life spills over into ours.

God is present everywhere all of the time, but His presence remains hidden for the most part. He is all around us, and yet we can remain ignorant of the love, joy, peace, and hope that characterize His manifest presence. Those who have experienced Him will never be satisfied with anything less. In this, they realize that the tidbits of life tasted during our short stay on the planet Earth will be fully realized on that last day when our everlasting hope becomes an experiential reality.

MESSAGES AND PRAYERS OF HOPE

It seems fitting to complete this chapter with a smattering of the many words and prayers of hope found in the Scriptures. Each provides a brilliant ray of light in even the darkest of circumstances. And we all know that the impact of darkness in our world is far-reaching.

"For I know the plans that I have for you," declares the LORD, "plans for welfare and not for calamity to give you a future and a hope. Then you will call upon Me and come and pray to Me, and I will listen to you. You will seek Me and find Me when you search for Me with all your heart." Jeremiah 29:11-13

"THINGS WHICH EYE HAS NOT SEEN AND EAR HAS NOT HEARD,

AND which HAVE NOT ENTERED THE HEART OF MAN,

ALL THAT GOD HAS PREPARED FOR THOSE WHO LOVE HIM." 1 Corinthians 2:9b

And we know that God causes all things to work together for good to those who love God, to those who are called according to His purpose. Romans 8:28

For I am confident of this very thing, that He who began a good work in you will perfect it until the day of Christ Jesus. Philippians 1:6

I pray that the eyes of your heart may be enlightened, so that you will know what is the hope of His calling, what are the riches of the glory of His inheritance in the saints, and what is the surpassing greatness of His power toward us who believe. These are in accordance with the working of the strength of His might which He brought about in Christ, when He raised Him from the dead and seated Him at His right hand in the heavenly places, far above all rule and authority and power and dominion, and every name that is named, not only in this age but also in the one to come. Ephesians 1:18-21

Now may the God of hope fill you with all joy and peace in believing, so that you will abound in hope by the power of the Holy Spirit. Romans 15:13

CONCLUSION

For some, hope will continue as little more than a vague idea. For others, temporal hope in money, government leaders, and sports heroes will one day lead to a shattered reality overflowing with regrets. But for those who manage to grasp the true genius of the Bible, our living hope will provide a secure anchor of stability in the midst of a tumultuous world. The wisdom and power of this hope will then be revealed to their fullest extent on the last day.

As a person's eyes are opened to the truth of God's eternal Word, he or she will discover a heavenly Father who is amazing beyond the reaches of human comprehension. Time and time again, the realization will dawn that while our Creator stands far beyond us in practically every way, He loves us with unbridled passion.

Viewing the Bible through the lens of a personal relationship with our heavenly Father provides a very different picture from the legalistic mindset that uses the Christian Scriptures as a rulebook to keep us bound by unattainable standards. As our hearts are captivated by the reality of our amazing Creator, we cannot help but be changed in the process.

But as our attitudes and subsequent actions are transformed, we'll also begin to see that our world's system—by which we were once enthralled—is entirely out of step with the eternal King's wise design. And as wonderful as it is to discover God and His ways, considerable conflict can result as we conform to the dynamics of His kingdom. Some friends and family members who were once soul mates in thought and deed will suddenly grow distant—if not contentious—due to our newfound life in Christ.

At some point, we will be left with a painful choice: abandon Christ and embrace the world's system, or embrace Christ and be at odds with people from whom we covet approval. This choice is not new or unique. In fact, it has been part of the Christian life ever since Jesus began His ministry. The faithful saints who have gone before us learned to persevere by laying hold of their everlasting hope in Christ.

The sixth chapter of John records a painful dialogue that took place between Jesus and a large number of His followers. In the end, many of them either couldn't understand or accept what He was trying to communicate. In spite of previous professions of faith, they really didn't believe Jesus to be the eternal Son of God. The result? They quit following Him.

Jesus then turned to His twelve hand-picked disciples and asked, "You don't want to go away too, do you?" Peter's response was one for the ages:

*"Lord, to whom shall we go? **You** have **words** of eternal life." John 6:68b (emphasis added)*

And so He does!

ACKNOWLEDGEMENTS

Writing a book can be relatively easy. Writing a good book is far more difficult. Approaching excellence—well, let's just say huge amounts of time and effort are necessary. Such an awesome group of people contributed to the painstaking effort of writing, editing, and publishing what I hope is an excellent work.

To begin, Dale Adams, Paul Edwards, Jason Hutchins, Brent MacDonald, Todd Stanley, and Ted Yohe sharpened me with their theological perspectives. Our growing team of volunteer editors—Mary Bonzo, Deb Croyle, Jeff Ference, Lynda Logue, Elaine Rice, Demi Richardson, Debi Santos, Judah Thomas, and Dr. Ruiess Van Fossen Bravo—also made huge contributions. Nat Davis provided the icing on the cake with her professional perspective.

I'm also thankful that Chris Ball, John Caton, and Philip Underwood, all took time out of their busy schedules to read the book (at least, I hope they did) and write endorsements. Finally, we leaned heavily on Steve Margita and Sean McGaughran for our design work.

I feel honored to do what I do, but none of it would be possible apart from those who serve, give, and pray for the sake of our ministry efforts.

SfMe Media Resources

Additional copies of **The TouchPoint** can be purchased through our SfMe Media website (www.sfme.org) and at major online retailers. Volume discounts are also available for paperback copies.

The Divine Progression of Grace: Blazing a Trail to Fruitful Living thoughtfully explores God's grace from a perspective of empowerment as well as acceptance. This book will take you deeper into a relationship with your Creator and also help to make you more usable for His purposes.

Each of the readings in **Champions in the Wilderness: Fifty-Two Devotions to Guide and Strengthen Emerging Overcomers** draws from a deep well of truth to encourage, strengthen, and instruct those who desire to walk with God but are struggling in the face of adversity. The format of **Champions** lends itself well to group discussion.

The Search for Me: A Journey Toward a Rock Solid Identity is a 12-part DVD study that boldly but lovingly touches many of the core issues that influence human behavior. This excellent small group resource makes for more than casual interaction as it interweaves the gospel with the issue of personal identity. The effects are multifaceted as participants grow together in faith, renew their love for God, and break free from sin. The audio files of the series are free for streaming from our sfme.org website for those who would like to review the study before purchasing.

Helping SfMe Ministries

SfMe Ministries burns with a vision to impact our world for Christ, but it's not something we could ever accomplish alone. *Honest online reviews of our books are always appreciated as they provide a cost-free way for our readers to contribute to our ministry efforts. Also, if your life has been impacted by one of our resources, please recommend it to others.*

Furthermore, we are a *faith* ministry, meaning that we seek to put our focus on God as our provider and do not aggressively solicit contributions. "Opportunity without pressure" is our motto when it comes to raising the necessary funds to fulfill our vision of forming and equipping a generation of world changers for Christ.

Those whose hearts move them to give financially are more than welcome to join us in advancing God's kingdom. The resources will be put to good use. We do not distribute contact information, nor do we badger our financial partners to give.

More information about financial partnership can be found on our ministry website (searchforme.info). SfMe Ministries is an IRS recognized 501(c)(3) non-profit organization. *Regardless of whether you feel led to give or not, your prayers for our ministry efforts are both coveted and appreciated!*